THE MEANING
OF GOD
IN MODERN
JEWISH RELIGION

THE MEANING OF GOD IN MODERN JEWISH RELIGION

Mordecai M. Kaplan

With an Introduction by Mel Scult

WAYNE STATE UNIVERSITY PRESS Detroit

First published 1937 by Behrman House.
Reprinted 1962 by Reconstructionist Press.
Reprinted 1994 by Wayne State University Press.

Copyright © 1962 by the Recontructionist Press.
Introduction copyright © 1994 by Wayne State University Press,
Detroit, Michigan 48201. All rights are reserved.
No part of this book may be reproduced without formal permission.
Manufactured in the United States of America.

Library of Congress Cataloging-in-Publication Data

Kaplan, Mordecai Manahem, 1881 -
        The meaning of God in modern Jewish religion/Mordecai M.
   Kaplan : with an introduction by Mel Scult.
            p.   cm.
        Previously published: New York : Reconstructionist Press,
   1962. With new introd.
        Includes index.
        ISBN 0-1843-2552-1 (pbk. : alk. paper)
        1. God (Judaism) 2. Judaism—20th century. 3. Reconstructionist
   Judaism. I. Title.
        BM610.K3   1994
        296.3'11—dc20   94-39779

CONTENTS

INTRODUCTION

Mel Scult

MORDECAI Kaplan (1881–1983), the father of Reconstructionism, has been called the prophet of Jewish renewal.
Throughout his life he searched for ways to help the modern Jew relate meaningfully to the Jewish tradition. In his
present work, published three years after his magnum opus
Judaism as a Civilization, Kaplan translates the major categories of traditional Jewish life into the compelling language of the present using the structure of the Jewish holy
days.

Kaplan was the preeminent teacher of American Jewry
during the first half of the twentieth century. A product of
Jewish civilization in Lithuania, he arrived here as a child,
was reared on the Lower East Side of New York, attended
City College, and graduated the Jewish Theological Seminary in 1902, a month after the arrival of Solomon Schechter. Kaplan's career was to be intimately tied to the Jewish
Theological Seminary. In 1909 he became the principal of
the Teachers' Institute, began teaching in the rabbinical
school, and remained on the staff for the next fifty-four
years.

It was during his graduate work at Columbia (1900–
1906) that the young orthodox Kaplan began to doubt the
primary doctrines of traditional Judaism. His professors, including the celebrated founder of Ethical Culture, Felix
Adler, and the pioneer in sociology, Franklin Giddings, encouraged his interest in the sociological underpinnings of

religous institutions and ideas, thus undermining Kaplan's beliefs in his own tradition as a God-given absolute.

Although not a full-time member of the Columbia University faculty, Felix Adler taught philosophy during these years and was a prominent personality on the campus. Deeply impressed by the founder of Ethical Culture, Kaplan attended his lectures and wrote his masters dissertation with the "great dissenter." The focus of his masters essay was the utilitarian philosophy of the nineteenth century, particularly the work of Henry Sidgwick. Sidgwick (1838–1900) was for many years professor of philosophy at Cambridge University; his book *The Methods of Ethics* is a significant treatise in the Benthamite tradition of utilitarian ethics. Kaplan's emphasis on function as well as some of his primary beliefs concerning religion are derived directly from Sidgwick.[1]

The course of Kaplan's intellectual development was significantly influenced by the cultural Zionism of Ahad Ha-Am (Asher Ginzberg, 1856–1927). Early on in his student years he was attracted to the writings of Ahad Ha-Am, the "secular rabbi" of Jewish nationalism. Ahad Ha-Am, Herzl's most passionate critic, awakened the Jews of his time to the possibility of their spiritual regeneration. He understood that the collective redemption of the Jewish people was a process, not an event, and would require the gradual transformation of the heart and soul of the Jewish masses. Ahad Ha-Am attributed the greatness of the Jews not to their having been chosen by God, but to their own creative genius. The principal agent in the life of the Jewish people, according to Ahad Ha-Am, was not God but the Jewish people themselves. Their genius expressed itself in the realm of morals and ethics; the Jewish spirit throbbed with a profound concern for the social responsibility of the individual. However, the national creative energy was dissipated when Jews were seduced by the values of their non-Jewish neighbors. Only a new Jewish center in Palestine could prevent this assimilation.

Felix Adler, Kaplan's teacher, also decisively shaped his thought, not only philosophically but also theologically. Adler maintained that when we talk of God we speak metaphorically: what we say is never literally true, but the metaphor nonetheless stands for something real. The gods, including Jehovah, are creations of the imagination, but the eternal is not. His "proof" derived from his understanding of morality and was similar to what is found in Kaplan's later works. "If then, I believe in the ultimate attainment of the moral end, I am forced to assume that there is provision in nature looking to the achievement of that end."[2]

Adler's appreciation of the transcendent made it easier for Kaplan to relate to his philosophy—though he never forgave Adler for leaving the Jewish fold and establishing a new religion. Despite his emphasis on the ethical, Adler possessed a genuine sensitivity for the transcendent: "the deepest experiences of life have been missed," he tells us, "if we have never been thrilled by the emotions which come from the thought of that vaster life of which ours is a part. It is wonder, evoked by the thought of the vastness, order and beauty of the world that has led men to the idea of God."[3]

In considering the experience of the transcendent, Adler emphasized not only wonder but righteousness. Adler paraphrased Matthew Arnold's approach, which may already have been familiar to Kaplan. Speaking of the demand for justice, Adler wrote, "on the other hand, if the demand for justice is realizable, then in the nature of things there must be provision that it shall be realized; then there must be as it has been expressed, 'a power that makes for righteousness.'"[4] This formulation, which dominates the structure of Kaplan's *The Meaning of God in Modern Jewish Religion*, is taken directly from Matthew Arnold's *Literature and Dogma*. Adler proceeded to explain Arnold's conception, emphasizing God as a power rather than a person.[5]

In 1905 Kaplan wrote in his journal of Arnold and of Ahad Ha-am: "I am more convinced than ever that Achad Ha-am's conception of nationality plus Arnold's interpretation of Israel's genius for righteousness contains that which could form the positive expression of the Jewish spirit. All it wants is definiteness and detail."[6] In his *Literature and Dogma*, Arnold set forth his goal of establishing the Bible on some basis other than that of revealed truth. Writing in the late nineteenth century, he assumed that religion was increasingly disregarded because most people could not accept the assumption that the Bible derived its authority from the "moral and intelligent governor of the universe." He argued that the authority of the Bible must be based "in something which can be verified instead of something which has to be assumed."[7]

The formulation "God as the power that makes for . . ." must also be understood against the background of Kaplan's knowledge of the social sciences. Kaplan may be described in his thinking as the sociologist qua theologian. It is widely believed that Kaplan's most important "teacher" was the sociologist Emile Durkheim. In fact, Kaplan had already formulated the primary principles of his approach before he read Durkheim's great work, *The Elementary Forms of Religious Life*. Durkheim confirmed his thinking but did not inspire it. In 1915 and 1916, in his diary and in a series of articles in the newly established *Menorah Journal*, Kaplan articulated the major assumptions of his ideology.

For Kaplan the group was essential in defining the nature of religion: "Religion is primarily a social phenomenon," he wrote in his journal in 1913; "to grasp its reality, to observe its workings and to further its growth we must study its functioning in some social group. The individual and his development or perfection may constitute the sole aim of religion, but the fact and substance of religion cannot exist completely and exhaustively in an individual."[8]

The essence of religion was not in belief, but in the "living energy which exists in all social groups."[9]

In his 1915–1917 *Menorah Journal* articles, Kaplan emphatically denied the existence of a specifiable set of doctrines incumbent on all Jews. The doctrines were everchanging. Not beliefs but the underlying life force—the life of the Jewish people—bound the generations one to the other. We must see Judaism "not in any one doctrine or sum of doctrines but in the innermost life force which has vitalized the Jewish people and has made of it the most self-conscious social group of any upon the face of the earth." Kaplan's basic thrust here suggests Bergson and his élan vital, but there is no direct evidence that he was influenced significantly by the philosopher of creative evolution.

Kaplan frequently used the concept of *energy*—a basic concept of the modern era and an emotionally, intellectually, and spiritually compelling one—in talking of the group or the nation or God. He maintained that considering Judaism a form of truth rather than a living reality was a radical misunderstanding. Rather, the living dynamic energy that produces the truths of Judaism is the core of Jewish reality.[10]

The novelty of Kaplan's formulation can be appreciated only if set beside the common approaches of this period. Both Reform and Conservative Jews were eager to show that Judaism was not merely a set of rituals and customs but also embodied a set of beliefs which constituted a rational picture of the universe. Judaism expressed an entire theology that was embedded in rabbinical dicta. (Thus the title and the purpose of Solomon Schecter's great work, *Some Aspects of Rabbinic Theology*.) Reform and Conservative leaders argued over the relative importance of this or that belief, but no one except Kaplan questioned the assumption that Judaism consisted of a series of rational beliefs about the world and the commandments that flowed from them.

Kaplan completely redefined Judaism, and in doing so he moved the discussion to a higher level. The question was not which belief to retain and which to discard, but how to nurture the life energy of the Jewish people—the life energy that constituted its essence. Moreover, the Jewish consciousness that sustained the vital energy could be fostered by many different means. "It may be the Synagogue, the Hebrew Language, the Zionist movement, Jewish education or even student societies," Kaplan wrote to his friend Henry Hurwitz in 1916.[11]

Kaplan, of couse, never confined his thinking to the sociological realm. When he looked out into the wider universe, the concept of energy continued to dominate his thinking. In an early diary entry from 1907, he wrote: "Prayer is communion. To commune with God is to put oneself in touch with the source of cosmic energy." He often talked of God as the "living universe." In the rare moments when Kaplan said that he believed in God as a transcendent Being, he did so tentatively. He once explained that while "I believed in God as a transcendent Being, I could not conceive of that Being having any meaning for us except through and in terms of human experience."[12]

Kaplan's use of the formulation "The power that makes for salvation" seems to denote more of a theological axiom required by his system than a compelling reality. "Power *that* . . . " instead of mere "power" is unnecessary reification. It would be better yet to use the concept of energy or life-energy, as Kaplan does in the following statement, in which he exhibits a fine sense of the numinous. "[Man's ability to triumph over evil] is spiritual and serves as a means of insight into the nature of the universal life compared with which our life is but an insignificant and passing moment." Kaplan believed that there exists a large reservoir of life-giving energy that we can tap into if we are sufficiently motivated. In the same passage he goes on to say, "calling upon Him to help us is a means of calling in to actuality whatever portion of that power is dormant within us."[13]

Kaplan's grand project, fully spelled out in his *Judaism as a Civilization*, can be described as a translation from one set of concepts to another. In the present work he uses the term "revaluation" to describe this process. Revaluation directs us to examine a traditional concept carefully to ferret out those elements that are of permanent significance and then to express those concepts in contemporary terms. With a successful revaluation we would express attitudes analogous to the ancients and see implications for our thoughts and behavior parallel to theirs without the necessity of adopting identical ideas.

The essence of Kaplan's theology is understanding that God is neither a being nor a philosophical abstraction. "We have to identify as godhood, or as the divine quality of universal being, all the relationships, tendencies and agencies which in their totality go to make human life worthwhile in the deepest and most abiding sense. The divine is no less real, no less dependable for our personal salvation or self-realization, if we think of it as a quality than if we think of it as an entity or being." This approach or methodology found throughout *The Meaning of God in Modern Jewish Religion* is what we would call today a predicate theology. Predicate theology states that God or divinity must be thought of as divine qualities rather than as a supernatural being. Thus we would speak of mercy or justice as divine and not of a being called God who is merciful or just.[14]

Kaplan the sociologist is more talented than Kaplan the metaphysician.[15] He incisively articulates what it means to believe in God, but becomes vague when it comes to describing what God is. It is tantamount to giving us an equation that delineates god-belief under any circumstances and requires us to fill in the blanks. Thus to believe in God is to believe that "human life is supremely worthwhile" and that "reality is so constituted so as to enable man to achieve salvation."[16] Although he moves beyond the "naive" conception of God as person, all conceptions of God fit his requirements of asserting the worthwhileness of life in the universe.

Salvation is a key term in the present work. Although it is usually associated with Christian theology, the word comes from the Hebrew Scriptures;[17] it is used frequently by the prophets and was employed by Solomon Schechter in explaining the theology of the rabbis.[18] As he does with "God," Kaplan gives us a functional definition of salvation, that is, the definition will fit many interpretations. Salvation is "life abundant," he tells us, whether we are talking about it in this world or the next. If the Sabbath, for example, is a foretaste of the world to come, as the rabbis believed, then it is obviously an embodiment of the concept of salvation.

A careful reading of *The Meaning of God in Modern Jewish Religion* will reveal that Kaplan is asserting much more than the easy equivalence between salvation and personal fulfillment. The Sabbath as a foretaste of the world to come is not about the enlargement of our life projects, but about superseding them. The Sabbath is about overcoming our petty concerns and our self-serving agendas. To truly celebrate the Sabbath, Kaplan insists, is to achieve a higher sense of self or a *neshama yeterah*[19] (literally, "additional soul"), as the tradition would put it. Kaplan teaches that during the Sabbath we are connected to a deeper sense of self, as was suggested to him by Ralph Waldo Emerson in his essay "The Oversoul." Kaplan's citation of Emerson allows us to use the sage of Concord as a commentary, though Emerson preceded him. "We live in succession, in division, in parts and particles. Meantime within man is the soul of the whole; the wise silence; the universal beauty, to which every part and particle is equally related; the eternal One."[20]

The Meaning of God in Modern Jewish Religion helps us to appreciate that Kaplan is not only the sociologist trying to understand how the Jewish people might flourish in the modern world. He is also an outstanding religious personality, following in a long line of charismatic rabbis who have struggled to rescue us from "Microcosmosis. [From] Drowning in the tiny tub of [ourselves]."[21]

Kaplan proceeds to reinterpret the connection between the Sabbath and the creation of the universe. The Sabbath traditionally is considered a "memorial of the creation," *Zeker lema'aseh bereshit*. He transposes the idea of God as creator into the idea of God as the creative life of the universe. We become holy to the extent that we express that creative urge. We *are* the creative life of the universe to the degree that we transcend our self-centeredness. As long as we remain self-absorbed we cannot be creative in any meaningful sense. Thus on the Sabbath we ought to be especially mindful of our creative function. Kaplan would say that the creation of the world is not complete unless the individual fulfills his or her creative function in it.[22]

To be creative is to be concerned with the other. We cannot regenerate ourselves in isolation, and of course everyone has an equal claim to be creative and to live under the conditions that would foster their creativity. Thus a primary function of religion is constant rededication to improving life and eliminating social evils. "Perfecting the world under the Kingdom of the Almighty, must mean the establishment of a social order that combines the maximum of individual self-realization with the maximum of social cooperation."[23] The holidays of Rosh ha-Shanah and Yom Kippur afford the principal opportunity for Jews to rededicate themselves to the process of self-transformation and self-regeneration. Sukkot, when Jews remember the sojourn in the wilderness, hopefully brings them face to face with the limitations of contemporary civilization, according to Kaplan.

The holiday represents a ritual return to an idealized past when the Jewish people were less materialistic and more directly bound to their natural environment.

It is in connection with *Shimini Azeret*, the holiday of solemn assembly, that Kaplan reveals his spiritual sensitivities most clearly. Lest we misunderstood what he has been saying throughout the work, Kaplan insists that "God must not merely be held as an idea; He must be felt as a presence. . . ." The translation into exalted qualities should not mislead us into thinking of God merely as a handmaiden of ethics or of human fulfillment. Kaplan is worth quoting here at length:

> Without the actual awareness of His presence, experienced as beatitude and inner illumination, we are likely to be content with the humanistic interpretation of life. But this interpretation is inadequate, because it fails to express and to foster the feeling that man's ethical aspirations are part of a cosmic urge, by obeying which man makes himself at home in the universe. Without the emotional intuition of an inner harmony between human nature and universal nature, without the conviction, born of the heart rather than the mind, that the world contains all that is necessary for human salvation, the assumptions necessary for ethical living remain cold hypotheses lacking all dynamic power. They are like an engine with all the parts intact and assembled, but lacking the fuel which alone can set it in operation. The dynamic of ethical action is the spirit of worship, the feeling that we are in God and God is in us, the yielding of our persons in voluntary surrender to those larger aims that express for us as much as has been revealed to us of the destiny of the human race. It is only this emotional reaction to life that can make humanity itself mean more to us than a "disease of the agglutinated dust."[24]

In the chapter entitled "God as Felt Presence," Kaplan's thinking to a surprising degree parallels the thinking of

Abraham Joshua Heschel, his colleague at the Jewish Theological Seminary. Prayer, which is so central to Heschel's thought, is profoundly understood by Kaplan the "rational sociologist" when he states that the person in the act of public worship "knows his life to be part of a larger life, a wave of an ocean of being. This is first-hand experience of that larger life which is God."

There is no more fitting way to illustrate Kaplan's religious understanding than through his liturgical abilities—in this case a prayer that he himself composed. In the summer of 1942 Kaplan was at the Jersey Shore editing his new service for the Society for the Advancement of Judaism. The Musaf, or additional service, consisted of a Hebrew section and some English prayers, which would be read in rotation. Kaplan believed that the Musaf should strike a universal theme, while the Shaharit, or morning service, would be more nationalist in tone. In seeking out an appropriate text he returned to Emerson, whom he profoundly admired and decided to take his famous "Address Delivered before the Senior Class in Divinity College, Cambridge, Sunday evening July 15, 1938" and transform it into a prayer. Kaplan intended this prayer to become a standard part of the Musaf service. Though the language here is Emerson, the prayer is Kaplan's.

NEEDED PROPHETS FOR OUR DAY
by
Rabbi Mordecai M. Kaplan
in the name of
Ralph Waldo Emerson

He who makes me aware that I am an infinite soul heartens me.
He who gives me to myself lifts me.
He who shows God in me fortifies me.
He who hides God from me destroys the reason for my being.
The divine prophets, bards and lawgivers are friends of my
    virtue, of my intellect, of my strength.
Noble provocations go out from them, inviting me to resist evil.

But let us not speak of revelations as something long ago given and done.

Only by coming to the God in ourselves can we grow forevermore.

Let us not say that the age of inspiration is past, that the Bible is closed.

Let us learn to believe in the soul of man, and not merely in men departed.

The need was never greater of new revelations than now.

The faith of man has suffered universal decay.

The heart moans, because it is bereaved of consolation and hope and grandeur.

We feel defrauded and disconsolate.

Our religion has become spectral.

It has lost its grasp on the affection of the good and on the fear of the bad.

What greater calamity can befall a nation than the loss of worship?

Then all things go to decay.

Genius leaves the Temple.

Literature becomes frivolous.

Science is cold.

The eye of youth is not lighted by hope of a better world.

Society lives for trifles.

In the soul let redemption be sought.

Let the keepers of religion show us that God is, not was.

That He speaketh, not spoke.

And thus cheer our fainting hearts with new hope and new revelation.

Notes

1. The thesis is written in Kaplan's hand and runs to ninety-five pages. It is entitled "The Ethical System of Henry Sidgwick" and was submitted on February 28, 1902. It can be found in the Rare Book Collection of Columbia University Butler Library.

2. Felix Adler, *The Religion of Duty* (New York: McClure Philips, 1905), 42.

3. Ibid., 35.

4. Ibid., 37.

5. Ibid, 39, 40.

6. Kaplan Journal, August 17, 1905.

7. Matthew Arnold, *Literature and Dogma* (London: MacMillan, 1892) Preface IX.

8. Kaplan Journal, February 24, 1913.

9. Kaplan Journal, March 3, 1913.

10. Judaism as a vital force: Kaplan Journal, January 26, 1914; Judaism as dynamic: *Menorah Journal* I:210.

11. Mordecai Kaplan to Henry Hurwitz, March 17, 1916, Hurwitz Papers, American Jewish Archives.

12. God as the living universe: Kaplan Diary, February 18, 1926. God as transcendent: Kaplan Journal, November 1, 1925.

13. Mordecai M. Kaplan, *The Meaning of Religion*, 93. Unpublished manuscript. Reconstructionist Rabbinical College.

14. Kaplan's work is being republished with a new introduction by Arnold Eisen. See *Judaism as Civilization* (Philadelphia: The Jewish Publication Society, 1994). On the matter of predicate theology, see Harold Schulweis, *Evil and the Morality of God* (Cincinnati: Hebrew Union College Press, 1984).

15. For a more extensive treatment of Kaplan's metaphysics, the reader should consult the following: William Kaufman, "Kaplan's Approach to Metaphysics" and Jacob J. Staub, "Kaplan and Process Theology," in *The American Judaism of Mordecai Kaplan*, ed. Emanuel Goldsmith, Mel Scult, and Robert Seltzer (New York: New York University Press, 1990).

16. Mordecai M. Kaplan, *The Meaning of God in Modern Jewish Religion* (Detroit: Wayne State University Press, 1994) pp. 25, 26.

17. While "Salvation" is a translation of the Hebrew word *Yeshua*, Kaplan in groping for the exact equivalent in the Scriptures uses the term *shalom*—meaning not only peace, but holiness and completeness.

18. Solomon Schechter, *Some Aspects of Rabbinic Theology* (New York: MacMillan Co., 1909); see index under salvation.

19. Kaplan, *The Meaning of God*, p. 60.

20. Kaplan cites Emerson's essay "The Oversoul" in *The Meaning of God* p. 60. Emerson's essay is reprinted in many editions. The most authoritative is perhaps *The Essays of Ralph Waldo Emerson—Text Established by Alfred R. Ferguson and Jean Ferguson Carr*, (Cambridge: The Belknap Press of Harvard University Press, 1979). Our citation is found on page 160.

21. Philip Roth, *Operation Shylock—A Confession* (New York: Simon & Schuster, 1993).

22. I have taken the liberty of paraphrasing Kaplan's statement on page 79 of *The Meaning of God*.

23. Ibid., p. 111.

24. *The Meaning of God*, pp. 244–45.

FOREWORD TO THE
1962 EDITION

AT FIRST BLUSH it might appear that any book written in
1936 would be hopelessly out of date in 1962. For, during this
fateful period, a second World War was fought, the first atomic
explosion occurred, the United Nations came into being and
the Cold War began. As for the Jewish People, six millions
were done to death in the Nazi extermination camps, and the
State of Israel was established.

Nevertheless, the reader of *The Meaning of God in Modern
Jewish Religion* will quickly discern that, if anything, Mordecai Kaplan's major work on Jewish religion is more relevant
today than it was when it first appeared. A quarter of a century ago, he found it necessary to plead for a scientific approach to religion, for the transformation of it from a system
of other-worldly salvation to one of this-worldly fulfillment,
for the assumption by religion of its central and sacred duty to
"release the powers of man and enable him to realize the
potentialities of ethical personality." In 1962 that appeal must
be articulated all the more strongly because, in the intervening
years a "religious revival" occurred which, in a sense, turned
back the clock of spiritual progress and invited men to accept
as virtually inevitable the evils of this world, and the impotence of a sin-ridden humanity to eliminate those evils. It bade
man throw himself upon the mysterious grace of a transcendent
God, to turn his eyes upward, away from the arena of human
struggle and to seek fulfillment in communion with the ineffable. The Orthodoxy of tradition was thus replaced by a neo-
Orthodoxy, the old doctrines were clothed in modern dress,
utilizing the vocabulary of the most recent scientific thought
but retaining the substance of supernaturalism.

The Jewish Reconstructionist movement, of which Dr. Kaplan is the founder, has devoted itself for the past twenty-five years to advocating a new approach to religion in general, and to Jewish religion in particular, designed to reinterpret the idea of God in such a way as to render it spiritually exalting, intellectually acceptable and ethically potent. Through *The Reconstructionist* magazine, and the Reconstructionist Press, Dr. Kaplan and his associates have sought to present the implications of this basic approach in books, pamphlets and articles. *The Future of the American Jew, Judaism Without Supernaturalism,* and *The Greater Judaism in the Making* are the titles of some of Dr. Kaplan's works which appeared after 1936. *Questions Jews Ask* appeared recently in a paper-back edition.

This new printing of *The Meaning of God in Modern Jewish Religion,* it is hoped, will introduce the reader, therefore, not only to Dr. Kaplan's brilliant interpretation of the Sabbath and Holidays but also to the total philosophy and program of Reconstructionism, the movement which is rapidly winning adherents on the American scene among those who are searching for a vital, meaningful and modern religious orientation.

IRA EISENSTEIN
President, Jewish
Reconstructionist Foundation

PREFACE

IRRELIGION among Jews is only one phase of Jewish maladjustment, and therefore cannot be treated apart from the whole of Jewish life, which is nowadays in an unhealthy state. In *Judaism as a Civilization* and in *Judaism in Transition,* I have attempted to formulate the organic and dynamic view of Jewish life, which is basic to a proper understanding of what must be done to set right anything that has gone wrong with that life. It was therefore inevitable that I should there discuss the place of religion in any civilization whatever, and particularly in the Jewish civilization. Of the conclusions there arrived at, those which underlie the thoughts developed in this book are the following:

1. Religion is a natural social process which arises from man's intrinsic need of salvation or self-fulfillment.

2. The need of self-fulfillment presupposes that reality is so patterned as to contain the means of satisfying it. This pattern of reality man has gropingly sought to envisage in his numerous, and often most absurd, conceptions of God.

3. Every civilization identifies the most important elements of its life as *sancta,* i.e., as media through which its people can achieve salvation, or self-fulfillment.

4. It is scientifically incorrect to say that there is a specifically Jewish conception of God. The correct way of stating the relation of the Jews to their religion is that there is a specifically Jewish application of the God idea. That application consists in associating the belief in God, which is determined by the general cultural and social level, with the *sancta* which belong to the Jewish tradition.

5. The Jewish religion has passed through three distinct

stages, and will enter a new and fourth stage in its career, if it will survive the present crisis.

6. To survive the present crisis, the Jewish religion will have to transform itself from an other-worldly religion, offering to conduct the individual to life eternal through the agency of the traditional Torah which is regarded as having been supernaturally revealed, into a religion which can help Jews attain this-worldly salvation. It will have to accept without reservation the validity of the scientific rather than the authoritative approach to reality, and make its objective the achievement of such conditions on earth as will release the creative powers of man and enable him to realize the potentialities of ethical personality.

What are the specific terms in which the Jewish religion must address itself to the modern Jew? What is the nature of this-worldly salvation to which the Jewish religion will have to relate its conception of God? Through which of its principal institutions can it best convey what God should mean to us? These are the questions which I have tried to answer in this book, in the belief that if they can be adequately answered, Jewish life would be rid of one of the main obstacles to its recovery.

I want to acknowledge my indebtedness to The Society for the Advancement of Judaism for having granted me the freedom of its pulpit, where during the last fifteen years I was stimulated to expound the ideas in this book. I also want to express my thanks to Rabbi Eugene Kohn for having recorded my discussions of some of the material which I had only in outline form, and for having thus facilitated my getting it ready for publication.

M. M. K.

December, 1936.

THE MEANING OF GOD IN MODERN
JEWISH RELIGION

I

INTRODUCTION: HOW TO REINTERPRET THE GOD IDEA IN THE JEWISH RELIGION

I

How to maintain the continuity of the Jewish religion in a changing world

TRADITIONAL Jewish religion belongs to an altogether different universe of discourse from that of the modern man. The ancients took for granted that the cosmos was maintained and governed not by forces which inhere in its very substance, but by a personal will which differed from the human will in being all-mighty and all-perfect. The will of God was conceived as operating in the world through the medium of invisible beings—angels, demons, satans and other incorporeal spirits.[1] In this mental image of the cosmos, heaven was pictured as an actual part of space reserved for the Godhead and His ministering angels.[2] Man's measurement of time by years, months and days was regarded as marking changes which were of significance to the whole of creation. Man's conduct was deemed so important that it was regarded as influencing the behavior of the physical elements of the universe. The Torah was taken to be literally the word of God. To obey its ordinances meant to earn life

[1] See Articles on "Angelology" and "Demonology" in *The Jewish Encyclopedia.*
[2] "On the whole, the old Rabbinic way of regarding Deity may fairly be described as at once childish and childlike." Solomon Schechter: *Studies in Judaism, Third Series,* 1924, 155.

eternal; to disobey them was to court suffering and extinction. The goal of life, that of "basking in God's presence,"
was assumed to be achievable only in the hereafter. The lack
of visible evidences of God's presence in this world was
regarded as part of this world's inherent imperfection and
as proof of the ultimate transformation of this world into
the world to come.

There are many who assume that religious truth differs
from the truth about the material world in being absolute
and immutable. Religious teaching, they maintain, must
belong to the eternal verities, otherwise it is delusion. According to them, no change in circumstances or in our pattern of thinking should affect a religious tradition. It is
futile to argue with those who subscribe to these assumptions; the very trend of all modern thinking is to repudiate
them as false. With our tendency to oppose the division of
truth into separate compartments and to insist that all our
ideas be mutually consistent and integrated, we cannot help
demanding of religion that it be organic with the rest of our
life and inherently relevant to it. Since the rest of human
life changes, religion must change with it. The religion of
one age cannot be transferred whole into a subsequent age
without being frozen into inertness. If we find that a religion manages to retain its vitality in a new age, we may be
sure that it has undergone transformation. If its teachings
and practices continue to have meaning long after the conditions of life and thought under which they arose have
changed, it is because that meaning is not the same they had
originally.

Even the technique for revitalizing the spiritual values of
the past is not the same in one age as it is in another. We
need a new technique for our day; neither the one employed
by the *Tannaim* and *Amoraim,* nor the one employed by the
Hellenist allegorists or the medieval theologians, will answer
our purpose. In the past, the process by which the continuity

of Jewish life and thought was maintained was an unconscious one. Before historic research or before any of the social sciences was born, men lacked the historic perspective which might have made them aware of the discrepancy between the original meaning of a sacred text or a ritual practice and their understanding of it, however unwarranted such understanding actually was. They were not troubled in the least by scruples about anachronism, and were therefore not inhibited from reading their own needs, beliefs and ideals into the religious traditions which had come down to them. We, on the other hand, must seek to maintain the continuity of the Jewish religion by a method which is in keeping with the modern historical sense, and which takes into account our repugnance to anachronisms. The method which the ancients employed may be termed *"transvaluation"*; the method we must employ may be termed *"revaluation."*

Transvaluation [*] consists in ascribing meanings to the traditional content of a religion or social heritage, which could neither have been contemplated nor implied by the authors of that content. The Jewish religious tradition often underwent this kind of transvaluation. The teachers and sages of a later period did not hesitate to read their own beliefs and aspirations into the writings of the teachers and sages of an earlier period. Both the sense of national continuity and the faith in the divine origin of the religious tradition made, transvaluation seem perfectly plausible. Practically any rabbinic rendering of a scriptural text reveals considerable disparity from the literal meaning of that text. To the *Tannaim* and *Amoraim* there was scarcely a verse in

---

[*] The term is here used in a different sense from that in which it is used in translations of Nietzsche's writings as the equivalent of "Umwerthung aller Werthe." Under the term "Umwerthung" Nietzsche advocated the deliberate overturn of traditional values and the adoption of other values in their place. The term "transvaluation" is needed to describe the practice which prevailed in the past, when men were in the habit of introducing radically new values under the guise of ancient tradition.

the Bible that retained merely its original significance.   Whole
mountains of teachings, to use a rabbinic figure, hang by a
hair to the text of the Bible. In ancient times the continuity
of the Jewish religion was attained by means of this process
of transvaluation. This is how the Jewish religion developed
from the henotheism, which it was during the First Commonwealth, into a religion based on a monotheistic and
universal conception of God; this is also how later it transformed itself from the theocratic religion which it was during the Second Commonwealth into a religion based on
otherworldliness.[*]

The full force of the foregoing statement can be made
evident only with the aid of a detailed examination of the
original sources of Jewish tradition. A few random illustrations, however, are necessary to make that statement
clear. In Exodus 20:21, we read the following: "An altar of
earth thou shalt make unto Me, and shalt sacrifice thereon
thy burnt-offerings and thy peace-offerings, thy sheep and
thine oxen; in every place where I cause My name to be
mentioned, I will come unto thee and bless thee." It is
apparent that this verse belongs to the legislation of the pre-
prophetic era when local sanctuaries were still legitimate.
Yet during the Second Commonwealth, this verse was undoubtedly interpreted in such a way as to negate the very
permission of local sanctuaries, which it granted. This is
transvaluation. Or, to take as an example an ancient narrative. The story of Jacob's wrestling, as told in the book of
Genesis, still has something of the primitive flavor; the mysterious being with whom Jacob wrestles is a god, an *elohim*,
perhaps YHWH Himself. But already to Hosea an *elohim*
is not a god, but an angel.[*] This transvaluation was made

---

[*] The Babylonian *Amora* Rav Kahana stated (*Shabbat* 63a) that he had
reached the age of eighteen and had studied all the six Orders of the Mishnah, without knowing that a biblical text retained its literal significance.
[*] This also explains how the Jewish religion could be transformed into
the Christian religion, as is evident from the kind of interpretation given
in the New Testament to texts in the Old Testament. *Cf.* The Acts 18:28.
[*] Hosea 12:4, 5.

necessary by the monotheistic and exalted conception that Hosea had of YHWH.

Coming to the rabbinic rendering of Scriptures, we are familiar with the interpretation of the law that demands eye for eye [7] as referring to monetary compensation.[8] This transvaluation was necessitated, on the one hand, by the change in moral standards, and, on the other hand, by the desire to retain the authoritative character of the traditional law. All those laws which have as their basis the principle of *gezerah shavah,* or inference from a similarity of phrases, are necessarily such as have no intrinsic connection with the literal meaning of the text, and therefore illustrate the process of transvaluation. The homiletic interpretations, or haggadic *midrashim,* are practically all of the same character. To take but one example, the fact that the story of creation begins with the letter *bet* is made the basis of a lesson. The *bet* is closed on three sides and open on the forward side. This, says a Palestinian *Amora,*[9] is a warning to man not to pry into the mysteries of creation but to limit his interest in the knowledge of what God would have him do. Surely, no such warning could have been contemplated or implied by the author of the first verse in the Torah. Resorting to the principle of inference from a similarity of phrases, another Palestinian *Amora* [10] reads into the verse, "And the Lord commanded the man, saying: 'Of every tree of the garden thou mayest freely eat,' " [11] the fact that God gave to Adam the six basic laws of human society.

The process of transvaluation is even more conspicuously illustrated by the work of the allegorists. The very term allegory, as its etymology indicates, suggests assigning to a statement a meaning other than that which its words convey. The lengths to which Philo goes seem absurd, as when, for example, he makes the four rivers in the story of the Garden of Eden symbolic of the four species of virtue which flow

---

[7] Exod. 21:24.
[8] *Cf. Mekilta,* Tractate *Nezikin.*
[9] Gen. *R.* I, 10.
[10] Gen. *R.* XVI, 6.
[11] Gen. 2:16.

from the genus virtue, *Pheison* is prudence, *Evilat* is graciousness, *Geon* is courage, and *Tigris* is self-mastery.[11] But it may be said that Philo stands outside the Jewish tradition. Yet when we turn to the *Akedat Yizhak* by Isaac Arama (1420–1494), we encounter the very same kind of allegorical interpretation; and the *Akedat Yizhak* served as the classic of traditional Jewish preaching down to our own day. Thus did the method of transvaluation function in the past as a means of giving to Jewish religion the element of continuity.

But the method of transvaluation cannot do that for the modern Jew. The very use of it implies that those who resort to it are themselves unaware that they are adjusting or reconstructing tradition to meet the needs of their own day. This resource, however, is no longer possible. The transition from traditional Judaism to the Judaism of the future can be effected only in the glaring light of complete awareness of the change involved. The problem of maintaining the continuity of the Jewish religion can be solved only in one way, and that is by being convinced that the continuity is genuine. Such conviction is compatible only with the certainty that whatever ancient meanings or values we choose to conserve and develop are read out of, and not into, the traditional teachings or practices. For that reason we have to avoid transvaluation and resort to revaluation.

Revaluation consists in disengaging from the traditional content those elements in it which answer permanent postulates of human nature, and in integrating them into our own ideology. When we revaluate, we analyze or break up the traditional values into their implications, and single out for acceptance those implications which can help us meet our own moral and spiritual needs; the rest may be relegated to archeology. It is highly essential that we acquire the ability of getting at the really significant implications. They need

[11] *Cf. Philo* (trans. by F. H. Colson and G. H. Whitaker), Vol. I, 187–189.

not necessarily be such as the ancients themselves would have been able to articulate,[18] but they should have psychological kinship with what the ancients did articulate. One advantage we surely have over those who lived in the remote past, when most of our religious teachings and practices took form; we are the heirs of all the experiences of the generations between them and ourselves. With the aid of these experiences, we should be able to unfold what is implied in the traditional teachings and practices.

To revaluate a religious idea or institution of a past age, one must, first of all, understand it in the light of the total situation of which it was a part. One must enter imaginatively into the thought-world of its authors, and try to grasp what it meant to them in the light of their experience and world-outlook. Then one should take into account the changes which have since taken place, and how they affect the validity of the idea or value of the institution under consideration. It may be that these changes have made the original idea or institution obsolete. But it is more likely that some modification of the original idea will suggest itself that might be related to the new situation and world-outlook in a way similar to that in which the original thought related itself to what was then the situation and world-outlook. As in mathematics any change in one term of an equation implies a corresponding change in the other, if the equation is to remain valid, so in interpreting any affirmation of relationship between two concepts any change in the one implies a change in the other.

When we say, for example, "God is a righteous judge," any change in our conception of the function and character of a righteous judge must be reflected in a corresponding

---

[18] "The religious side of Plato's thought," says Gilbert Murray, "was not revealed in its full power till the time of Plotinus in the third century A.D.; that of Aristotle, one might say without undue paradox, not till its exposition by Aquinas in the thirteenth." (*Five Stages of Greek Religion*, N. Y., 1925, 17.)

change in our conception of God, if the proposition is to remain valid. Thus in an age when a righteous judge is conceived as one who "makes the punishment fit the crime," God will be conceived, in His attribute of justice, as punishing the wicked and rewarding the righteous. If life on earth gives no evidence of such reward and punishment, faith in God's justice will create a heaven and a hell of the imagination. But in an age which has come to recognize that factors of heredity and environment so condition the behavior of the individual that no crime and no virtuous deed can be traced to his exclusive responsibility, the true judge ceases to be one who metes out measure for measure. He is conceived instead as one who, within the limits of the authority vested in him, so administers the law that all the conflicting claims of men that come before him are adjusted on the basis of the equal right of every one to self-realization. Such a view of the function of the judge makes faith in God as the true judge identical with faith in Him as the Power in the world that makes for self-realization. Reward and punishment become irrelevant, and heaven and hell drop out of the picture.

A law or institution which has become obsolete through a changed social situation may be given significance, if we realize that the fact of its having become obsolete does not necessarily mean that the needs which gave rise to it have ceased to exist. By substituting the modern psychological equivalent for that which has become obsolete, its implications may be made plain. If we take idolatry in its literal sense, the denunciation of it or the prayer for its eradication (*'al ken nekaveh*) can have only historic interest. But may we not treat as idolatry any form of worship directed to a god who is conceived in terms that no longer satisfy the deepest spiritual insights of the age? So conceived, who will deny its existence today, or the obligation to extirpate it? Under such methods of interpretative analysis, religious traditions yield significant values which have hitherto been dormant. It is through these implied values that the Jewish religion can be revitalized, and its identity maintained.

The Jewish religious content which is in need of being subjected to the process of revaluation may be divided into three distinct layers. The first layer consists of the greater part of the material recorded in the Bible. It reflects the formative period, or the first stage, of the Jewish religion. To be recognized, it has to be retrieved through the scientific study of the Bible. The second layer which reflects the religious development of the Jews during the Second Commonwealth to about the beginning of the common era is, in part, also found in the Bible, but, on the whole, is contained in the Jewish literature later described as "extraneous books." The third layer consists of the rabbinic and theological writings which cover the period of about two thousand years preceding the modern era. The last two layers would never have been produced out of the first, were it not for the process of transvaluation. Yet they are representative of the Jewish spirit in their own right. Though they are not, as the ancients believed, part of the pristine revelation to Israel, they are, nonetheless, the creation of the Jewish spirit, and must therefore function in any Jewish life in which that spirit is to be continued. The only way, however, in which the second and third layers of the Jewish religious tradition can be made to function in our day is by our *revaluating*, not by our transvaluating, their content.

2

Refusal to recognize the chasm between the traditional and the modern world-view responsible for ambiguous theology of Conservative Judaism

To carry through the process of revaluation effectively, it is necessary to reckon frankly and whole-heartedly with

the modern man's orientation to life. The chasm that separates the religious outlook of Jewish tradition from the one
which is in keeping with modern thought is not at all un-
bridgeable. But *to construct a firm and wide-gauged bridge
between the past and the present, nothing should be done to
underestimate the distance that separates them.* There is a
tendency in certain circles to blur the sharp outlines of the
traditional ideology by surrounding it with a fog of words.
This is probably motivated by the desire to prove that there
is no need for emphasizing the fact that the Jewish religion
is undergoing a radical change. This has given rise to a kind
of hybrid theology which would not be recognized by the
ancient authorities as true, nor by cultivated men and women
of the present as answering their needs. Its sterility is
responsible for its failure to elicit stimulating thought and
intelligent guidance from the teacher, inspiring ritual from
the poet, and enthusiasm in living a Jewish life from the
men and women of our people.

The following passage from Morris Joseph's *Judaism as
Creed and Life* may serve to illustrate the way vague language is used by this type of theology in the hope that it
may, at the same time, mean modernism to the modernist
and traditionalism to the traditionalist:

"The Bible is the great source of our knowledge of Religion, as Israel has conceived it. To its pages we must
chiefly turn in order to know what we ought to believe and
how we ought to live as Israelites." [14]

It is easy to recognize the phrases in this brief passage,
which are meant to serve as sops to the modernist conscience.
To speak of the Bible as "the source of our knowledge of
Religion" rather than as the authentic revelation of God to
Israel is meant to satisfy the historical spirit of the age. It
tries, by innuendo, to shift the basis of the Bible's authority
from a supernatural sanction to a natural, institutional one

[14] Joseph, Morris: *Judaism as Creed and Life,* London, 1903, 14.

by basing it on the part that the Bible has historically played in Jewish life and thought as undeniably the source of Jewish law and doctrine. Again, the qualifying expression "as Israel conceived it" is intended to hint, what the author lacks the courage positively to affirm, that other alternative conceptions of religion are possible which may be just as valid. Then the author, in timid retreat, immediately undoes all the effect that these indefinite phrases may have produced in suggesting the compatibility of tradition with modernism, by saying that we turn chiefly to the Bible "in order to know what we ought to believe and how we ought to live as Israelites." The very notion that any text written hundreds of years ago, at a time when the social situation was radically different from what it is today, can give us clear and valuable guidance in deciding, ethically, issues that did not arise until recent times is utterly antagonistic to the modern evolutionary outlook. No matter how we may reverence the authors of the biblical books as teachers of justice and righteousness, we cannot today determine what is right in the ethical problems that come before us by reference to a biblical text.

But if the author's method of using the biblical text is unsatisfactory to modern-minded people, it is no more satisfactory to the genuine traditionalist. To speak of the Bible as "the source of Religion, as Israel has conceived it" rather than as the word of God, is from the viewpoint of Orthodoxy an offensive understatement. It implies that the authority of the Bible is validated by its being a source of religion, i.e., of our "ideas about God and our responsibility to Him," to use the author's own definition, ideas which can also be derived by reasoning from general experience. But to the genuine traditionalist it is precisely his feeling of the inadequacy of human reason to achieve salvation that makes him seek authority in the Bible. For him the Bible is valid not because it coincides with reason, but because of its super-

natural origin. The law prohibiting the wearing of a gar-
ment of mixed wool and linen rests for him on the same
authority as the law forbidding murder. He does not regard
it as a mere symbol or ceremony. Until the time of Maimonides, no comprehensive attempt had been made to interpret the reasons for all the ritual laws of the Torah, and
even he did not regard awareness of the reason as essential
to Jewish religious living, but did regard obedience as essential. The Mishnah voices definite objection to interpreting
the reason for the prohibition of taking the mother-bird with
the young.[16] "If one says: 'Thy mercies extend over the
bird's nest' . . . he is to be silenced." [16]

Such reasoning as is represented in the quotation from
Judaism as Creed and Life is not limited to the particular
book from which it is taken, nor to the writings of its
author. It is quite characteristic of the apologists for tradition in our day. We cite two more quotations from other
works of more recent date to illustrate our point. The first
of these is taken from the introduction to Isidore Epstein's
Judaism of Tradition.

"And what is revelation? It is the conception of God
revealing Himself in no uncertain manner to prophet and
people in order to help man along in his quest of the Divine.
. . . I have advisedly said 'God revealing Himself in no
uncertain manner.' For it is this sense of *sureness,* this sense
of overmastering certainty which grips the spirit that distinguishes the knowledge that comes by means of Revelation
from all other branches of knowledge, like art, literature,
to which the term revelation or inspiration is loosely
applied." [17]

The modernist must take exception in the above passage
to the illogicality of using the word "revealing" to define the
noun "revelation," and to the folly of making sureness a

[16] Deut. 22 :6, 7.   [16] *Mishnah Berakot* V, 3.
[17] Epstein, Isidore: *Judaism of Tradition,* London, 1931, 20.

criterion of truth, since stupidity is almost invariably sure of its own wisdom. On the other hand, the traditionalist will take exception to making the only distinction between what we loosely call inspiration in literature and art and what tradition means by revelation lie in the *certainty* with which the prophet or lawgiver apprehended the truth which he claimed to have been revealed to him.

Another illustration may be taken from Maurice H. Farbridge's *Judaism and the Modern Mind*. The author undertakes to resolve the difficulties encountered by the modern mind, in that the ethical standards of the Law are not always on as high a plane as the best ethical standards of modern times. This is his apologia:

"Historical revelation cannot at a stroke annihilate existing traditions and create a world of new ones. Revelation can only work in accordance with the laws of historical development . . . it has to content itself with bearing patiently with considerable evil, and replace the old whilst the good which it implants has time to grow and develop." [18]

The modernist on reading this passage wants to know why, if revelation can work only in accordance with the laws of historical development, it is at all needed, why the laws of historical development themselves cannot suffice as evidence of God's work in human history. The traditionalist, on the other hand, would probably feel it to be damning with faint praise to pronounce the Torah only as true as the limited understanding of those to whom it was communicated permitted it to be.

Are any more quotations necessary? Can we not recognize in the above statements the sort of traditional apologetics that we hear repeatedly from the pulpits by preachers who try to be modern, but whose thinking is fettered by

[18] Farbridge, Maurice H.: *Judaism and the Modern Mind*, N. Y., 1927, 100–101.

traditional attitudes? Sentimentally attached to the old and distrustful of the new, they try to persuade themselves and others that no radical change has taken place in human thinking, and that none is necessary in the Jewish religion. But if we are to do justice to the problem which confronts the Jewish religion, we must not minimize the revolutionary character of the changes in the very assumptions on which men have come to base their world-outlook.

3

Reformist theology irrelevant because of its failure to realize that religion must express itself in the context of a civilization

Those familiar with the Reformist theology, especially as developed by the late Kaufmann Kohler in his *Jewish Theology*, will find that to a large extent it answers the two requirements of Jewish religion for our day. First, it realizes the wide gap that divides the world-outlook of traditional religion from the one with which modern religion must reckon, and secondly, it has formulated some highly valuable spiritual and ethical truths, though many of these truths are themselves in need of being reformulated to fit into the framework of latter-day thought. But there is something radically wrong with the Reformist theology. It starts with a false premise as to what it is that makes one a Jew. It assumes that what unites Jews to one another, and differentiates them from the rest of mankind, is their religion. Thus conceived, the Jewish religion comes to be a series of general or universal teachings about God and man, apart from the specific social realities of the Jewish people. Conceiving the Jewish religion as the soul of the Jewish people, Kohler makes the mistake of hypostatizing the soul and treating it as an entity independently of the body. This error he, in common with all Reformist theorists, falls into,

because like them he insists upon denying the fact that what
unites Jews to one another is their nationhood, and what
differentiates them is a civilization of which religion is only
an element, though undoubtedly the most significant. This
error leads him to regard Judaism and Jewish religion
merely as different names for the same thing, with the consequence that every aspect of Jewish life must justify itself
by its relation to the God idea, and God comes to be a
hypostatized abstraction moving in a vacuum.

Kohler realizes that the philosophical emphasis upon the
unknowability of God leaves one cold. "A divinity void of all
essential qualities," he rightly says, "fails to satisfy the religious soul. Man demands to know what God is—at least,
what God is to him." We wonder how much satisfaction
the religious soul can derive from the answer which Kohler
gives when he says: "God is not merely the supreme Being
but also the supreme Self-consciousness. As man, in spite of
all his limitations and helplessness, still towers high above
his fellow creatures by virtue of his free will and self-conscious action, so God, who knows no bounds to His wisdom
and power, surpasses all beings and forces of the universe,
for He rules over all as the One completely self-conscious
Mind and Will. In both the visible and invisible realms, He
manifests Himself as the absolutely free Personality, moral
and spiritual who allots to everything its existence, form and
purpose. For this reason Scripture calls Him 'the living God
and everlasting King.'

"Judaism, accordingly, teaches us to recognize God, above
all, as revealing Himself in self-conscious activity, as determining all that happens by His absolutely free will, and thus
as showing man how to walk as a free moral agent. In relation to the world, His work or workshop, He is the self-
conscious Master, saying 'I am that which I am'; in relation
to man, who is akin to Him as a self-conscious rational and
moral being, He is the living Fountain of all that knowledge

and spirituality for which men long, and in which alone they may find contentment and bliss." [19]

All this, translated into the poetic language of liturgy, might awaken an emotional response. But one fails to see why the God thus described need necessarily be the God of Judaism. If those words convey any meaning, they do so irrespective of what Judaism has to say. But actually they are merely a rehash, not even warmed over, of medieval verbalism; of a verbalism divorced from facts and realities as known and experienced in everyday life.

What more important function can religion have than to serve as antidote to the harm that the evil in the world might do to our personalities? The least we should expect of any acceptable statement we make about God is that it should bolster up our morale. In the light of this criterion how much value can we attach to the following?

"None of the precious truths of Judaism has become more indispensable than the belief in divine Providence, which we see about us in ever new and striking forms. Man would succumb from fear alone, beholding the dangers about him on every side, were he not sustained by a conviction that there is an all-wise Power who rules the world for a sublime purpose. We know that even in direst distress we are guided by a divine hand that directs everything finally toward the good. Wherever we are, we are protected by God, who watches over the destinies of man as 'does the eagle who hovers over her young and bears them aloft on her pinions.' Each of us is assigned his place in the all-encompassing plan. Such knowledge and such faith as this comprise the greatest comfort and joy which the Jewish religion offers. Both the narratives and the doctrines of Scripture are filled with this idea of Providence working in the history of individuals and nations." [20]

The foregoing reads like an ancient text which is itself

[19] Kohler, Kaufmann: *Jewish Theology*, 73.   [20] *Ibid.*, 167.

in need of interpretation, and poses a series of questions instead of answering them. But the most serious fault with it is that, as stated, one sees no reason why it should be interpreted at all. It is unattached to any institution or situation which is in need of being explained and therefore entirely irrelevant.

The very attempt to abstract Jewish religion from all the other aspects of Jewish life shows a woeful misunderstanding of the vital and organic relationship between religion and the other elements of a civilization. *The civilization of the Jewish people, with its long history and idealized future, has hitherto been the matrix of the ideas and practices by means of which the Jew expressed his relationship to God.* All the components of that civilization, namely language, literature, social norms, folkways and the arts, have always entered into every texture of the Jewish religion. We can no more think of that religion apart from them than we can think of the soul or personality of any human being without reference to his appearance, voice, acts and words.

Reformist theology, by divorcing the element of religion from the secular aspects of the Jewish civilization, has furnished the Jewish secularists a most convincing argument in support of complete secularization of Jewish life. Religion abstracted from the other human interests that express themselves in a civilization becomes irrelevant and pointless, a way of speaking rather than a way of living. From being a medley of anemic platitudes, which no one would ever take the trouble of disputing, to becoming superfluous altogether, is but one step. The secularists, to be sure, commit the same error as the religionists who deprecate all Jewish secular interests, for, like them, they fail to see the organic relationship between the secular and religious aspects of life. The only difference between them is which aspect they choose to identify themselves with. The secularist may take an affirmative attitude toward the survival of the Jewish group, but he fails to realize that group life, which is rooted in the past and which is held together by common purposes and ideals, must have an outlet in specific beliefs, emotions and actions.

If we try to envisage the way religion actually functions when it is not a mummified affair but part of human experience, we realize that in the life of a group there naturally arise conflicts between the desires, purposes and interests of the individuals composing it. These conflicts have to be resolved, and the effort at resolving them gives rise to laws, customs and social habits of the people and to standards of value which these express. These standards, norms and mores require some sanction to validate them. Personal advantage is not enough of a sanction to justify the duty of conforming to them under all circumstances. Resort is had to the God idea, for that idea inherently endorses the rightness of that which we regard as right. This is its chief pragmatic significance.

Likewise every nation develops in its own language a literature that reflects the mind of the group. Certain works of this literature assume a special importance as expressing supremely what the group has felt to be the meaning of its history and the purposes that should inspire its actions. Such books become holy or sacred scriptures, that is, they are ascribed to God, or, let us say, by ascribing them to God their holiness is stressed; for, the pragmatic significance of the God idea is the recognition of certain elements in life as supremely important.

Great personalities arise in crises of a nation's history and render services that seem to make them the embodiment of the nation's will and aspiration. They are then held up as examples for the people to follow in molding their own characters to a pattern in harmony with purposes and aspirations of the group. Such men become the heroes of the nation. To emphasize their heroism, they are described as indebted for their superiority to God, Whose spirit alone enabled them to accomplish great deeds. Thus the God idea plays its part as accounting for human leadership and heroism.

Epoch-making events in the national history which are felt to have meaning for the nation's future are celebrated, and methods are devised to insure that they be not forgotten. As they are recalled year by year and their significance is reinterpreted in accordance with the cumulative experience of the group, there is evolved a ritual which associates their observance with ideals which express the highest aspirations of that group. They thus become holy days, when the people seek communion with God for renewing their faith in those ideals which are associated with the day. Thus the God idea functions to emphasize and validate a people's sense of its historic destiny, and its collective responsibility for achieving the salvation of the individual and of society.

The frustration of many of the desires and purposes of the collective consciousness of the group leads to an imaginative reconstruction of the social order more in harmony with these purposes. Such utopias, as the term implies, exist nowhere and would remain mere idle fancies were it not for the fact that the people recognize in them a manifestation of divine creativity, an insight into life's boundless possibilities. The God idea thus functions to convert what might otherwise have remained an idle fancy into a prophetic vision that assigns objectives to collective effort. The association of prophecy with divination of the future is based on the fact that prophetic insight into future possibilities, combined with the faith that whatever ought to be can be, is a potent force in shaping the future. That faith is definitely implied in the God idea, and can have no other validation.

The sum of all these ways in which the God idea functions pragmatically in the civilization of a people is what we mean by its religion. Apart from all the other aspects of a civilization, religion is nothing. Its very life depends upon them.

It cannot be preserved as a glass-encased exhibit in a museum. But all the secular aspects of a civilization need the sanction of religion. None of them can function vigorously in a civilization that is world-weary, cynical and depressed. Only the tonic faith which is expressed in the intuitive acceptance of the God idea can stimulate them to achieve the utmost of their potentialities.

4

The synthesis of incompatible notions about God a heritage from the past

We cannot expect to understand the nature of God. Who of us even knows the nature of man, or for that matter his own nature? We cannot even predict what we will be doing and thinking ten minutes from now. But we must be able to state definitely what experiences or phenomena we are prepared to identify as manifestations of God, and why we identify them as such.

The fact that the nature of God is beyond our understanding does not mean that we can afford to conceive of Him in terms that are clearly not true in accordance with the highest standards of truth. Our conception of God must be self-consistent and consistent with whatever else we hold to be true. That this conception will not describe Him we know, just as our conception of life does not begin to give us the faintest idea of what life means to the infinite variety of living creatures that inhabit our earth. But we do not plead our inability to understand all that life means as an excuse for making assertions about life which are inconsistent with experience. Just so we must insist that whatever we say or think about God shall be in harmony with all else that we hold to be true. We cannot, for example, believe that God performs miracles, and at the same time believe in the uniformities of natural law demanded by scientific theory.

In our thinking about God we must avoid all those mental habits which issue in logical fallacies. The most common of these is the habit of hypostasis, or assuming the separate identifiable existence of anything for which language has a name. There is a considerable difference, for example, between the way a scientist thinks of gravity and the way most laymen think of it. A scientist regards it as a property or quality of matter, a descriptive term for the way masses of matter behave in relation to one another. The average layman, however, thinks of it as a force, an invisible something that acts upon masses of matter pulling them together. According to both conceptions, gravity is real and must undeniably be reckoned with, but the layman finds it difficult to regard gravity as real without at the same time thinking of it as a thing, an object, a self-existent being or entity.

When we study the historical development of the God idea, we realize to what extent the mental habit of hypostasis (the tendency to treat qualities, attributes, relationships as though they had a separate existence) has been responsible for the contradictions and ambiguities that have discredited the conception of God and driven many to atheism. Before the origin of monotheistic religion, people spoke not of God but of gods. What was then the meaning of the word "god"? A god was a being, mostly non-human, but at times also human, to whom worship was accorded because he was regarded as possessing the power to help men realize their aims and achieve their desires. The existence of other non-human beings was taken for granted. But a "god" was a being that stood in reciprocal relationship with a group like a family, clan, tribe, or nation. That relationship involved, on the part of the god, a claim to worship, and on the part of his worshipers, a claim to protection. Just as in their secular and political life, men were concerned with the question of who should be king, long before they asked themselves what the nature of sovereignty was, and how it should be asserted, so ancient peoples were concerned in their religious life not with the question of *what* God was, but with the question of *who* their God was. Some real or imagined beings were identified as those to whom worship was due; the others were rejected. Such is the background of the verse: "I will take you to me for a people, and I will be to you a God; and ye shall know that I YHWH, am your God who brought you out from under the burdens of the Egyptians." [21]

There can be no question that the *Shema Yisrael*,[22] whatever meaning it may have subsequently acquired, meant originally nothing more than that Israelites should worship YHWH, and YHWH alone, as their God. It contained no implication that the beings whom the other nations worshiped were non-existent, but merely that they were not to be considered as gods, or as entitled to worship. They were not gods; YHWH alone was God. He alone held sway in the heavens and on the earth.[23] Christianity and Mohammedanism similarly in their origin did not think of God generically. They did not ask themselves what God was or meant, but answered the question, "Who is God?" by answering, in the one case, "Jesus is God," and in the other, "Allah is God," Allah being the name of one of the many deities worshiped by the Arabs before the advent of Mohammed. In the Greco-Roman world of classic antiquity, the gods who were worshiped were personifications of forces of nature—the rain, the sun, the sea, the earth, etc.—which were thought of not as natural phenomena, but as beings whose aspect and behavior the imagination of the Greeks conceived in anthropomorphic terms.

It was only with the development of the philosophic movement among the Greeks that men began to think generically about God. The Greek philosophers were supremely interested in the formulation of generic concepts, in such ques-

[21] Exod. 6:7.   [22] Deut. 6:4.   [23] *Ibid.*, 4:39; *Cf.* Ps. 97:7, 9.

tions as: What is an animal? How is it that dogs, horses and cats can all differ from one another and yet be animals? What constitutes the essence "animal" in the dog, and what is merely the "dog" in him? Similarly, they were interested in problems of human psychology, in an analysis of human nature. They did not look upon men merely as individuals, but were interested in the question of what qualities are common to the genus man, and distinguish it from, let us say, the genus beast. This same interest in the generic led them to the question: what constitutes the godhood of the gods? They were less interested in Zeus as Zeus, or in Athene as Athene, than they were interested in the *god* in Zeus and in Athene. One finds them frequently, therefore, speaking of God in the singular, and it would be easy to imagine that they were really at heart monotheists like the Jews. But that would be an erroneous conclusion. When we say, "Man is a biped," we do not mean that there is only one man; and when a Greek philosopher said God was perfect, he was talking in a similar generic sense, using the term "God" to express a concept of godhood in all its manifestations. There is no reason to believe that Aristotle did not worship the same individual gods as his fellow Greeks, or that he even doubted their existence.

In Alexandria, during the second and first centuries before the common era, the Jewish religion came into contact with Greek philosophy. It was then that a synthesis took place. The idea of God, conceived individually as a superhuman Person to whom worship is exclusively due, was combined with the idea of God, conceived generically, as a concept embracing all those qualities and attributes that make men regard certain objects and persons as divine. The religious philosophers effected this synthesis by the process of hypostasis. God became the personification of the generic concept of godhood, and YHWH, the God of Israel, was assumed to have always possessed as personal traits the perfection of whatever qualities were associated with deity: power, wisdom, love, justice, sovereignty. These qualities in their perfection made God eternal, omnipotent, omnipresent, omniscient. At the same time the synthesis with the individual God of tradition endowed Him with such human attributes as loving, rewarding, punishing, being influenced by prayer and praise and a host of other personal qualities which, when analyzed, are meaningless as applied to an eternal and infinite being. These contradictions emerge again and again in the writings of the religious philosophers from Philo down to the theologians of our day.

Some appreciation of the dilemma in which the religious philosophers found themselves as a result of this synthesis of a personal God with a generic God shows itself in the difficulty they experienced in interpreting the simple declaration of Jewish faith, "YHWH is our God, YHWH alone." If YHWH is to be considered a superhuman Being, its meaning is clearly that only this one superhuman Being is God and should be worshiped. But if God is to be thought of generically, there is no point to saying that He is one, for any general concept, such as man, beast, bird, triangle, is not subject to number. They are, therefore, at great pains to tell us that not only is God one, but He is one with a unique unity, a unity that is not a term of a numerical series nor composed of fractional parts. But, obviously, if the term "unity" when applied to God has an utterly different meaning from that which it has when applied to anything else, the affirmation of God's unity conveys no meaning to us at all. It is as if one were to say of a certain object that it is red, but not red in the sense of the color red, but in a totally different sense of the term, that applies to that object alone.

Such is the confusion into which we are led by the tendency to combine two incompatible ways of thinking about God, one, that of naïve personification, the other, that of philosophical abstraction. If we want to get at the reality behind genuine religious experience, we must steer clear of both these ways of thinking. We have to identify as godhood, or as the divine quality of universal being, all the relationships, tendencies and agencies which in their totality go to make human life worthwhile in the deepest and most abiding sense. The divine is no less real, no less dependable for our personal salvation or self-realization, if we think of it as a quality than if we think of it as an entity or being. Human personality may serve as an illustration. It is no less real, if we think of it in psychological terms, as a system of behavior patterns in which the human organism reacts to the world, than if we think of it as a sort of invisible spiritual man that inhabits the visible physical man and determines his behavior.

5

What belief in God means, from the modern point of view

To the modern man, religion can no longer be a matter of entering into relationship with the supernatural. The only kind of religion that can help him live and get the most out of life will be the one which will teach him to identify as divine or holy whatever in human nature or in the world about him enhances human life. Men must no longer look upon God as a reservoir of magic power to be tapped whenever they are aware of their physical limitations. It was natural for primitive man to do so. He sought contact with his god or gods primarily because he felt the need of supplementing his own limited powers with the external forces which he believed were controlled by the gods. He sought their aid for the fertility of his fields, the increase of his cattle, and the conquest of his foes. In time, however—and in the case of the Jewish people early in their history—men began to seek communion with God not so much as the source of power but rather as the source of goodness, and to invoke His aid to acquire control not over the external forces but over those of human nature in the individual and in the mass. With the development of scientific techniques for the utilization of natural forces, and with the revision of our world-outlook in a way that invalidates the distinction between natural and supernatural, it is only as the sum of everything in the world that renders life significant and worthwhile—or holy—that God can be worshiped by man. Godhood can have no meaning for us apart from human ideals of truth, goodness, and beauty, interwoven in a pattern of holiness.

To believe in God is to reckon with life's creative forces, tendencies and potentialities as forming an organic unity, and as giving meaning to life by virtue of that unity. Life has meaning for us when it elicits from us the best of which we are capable, and fortifies us against the worst that may befall us. Such meaning reveals itself in our experiences of unity, of creativity, and of worth. In the experience of that unity which enables us to perceive the interaction and interdependence of all phases and elements of being, it is mainly our cognitive powers that come into play; in the experience of creativity which we sense at first hand, whenever we make the slightest contribution to the sum of those forces that give meaning to life, our conative powers come to the fore; and in the experience of worth, in the realization of meaning, in contrast to chaos and meaninglessness, our emotional powers find expression. Thus in the very process of human self-fulfillment, in the very striving after the achievement of salvation, we identify ourselves with God, and God functions in us. This fact should lead to the conclusion that when we believe in God, we believe that reality—the world of inner and outer being, the world of society and of nature—is so constituted as to enable man to achieve salvation. If human beings are frustrated, it is not because there is no God, but because they do not deal with reality as it is actually and potentially constituted.

Our intuition of God is the absolute negation and antithesis of all evaluations of human life which assume that consciousness is a disease, civilization a transient sickness, and all our efforts to lift ourselves above the brute only a vain pretense. It is the triumphant exorcism of Bertrand Russell's dismal credo: "Brief and powerless is man's life. On him and all his race the slow sure doom falls pitiless and dark." It is the affirmation that human life is supremely worthwhile and significant, and deserves our giving to it the best that is in us, despite, or perhaps because of, the very evil that mars it. This intuition is not merely an intellectual assent. It is the "yea" of our entire personality. "That life is worth living is the most necessary of assumptions," says Santayana, "and were it not assumed, the most impossible of conclusions." The existence of evil, far from silencing that "yea," is the very occasion for articulating it. "The highest type of man," said Felix Adler, "is the one who in *articulo mortis* can bless the universe."

The human mind cannot rest until it finds order in the universe. It is this form-giving trait that is responsible for modern scientific theory. That same need is also operative in formulating a view of the cosmos, which will support the spiritual yearnings of the group and make their faith in the goals and objectives of their group life consistent with the totality of their experience as human beings. Out of this process of thought there arise traditional beliefs as to the origin of the world, man's place in it, his ultimate destiny, the role of one's own particular civilization in the scheme of human history, and all those comprehensive systems of belief that try to bring human experience into a consistent pattern.

But there is one underlying assumption in all these efforts at giving a consistent meaning to life, whether they are expressed in the naïve cosmologies of primitive peoples or in the most sophisticated metaphysical systems of contemporary philosophers, and that is the assumption that life is meaningful. Without faith that the world of nature is a cosmos and not a chaos, that it has intelligible laws which can be unravelled, and that the human reason offers us an instrument capable of unravelling them, no scientific theorizing would be possible. This is another way of saying that science cannot dispense with what Einstein has appropriately named "cosmic religion," the faith that nature is meaningful and hence divine. And just as our inquiry into natural law demands the validation of cosmic religion, so also does our inquiry into moral law and the best way for men to live. It implies the intuition that life inherently yields ethical and spiritual values, that it is holy. The God idea thus expresses itself pragmatically in those fundamental beliefs by which a people tries to work out its life in a consistent pattern and rid itself of those frustrations which result from the distracting confusion of ideals and aims, in a word, beliefs by which it orients itself and the individuals that constitute it to life as a whole.

The purpose of all education and culture is to socialize the individual, to sensitize him to the ills as well as to the goods of life. Yet the more successful we are in accomplishing this purpose, the more unhappiness we lay up for those we educate. "As soon as high consciousness is reached," says A. N. Whitehead, "the enjoyment of existence is entwined with pain, frustration, loss, tragedy." Likewise, the more eager we are to shape human life in accordance with some ideal pattern of justice and cooperation, the more reasons we discover for being dissatisfied with ourselves, with our limitations, and with our environment. If, therefore, culture and social sympathy are not to break our hearts, but to help us retain that sureness of the life-feeling which is our native privilege, they must make room for religious faith which is needed as a tonic to quicken the pulse of our personal existence.

Faith in life's inherent worthwhileness and sanctity is needed to counteract the cynicism that sneers at life and mocks at the very notion of holiness. Against such a cheapening of life's values no social idealism that does not reckon with the cosmos as divine is an adequate remedy. How can a social idealist ask men to deny themselves immediate satisfactions for the sake of future good that they may never see in their lifetime, when he leaves them without any definite conviction that the universe will fulfill the hopes that have inspired their sacrifice, or is even able to fulfill them? If human life does not yield some cosmic meaning, is it not the course of wisdom to pursue a policy of "Eat, drink and make merry, for tomorrow we die"?

Belief in God as here conceived can function in our day exactly as the belief in God has always functioned; it can function as an affirmation that life has value. It implies, as the God idea has always implied, a certain assumption with regard to the nature of reality, the assumption that reality is so constituted as to endorse and guarantee the realization in man of that which is of greatest value to him. If we believe that assumption to be true, for, as has been said, it is an assumption that is not susceptible of proof, we have faith in God. No metaphysical speculation beyond this fundamental assumption that reality assures both the emergence and the realization of human ideals is necessary for the religious life.

6

God not known unless sought after

Once this idea is clear in our minds, the next step is to identify those elements in the life about us, in our social heritage and in ourselves, that possess the quality of Godhood. The purpose in setting forth in concrete ethical and rational terms the meaning of God should be twofold: first, to forestall the denial of the divine aspect of reality, and secondly, to counteract the tendency to exaggerate the significance of God-awareness as such, regardless of the irrationality or the immorality of the conduct which accompanies that awareness. *While the immediacy and the dynamic of God-awareness are, no doubt, indispensable to vital religion, their value is dangerously overstressed by those of a romantic or mystic turn of mind.*

Nothing less than the deliberate refusal to be satisfied with the negation of life's inherent worth is likely to keep our minds in a receptive mood for the belief in God. But being in a receptive mood is not enough. We shall not come to experience the reality of God unless we go in search of Him. To be seekers of God, we have to depend more upon our own thinking and less upon tradition. Instead of acquiescing passively in the traditional belief that there is a God, and then deducing from that belief conclusions which are to be applied to human experience and conduct, we must accustom ourselves to find God in the complexities of our experience and behavior. "Seek ye me and live." [**] To seek God, to inquire after Him, to try to discern His reality is religion in action. *The ardent and strenuous search for God in all that we know and feel and do is the true equivalent of the behest, "Thou shalt love the Lord thy God with all thy heart, with all thy soul and with all thy might."* [**] Only by way of participation in human affairs and strivings are we to seek God.

We seek God, whenever we explore truth, goodness and beauty to their uttermost reaches. We must take care, however, not to treat these objects of our striving as independent of one another, for then we are likely to pursue some partial truth, some mistaken goodness, or some illusory beauty. The pursuit of truth, unwedded to an appreciation of goodness

[**] Amos 5:4.   [**] Deut. 6:5.

and beauty, is likely to issue in the sort of personality that can be absorbed in the scientific investigation of the explosive properties of certain chemicals, wholly indifferent as to whether one's conclusions be made to further war or peace, construction or destruction. The well-meaning fanatics of virtue, who inspired the title of one of Bertrand Russell's essays, "The Evil Good Men Do," are typical of the results of seeking goodness while underestimating its relationship to truth and beauty. Their intentions are good, but their behavior reminds us that "the road to hell is paved with good intentions." The exclusive pursuit of beauty results in the type of decadent estheticism that fiddles while Rome burns. It issues in an art that is for art's sake rather than for life's sake, and that reaches a *reductio ad absurdum* in forms of artistic expression which communicate no meaning to any except the few artists who happen to subscribe to the same set of artistic dogmas, and to be interested in experimenting with the same techniques.

The penalty for the failure to deal with truth, goodness and beauty as organically related to one another is the failure to reach the conviction of life's true worth. The attainment of that conviction is vouchsafed only to those to whom truth, goodness and beauty are but partial phases of life's meaning. Religion has the one word which seeks to express that meaning in all its depth and mystery. That word is "holiness." It is folly to try to eliminate the concept of holiness from our vocabulary. It is the only accurate term for our deepest and most treasured experiences. The moment any situation evokes from us the awareness that we have to do with something to which no other term than "sacred" is adequate, we are on the point of discovering God. In fact, we already sense His reality.

The part to be played by our religious tradition is to bring to our attention the *sancta* through which the God-awareness has been actualized. But we must take care not to adopt the attitude of the philistine who departmentalizes life into the secular and the holy, and who thereby misses the main significance of holiness, which is compatible only with the wholeness of life. The philistinism which associates sanctity only with certain places and occasions and regards all others as secular is, in effect, a reversion to the primitive magical conception of holiness. Certain sites that, for one reason or another, impressed themselves particularly on the imagination of primitive peoples seemed the special haunts of deity; certain times seemed particularly propitious, others unpropitious for approaching him. Those were then pronounced holy. In our logical thinking we reject such notions as superstition, having been taught by our Prophets to associate the holiness of God with the thought that "the whole earth is filled with His glory." But our emotional reactions often revert to the attitude of primitive religion, and we then associate holiness only with persons, places and events which have been sanctified by traditional rituals. If, however, we relate the ideal of holiness to the worthwhileness and sanctity of life as implicit in the God idea, we invest places, persons and events with sacredness only as they contribute to our awareness of the sanctity of life as a whole, only as they symbolize the holiness that is in all things.

Every effort to articulate our sense of life's worthwhileness in ritual and prayer is a means of realizing the godhood manifested in our personal and social experience. The same appreciation of whatever contributes to our joy in living which is voiced in the traditional prayers of praise and thanksgiving still calls for expression. The same hopeful yearning for unrealized good that is voiced in the traditional prayers of petition needs to be articulated, as one of the means toward its ultimate realization. We may have to revise our liturgy to express with greater truth what we sincerely think and feel when we have God in mind, but we cannot dispense with worship. The departure from the traditional idea of God as a self-existent entity necessarily changes the function of prayer, but by no means destroys it. The institution of worship and the resort to prayer did not have to wait for our day to suffer change in their meaning and functioning. From the time that the conception of God as a kind of magnified human being in form or feeling was banned, prayer could not possibly mean what it did in the earlier periods of Jewish religion, when men naïvely believed that God acted directly in answer to any petition that was addressed to Him. Ever since philosophy invaded the field of Jewish religion, it became difficult to pray in the spirit of those who had never been troubled by philosophic scruples. It is unfortunate that medieval Jewish theologians who took such pains to deprecate the naïve idea of God failed to indicate that prayer must undergo changes both in form and meaning to correspond with the more philosophical conception of God that they were urging. But their omission does not alter the fact, first, that any affirmative conception of God must necessarily find expression in prayer, and secondly, that the content of the prayer must correspond with the particular conception of God to which we can whole-heartedly ascribe.

Religious prayer is the utterance of those thoughts that imply either the actual awareness of God, or the desire to attain such awareness. To those who formerly prayed for rain, God was a being who gave or withheld rain as it suited His purpose. There is no room for such prayer in a conception of God in which giving or withholding rain at will does not enter. There will always be need, however, for prayer which voices a yearning for those abilities of mind and body, or for that change of heart and character which would enable us to avail ourselves of such aspects of life as in their totality spell God. By voicing that yearning we take the first step—though only the first step—to its realization. Moreover, there is need for that equivalent of praise of God, which, even more than petition, constituted in the past the principal element of prayer. That equivalent is the affirmation in song, liturgy and symbol of the aspects of life that spell God. Study and work, however, as well as prayer and praise, must express our faith in God, and the whole of life must contribute to *kiddush hashem,* the sanctification of God's name, and to the demonstration of the reality and glory of the divine.

7

The Jewish Sabbath and Festivals as focal points in the context of Jewish life, which can yield a conception of God that is Jewish, modern, and relevant

No creed that means to be vital can afford to ignore the requirement of being relevant to the best in contemporary life and social idealism. Why teach the Prophets' denunciation of the social injustices of their day, if not to inspire us to remedy the glaring injustices of our own social order? Why pray for forgiveness of the sins that troubled our forefathers at the time that the *al het* of the *Yom Kippur* liturgy was written, and not seek atonement for the specific sins that vitiate the social behavior of the modern world? Why teach as part of religion the ancient mythical theories of the origin of the natural world and of human society, and deem irrelevant to religion all that modern science has taught us with regard to the origin of life, of animal species, of the human race, of civilizations? New experiences acquire meaning for us as individuals only as they relate themselves to our past experiences, and our past experiences are recalled only as some new situation calls up their memory as an aid to its interpretation. Similarly, the collective mind of the group, as long as it functions healthily, keeps assimilating new knowledge by the aid of past experience and reinterpreting past experience in the light of new knowledge. It is a morbid symptom when the traditions of a people offer no inspiration that might help them deal effectively with current problems, or when contemporary thought does not lead to a reconstruction of inherited tradition. Yet most Jews today live in two worlds that seem to have no connection, a modern week-day world of business and pleasure-seeking which is uninfluenced in any conscious way by Jewish tradition, and a Sabbath-and-holy-day-world permeated with memories of the remote past and hopes for the distant future, but segregated from the activities and interests of a work-a-day world.

But how proceed with our reinterpretation of Jewish religion in terms that would make it relevant to the needs and experiences of modern Jews? To attempt a reconstruction of Jewish ideology in a logical schematic arrangement would be to repeat the mistakes of the theologians, which have been dwelt upon at some length. It would mean abstracting Jewish religious ideas from the context of the civilization in which they functioned. This would both destroy their vitality and distort their meaning, as always happens with ideas that are torn from their context. The subjective preferences of the author would be more clearly apparent than the implications of the tradition which he is trying to interpret. It, therefore, seems a wiser course to study some context of Jewish religious observance that has survived the ravages of time, and to work out its implications. If there are any traditional observances which are generally practiced by religious Jew regardless of their theories of Judaism, we may safely assume that they express certain deep and abiding strivings and ideals within the Jewish soul. If then we can discover just what wants these observances seem to satisfy, if we can analyze what they have meant to the Jewish people in the past, and can work out the implication of these meanings in terms of aspirations and desires appropriate for our day, we have a method of approach to the formulation of

Jewish belief that is far superior to the discredited scholastic method of systematic theology.

Now, an analysis of the ideas associated with the Sabbaths and Festivals of the Jewish year, and expressed in the traditional liturgy and ritual associated with them, affords the best opportunity for applying this method of approach, since these occasions are sacred alike to every school of Jewish thought, in one form or another. Orthodoxy, Reformism and Conservatism agree in hallowing them. Even secular nationalism, from its own point of view, ascribes importance to them. They still stir in the heart of the Jew emotions which awaken in him his love for his people and his feeling of identification with them in the pursuit of certain ideal ends. It is through them, therefore, that we must seek to arouse the Jewish consciousness to an awareness of itself. They should become the great educational occasions in the Jewish year. They should be dedicated to the clarification and interpretation of the religious values in the Jewish heritage. Only thus will the life of the Jew be enhanced ethically and spiritually. *The Sabbaths and Festivals of a people reflect its highest interests and ideals. By celebrating a natural or an historic event, a people directs attention to that phase of the event which to it is of vital import.*[20] The Jewish Sabbath and Festivals especially are rich in ideas which reveal the hopes and strivings of the Jewish people. To know those ideas and to be aware of their implications is to know what ends the Jew cherishes.

The effect of reinterpreting the Sabbath and the Festivals of the Jewish calendar in the spirit here suggested will, therefore, be not only to bridge the chasm between the past and the present, but also to span the gulf that separates the

[20] R. Eleazar of Modin includes the disparagement of the Festivals among the cardinal sins which cause one to forfeit salvation. *Abot* III, 11. R. Sheshet in the name of R. Eleazar b. Azariah said: "To disregard the appointed seasons is like practising idolatry." *Makkot* 23a (Rashi's interpretation that this refers to intermediate days is not in accord with the original meaning of the statement.)

two worlds in which the modern Jew lives—the world of Jewish memories and hopes and the world of his everyday occupations and cares. Such revaluation, if successful in its purpose, should bring healing to the sick soul of the Jewish people now suffering from the morbid state of dual personality. The sound instinct of the Jewish people still regards its Sabbaths and Festivals as sacred in theory, although in practice they function but feebly and, in many circles, have almost fallen into desuetude. The main reason is the irrelevancy to modern life of the ideas that people commonly associate with these days and of many of the forms of their observance. But the very need for revitalizing the Jewish holidays, a need experienced by almost all Jews to whom Judaism is still dear, may be made to contribute to Jewish revival. The "days of solemn assembly," as the Torah calls them, still have a powerful appeal as media of spiritual instruction, and exert an influence as few other elements do in the life of our people. If, therefore, the Jewish Sabbath and Festivals were to have those latent meanings which have relevance to modern needs made explicit, they would no doubt infuse new health and vigor into the body of Jewish tradition.

Unless we effectively reinterpret these meanings in relevant terms, the obsolescence of the sacred days of the Jewish calendar, the last stronghold of the Jewish religious life in modern times, seems imminent. The changes which have come about in the relationship of the Jew to the rest of the world, both in his ideas and in his interests, make it impossible for the values associated with the Sabbath and the holy days in their traditional form to function as a stimulus to the life of the spirit. The effect of these changes upon the observance of the Sabbaths and Festivals has been to reduce them at best to occasions merely for suspending the daily routine and experiencing a vague feeling of religiosity. If they are observed at all, it is due to the rituals which are associated with them. The *Shofar,* the fasting, the *Sukkah,* the *Seder* have an inherent appeal. And the public worship of which they are the occasion still has something about it that attracts the Jew who does not want to lose all touch with his people.

It is doubtful, however, whether these rites can retain their hold upon the Jew much longer, unless they are deliberately made to reflect and symbolize spiritual values which have a direct bearing on the life and thought of today. While it is true that abstract ideas are not likely to make a profound impression on the minds of most people unless accompanied by some activity, meaningless activities dissociated from any significant ideas are no less ineffectual. It is dangerous to entrust the fate of so important a series of religious institutions as the Sabbath and Festivals to activities and rites which have no meaning beyond themselves. Even rendering them more pleasing to the esthetic sense is not enough. They must have meanings which will guide and inspire. It is, therefore, necessary to identify the Sabbath and Festivals with specific ideas and ideals which play an important part in the psychology of the modern man. Not alone the preaching but also the liturgy, the music and the rituals should all be focused upon what to us are the highest ethical and religious needs so as to evoke from them a rich and manifold Jewish folk expression.

Thus does the very need of rendering the sacred days of the Jewish calendar meaningful solve the problem of the kind of scheme into which the teachings of the Jewish religion should be cast. By associating these teachings with the observance of the Sabbath and the Jewish holy days, we take cognizance of their organic relation to the historic consciousness of the Jewish people. We thus avoid a danger that has vitiated many an earnest effort to reinterpret the principles of the Jewish religion. For we need not fear lest, in our zeal to incorporate into the Jewish religion the most ethical and spiritual truths of our day, we confuse our own pet metaphysical and ethical theories with those fruitful ideas and ideals that are at once implicit in our tradition and relevant to modern life. The ideals they represent will have the abiding quality of all ideals that have sunk deep roots in the tradition of a people. But they will not have that timelessness which is characteristic only of abstract concepts like those of geometry. *Not timelessness but timeliness is the desideratum. Religion is necessarily rooted in the soil of tradition, but its life depends on its ability to send forth new shoots into the light of our own day.* We need not be apprehensive, however, that such innovation as is involved in our effort to make the Jewish religion relevant to modern needs and aspirations will introduce alien and unassimilable elements into the body of Jewish civilization, for the pattern into which any philosophy of life based on the significance of the sacred days of the Jewish calendar must fall cannot be other than a Jewish one.

II

GOD AS THE POWER THAT MAKES
FOR SALVATION

THE Sabbath is named as the first of the "appointed seasons of the Lord, holy convocations," [1] whose purpose it was to bring Israel into closer kinship with its God. Although archeologists may identify the origin of the Sabbath with a superficially similar institution of ancient Babylonian civilization, associated with the worship of the moon, its significance must be judged by what it came to mean to the Jewish people. It became for them preeminently the occasion not only for rest from their labors, but for seeking satisfaction in that knowledge of their God which helped them to live and to achieve the purpose of life.

From the point of view of tradition, the Sabbath enjoys a measure of sanctity beyond that of any other occasion in the year, with the single exception, perhaps, of the Day of Atonement.[2] The prohibition of work, one of the methods of hallowing a day, is stricter and more inclusive in regard to the Sabbath than in regard to any of these other "appointed seasons." The negative precepts are significant as reflecting the intensity of the Jew's devotion to the Sabbath, a devotion which derived from his experience of its sanctity. Note the emphasis given to the Sabbath in Nehemiah's résumé of God's dealings with Israel. "Thou hast made known to them Thy holy Sabbath, and didst command them ordinances and statutes, and a law by the hand of Moses Thy Servant." [3]

[1] Lev. 23:2, 3.
[2] Cf. *Makkot* 23b; Sabbath and Yom Kippur compared in Lev. *R.* XXXIV, 16.
[3] Neh. 9:14.

40

The Sabbath is thus made coordinate with the whole system of Mosaic law.[4] *Since the Sabbath attained such primacy among Jewish religious practices, we may properly regard it as symbolizing the most significant and comprehensive spiritual purpose which the Jewish religion sought to help the Jew achieve.*

What more comprehensive purpose can there be to human life than the complete and harmonious fulfillment of all the physical, mental and moral powers with which the human self as a social being is endowed? The conception of that purpose and of the means of attaining it has varied with every people, civilization, religion and age. But the purpose itself is as old as man, for, the very idea of having a self which is in need of fulfillment differentiates man from the subhuman. Self-fulfillment or self-realization is nothing more than the modern equivalent of what in general life is expressed by the term "salvation," and in traditional Jewish life by the phrase "having a share in the world to come."

That the Sabbath was regarded as representative of the all-comprehensive purpose of self-fulfillment or salvation is attested by the significance which the Prophets attached to its observance, and by the rabbinic identification of it as a veritable modicum of the world to come.

Thus in the book of Isaiah we read:

> "If thou turn away thy foot because of the Sabbath
> From pursuing thy business on My holy day;
> And call the Sabbath a delight,
> And the holy of the Lord honorable . . .
> Then shalt thou delight thyself in the Lord,
> And I will make thee to ride upon the high places
>   of the earth." [5]

That the Prophets deemed the Sabbath of such high worth as to make self-fulfillment possible even to those who might

----
Jer. Nedarim III, 14 (38b).   [5] Is. 58:13, 14.

regard their lives as frustrated is borne out by the following
also from the book of Isaiah:

> "For thus saith the Lord
> Concerning the eunuchs that keep My Sabbaths,
> And choose the things that please Me,
> And hold fast by My covenant:
> Even unto them will I give in My house
> And within My walls a monument and a memorial
> Better than sons and daughters;
> I will give them an everlasting memorial
> That will not be cut off." [6]

What the Sabbath meant to the Rabbis is set forth in the
following from the tannaitic *Midrash*: "We read in the
Torah, 'Verily ye shall keep my Sabbaths, for it is a sign
between me and you throughout your generations, that ye
may know that I am the Lord who sanctifies you.' [7] This
reflects the future world, which is characterized by a kind of
holiness possessed by the Sabbath of this world. · We thus
learn that the Sabbath possesses a holiness like that of the
future world. And thus it says: 'A Psalm; a song of the
Sabbath day,' referring to the world in which there is Sabbath all the time." [8]

It may therefore with justice be asserted that the Sabbath
came to function in the Jewish consciousness as a symbol of
salvation. It was designed to make the Jew aware that God
provided him with the means and opportunities for the satisfaction of those desires that gave meaning and purpose to
his life. The Sabbath is calculated to impress the Jew with
the fact that the world is so constituted as to enable man to
achieve salvation. It is to this function of the Sabbath as the
symbol of salvation that the reasons given in the Torah for
the observance of the Sabbath will have to be related in our
day, as they were throughout the eighteen centuries of rab-

---

[6] *Ibid.*, 56:4, 5.   [7] Exod. 31:12, 13.
[8] *Mekilta,* Tractate *Shabbata* (*Cf. Berakot* 57b; Gen. *R.* XVII, 5).

binic Judaism. That God rested on the seventh day after having created the world in the course of the six preceding days, that God endowed the day with a sanctity all its own, and that the Sabbath is to serve as a reminder of the covenant between God and Israel, all these reasons will have to be integrated into the all-comprehensive purpose of serving as a symbol of salvation. But before doing so we must understand clearly the meaning of salvation and realize what it has to do with the conception of God.

I

The traditional conception of salvation

During the entire period between the destruction of the second Temple in the year 70 and the initiation of the modern phase of Jewish history with the movements of Emancipation and Enlightenment, the conception of salvation held by Jews was other-worldly. This simple fact cannot be properly understood or appreciated without some knowledge of the general world-outlook to which it was integral. The prospect of salvation in the world to come, or of other-worldly salvation, must not be regarded as belonging, for example, to the same universe of discourse as what we commonly understand by the belief in immortality. To be sure, most religious people still profess belief in the immortality of the soul. They accept this belief, either because it was included in the stock of beliefs that were taught to them in their childhood as Jewish doctrine, or because it offers a certain solace in the face of bereavement. But such a belief in the immortality of the soul as is held by modern men is something very different from the conception of the world to come as held by our fathers. It is different, because, not being associated in any vital way with the conception of salvation, it does not to any extent motivate the behavior of people. It has more in common with the ancient belief in the

continued existence of the soul in Sheol or Hades, a belief
that prevailed before the thought of the world to come took
hold of men's minds. The question under consideration is
not whether people still believe in some kind of survival after
death, but where and how they expect to achieve their self-
fulfillment or salvation. The point is that the conduct of
people today is motivated not by the desire to win for themselves a "share in the world to come," which would reward
all their earthly efforts and compensate all their earthly
suffering, but by the desire to win for themselves a share of
life in this world, to win success, honor, love and everything
that contributes to human well-being and self-fulfillment on
earth.

It was not so in the past. When R. Jacob said: "This
world is like a vestibule before the world to come; prepare
thyself in the vestibule that thou mayest enter into the hall," [9]
he expressed in a simile the practical significance of believing
in the world to come as the scene of human salvation. Nothing that happened to a man during his sojourn on this earth
was deemed as being of any consequence, except as it impeded or aided his pursuit of salvation in the world to come.
His earthly joys were but a symbol and an anticipatory token
of "the abundance of Thy bounty that Thou hast laid up for
them that fear Thee." [10] His sorrows and tears were destined
to pass away with his transitory world on the day when God
would "destroy death for ever" and would "wipe away tears
from off all faces," [11] and the pious resignation with which
he bore his sorrows would be rewarded by compensatory joys
proportionate to his suffering on earth. The religious regulations and moral laws of his social heritage were not regarded
as methods of achieving an integrated personality and a cooperative society, but as defining the conduct by which he
might qualify himself for heavenly bliss in the hereafter.

The terms in which our fathers conceived of this bliss

[9] *Abot.* IV, 16.   [10] Ps. 31:20.   [11] Is. 25:8.

were very concrete, and were projections of whatever men found desirable on earth. The idea that there would be a new world originated from the biblical descriptions of the glorious future that awaited Israel at the end of days, and from the various allusions to the great upheaval that would herald that future. Those descriptions portray the future as an era when God's sovereignty over Israel and the world would be made manifest through the restoration of Israel to a position of preeminence and security, and the establishment of universal righteousness and peace. Even nature would respond to the new order; carnivorous beasts would lose their ferocity; "the wolf shall dwell with the lamb, and the leopard shall lie down with the kid . . . and the lion shall eat straw like the ox. . . . They shall not hurt nor destroy in all my holy mountain; for the earth shall be full of the knowledge of the Lord as the waters cover the sea." [18] The longer Israel had to wait for the realization of its dream of preeminence, and the greater the disparity between its hopes and its earthly status became, the more emphasis did it give to the miraculous and supernatural elements in this dream of the future, until the awaited Day came to be utterly dissociated from reality as experienced on earth and to require the creation of a "new heaven and new earth" as its proper setting. Thus was the awaited future transformed into the world to come, which became a dominant idea in the Jewish religion and in the religions that sprang from it.

To understand the hold that this idea of the world to come had on men's thinking, we must realize that, fanciful as this idea was, and colored by what we today characterize as wishful thinking, it fitted with admirable logic into the general view of the cosmos that our ancestors held. They assumed that whatever thwarted men's efforts at self-fulfillment represented a corruption or deviation from the original plan of the universe as it emerged from chaos at God's command.

[18] *Ibid.*, 11:6-9.

For when God had created the world, "God saw all that He had made, and behold! it was very good." [13] He made man and placed him in the Garden of Eden where he could obtain, without pain or toil, all that he needed for his maintenance and happiness. And God intended that man live forever, for in the midst of the Garden was the Tree of Life, and the first man and woman were not debarred from eating of its fruit. But in their desire to become "like God, knowing good and evil," they transgressed the one command which it was necessary for them to fulfill in order to continue in the enjoyment of a life of unadulterated happiness. In consequence, there came into the world death, sin, toil, pain and strife. The generations of man became more and more corrupt, necessitating the destruction of all life by the Flood, save that which Noah was able to preserve with him in the Ark. But the covenant that God made with Noah never again to destroy all mankind with a flood was predicated on the assumption that the sinfulness of man was ineradicable, since "the inclination of the heart of man is evil from his youth." [14] Man therefore cannot achieve salvation unaided.

But this pessimism with regard to the possibilities of human nature, as our fathers knew it, could not destroy their optimism as to the ultimate intention of God and the eventual destiny of man. Man's state of corruption was not to last forever, since the divine grace, God's attribute of mercy, would itself intervene. It was for the purpose of freeing man from that corruption that God chose the Patriarchs, and revealed the Torah to their descendants. The Torah was intended as the way of life by which Israel and the world would eventually be redeemed. In the world to come the conditions that existed in Eden would again prevail throughout the world, and all who followed the precepts of the Torah would have a share in the regenerate life forever.

Commonly associated with the ushering in of the world to

[13] Gen. 1:31.   [14] *Ibid.*, 8:21.

come are the following: (1) the coming of the Messiah, God's anointed, who would establish the preeminence of Israel among the nations, and who would rule over Israel in righteousness, so that the whole earth would acknowledge Israel's God; (2) the resurrection of the dead to give to all who in this life had been loyal to the Torah a share in the deathless life of the world to come; (3) the Day of Judgment, when all the resurrected dead will be judged, the wicked consigned to destruction and the righteous to everlasting bliss. Meanwhile the Garden of Eden or Paradise, the original abode of man, which alone of all regions on earth was unaffected by man's fall, is reserved as the temporary abode of the souls of the righteous after death, where they await resurrection in happiness. (The counterpart of the Garden of Eden is the subterranean region, *Gehinnom* or hell, where the souls of the wicked await resurrection and the Day of Judgment.)

But none of these concepts must be confused with that of the world to come itself.[15] In the world to come, there would not only be no death, but there would be no toil. Life would sustain itself, according to one version, without food or drink. There would, of course, be no begetting of children,[16] all the created souls having had their due incarnation,[17] so that the curse of Eve as well as the curse of Adam would be removed.[18] According to another version, men would eat in the future world as well as in the present, but they would eat no ordinary food but *manna*,[19] a heavenly food which both delighted the palate and nourished the body to perfection. According to a third version, it was conceived that men would eat the fruits of the earth as in this life,[20] but these would be brought forth in abundance, without men's having to toil to produce them. As prophesied in the book of Isaiah in the passage quoted above, the nature of the beasts would

[15] Cf. *Pirkë De-R. Eliezer* LI.
[16] *Berakot* 17a.   [17] *Yebamot* 62a.   [18] Gen. 3:16-17.
[19] *Mekilta Va-Yassa'* 4; *Mekilta R. S.* 78.   [20] Exod. *R.* XV, 21.

be changed so that none would be hostile to man, and all would be domesticated to minister in one way or another to his happiness. The world would be illuminated by the original light that shone during the first seven days and that flowed directly from the Divine Presence, a light of incomparable brightness which would make the sun unnecessary for purposes of illumination, though it would continue to shine, because its rays bring healing to the righteous."[11]

But more significant than any of these changes in the physical environment of man in the world to come were the anticipated changes in human nature itself. For, it was assumed that in initiating the world to come, God would destroy the Evil *Yezer*, all those passions and appetites that tempted man to evil-doing, so that he would no longer be in danger of falling from grace, and there would be no bar to his perfect and direct communion with God. Israel at Sinai could not endure hearing the voice of God; they, therefore, asked Moses to deliver God's message to them. But they soon realized what a high privilege they forfeited, and they pleaded to hear God's voice once more. The answer came: "Not in this world, but in the world to come, at which time the Evil *Yezer* will depart from them forever."[12]

It was this picture of the world to come that figured prominently in the consciousness of the masses of the Jewish people from about the beginning of the common era down to the end of the Jewish Middle Ages, less than a century and a half ago. The picture, however, was modified, and the texts on which it was based were reinterpreted by the religious philosophers of the Middle Ages who had come under the influence of Greek thought. Under the influence of Greek philosophy everything material was conceived as transitory, and only the spiritual was regarded as abiding. Hence it became necessary to interpret as figures of speech all the

[11] *Ibid.*   [12] Cant. *R.* on 1 :2.

promises that had reference to the gratification of any of the senses. The religious philosophers found support for such an interpretation in the passage, "in the world to come there will be no eating, drinking or procreation," [**] by interpreting these words to mean that it is to be a life adapted to disembodied spirits.

Maimonides went so far as to identify the world to come not with any cosmic future event, but with the everlasting bliss which the individual soul of the righteous enjoys when death delivers it from bondage to the body. He says: "The reason that the Sages speak of it (i.e., life after death) as the world to come, is not because it does not exist in the present, and because this world will be destroyed and, thereupon, the other will be ushered in; for, verily, it exists and is established, as is attested by the verse: 'How abundant is Thy bounty which Thou hast laid up for them that fear Thee, which Thou hast wrought for them that it would take refuge in Thee.' [**] But they called it the world to come, because that life comes to a man after the life of this world in which we exist as body and soul, such as is the original state of all human beings." [**]

But this identification of the world to come with personal immortal bliss immediately after death brought Maimonides into intellectual difficulties which led to no end of controversy. For he could not deny that the hope of bodily resurrection is voiced repeatedly in authoritative traditional sources and finds emphatic statement in the traditional liturgy. He himself found it necessary to include the belief in resurrection among his thirteen principles of faith. But he leaves the resurrection without any specific function, for the righteous who will be resurrected will again have to die, "For know," he says, "that man must of necessity die and decompose and return to his component elements." [**] Con-

[**] *Berakot* 17a.   [**] Ps. 31:20.
[**] *Mishneh Torah, Hilkot Teshubah*, VIII, 8.
[**] Commentary on *Mishnah Sanhedrin*, X, 1.

sequently his opponents accused him of not believing in the resurrection.

But our fathers, whether they held the popular traditional view of the world to come as indeed a new heaven and a new earth, or accepted the philosophic version of it as the blissful state of the disembodied soul after death, were all agreed in seeing the possibility of human salvation in a posthumous existence of an entirely different order from life as it is encountered here on earth. For them, in contradistinction to the men of our age, the center of gravity of their lives was not in this world but in the world to come.

We can understand such a faith better when we remember that only in comparatively recent times has it dawned upon man that he can transform his physical and social environment and deliberately change the conditions under which he lives. The mere notion of such a possibility would have seemed both ridiculous and dangerous in former times, because it was deemed tantamount to measuring oneself against God, and therefore an expression of rebellion against Him. Since man knew too little about his environment to be able to change it, he made a virtue of the necessity of accepting the evils he found in it as inevitable, and as capable of being eliminated only by God through superhuman means and agencies.

When men suffer from evils that are apparently irremediable, they are confronted with the alternative of utter pessimism and demoralization, or of fitting their experience of evil into some pattern of thought that will enable them to see in it at least an opportunity for future good. Faith in the possibility of heavenly reward after death is, therefore, an expression of this psychic need for an outlook on life that would make evil appear other than inevitable defeat and frustration. Salvation meant the ultimate realization of all the joy that eluded our pursuit on earth, a state in which the ego was no longer rebuffed, inhibited and frustrated in its desires, but achieved at last self-fulfillment so complete and transfiguring that it glorified all that had gone before. It also meant a regenerate society of souls living together in happy communion, without strife or discord. It meant the ultimate fulfillment of all human yearnings for a harmonious and co-operative social order, one in which every man would have his appropriate place and in accordance with his own merits, regardless of the humble or exalted position he may have occupied while on earth.

2

What salvation must mean in our day

Although faith in other-worldly salvation no longer functions as it did in the past, this does not mean that we can dispense with the faith that the world affords men an opportunity for salvation, or with the institution of the Sabbath that expresses and confirms this faith. However conditions of life may have changed and however different our modern conception of the cosmos may be from that held by our fathers, the need for a faith that will save us from a sense of the vanity and futility of human life remains with us. For man is not a self-sufficient entity. His interests cannot be confined in space or time to his immediate physical environment and the brief span of his life. And it is these larger interests that, above all, he identifies with his selfhood or personality.

Man's immediate unconscious responses to the physical stimuli of his environment, while indispensable to his life, do not spell for him the meaning of life; they are not the experiences that make him want to cling to life. It is of his purposive acts, his awareness of wants and his attempts to satisfy them that a man thinks, when he thinks of his life. The summoning of all our resources of memory and imagination in response to consciously felt needs gives us our sense of personality. As part of the process of satisfying our wants we conceive a future situation in which these wants shall have been satisfied; and we endeavor to affect our environment or our own behavior in ways that conform to that concept. Such concepts are what we mean by ideals.

The fact of human mortality puts no temporal limit to the objectives of our idealization. Men are concerned that, even after their death, their world be a safe one for their children to grow up in. But the fact of human mortality does put an end to the opportunity of men to achieve the purpose that the ideal expresses; it is this which often overwhelms men with the sense of human impotence and the futility of living. This sense of frustration can be counteracted only by faith in a God of salvation, faith that inherent in the world as it is constituted is the Power that makes for the fulfillment of all valid ideals. We shall learn in the sequel what constitutes validity.

We cannot today think of salvation in the same other-worldly terms as did our fathers. But in the terms in which we can think of it, it remains an indispensable element of our religion. Fortunately, the very forces that have destroyed the illusion by which the medieval mind saved itself from despair and weariness of life give us a substitute for our lost paradise. The extent to which man has, by scientific techniques, changed the face of nature for the satisfaction of his own physical needs has released him from the feeling of helplessness in the face of other obstacles to the satisfaction of his desires and purposes. True, psychology and the social sciences have lagged behind the physical sciences in their development, and we are not yet able to change our social environment in conformity with human needs with the same facility with which we have changed our physical environment. "Knowledge comes but wisdom lingers." Nevertheless, we look to these sciences to point the way to the eventual abolition of the inveterate evils of human life.

The salvation that the modern man seeks in this world, like that which his fathers sought in the world to come, has both a personal and a social significance. In its personal aspect it represents the faith in the possibility of achieving an integrated personality. All those natural impulses, appetites and desires which so often are in conflict with one another must be harmonized. They must never be permitted to issue in a stalemate, in such mutual inhibition as leaves life empty and meaningless, without zest and savor. Nor must they be permitted to issue in distraction, in a condition in which our personality is so pulled apart by conflicting desires that the man we are in certain moments or in certain relations looks with contempt and disgust at the man we are in others. When our mind functions in such a way that we feel that all our powers are actively employed in the achievement of desirable ends, we have achieved personal salvation.

This personal objective of human conduct cannot, however, be achieved without reference to a social objective as well. Selfish salvation is an impossibility, because no human being is psychologically self-sufficient. We are impelled by motives that relate themselves to the life of the race with as imperative an urge as by any that relate themselves to the preservation of our individual organism. "Love is strong as death," [87] and frequently sacrifices life itself for the object of love. Although to every individual the achievement of personal salvation is his supreme quest and responsibility, it is unattainable without devotion to the task of social salvation. The thought, "If I am not for myself, who will be for me?" in this striving for salvation always carries with it the implication, "If I am but for myself, what am I?" [88] because we cannot even think of ourselves except in relation to something not ourselves.

In its social aspect, salvation means the ultimate achievement of a social order in which all men shall collaborate in

[87] Cant. 8 :6.   [88] *Abot.* I, 14.

the pursuit of common ends in a manner which shall afford to each the maximum opportunity for creative self-expression. There can be no personal salvation so long as injustice and strife exist in the social order; there can be no social salvation so long as the greed for gain and the lust for domination are permitted to inhibit the hunger for human fellowship and sympathy in the hearts of men. There is a sense in which it is still true that salvation is of the world to come, for its attainment is clearly not of today or of tomorrow. That it will ever be attained can never be demonstrated, but faith must assume it as the objective of human behavior, if we are not to succumb to the cynical acceptance of evil, which is the only other alternative.

The goal to be reached need not necessarily be conceived as a static and final goal. Life can always be depended upon to create new wants that call for satisfaction and give birth to new ideals. But the measure of our self-fulfillment as individuals and as a society will ever be the extent to which our lives are oriented to valid ideals. In this sense the center of gravity of our lives remains in the world to come, for it is ever the potentialities of the future that redeem the efforts of the present from futility, and that save our souls or ethical personalities from frustration. The self-indulgent sensualist who spiritually lives a hand-to-mouth existence can never find self-fulfillment, because such a life does not begin to bring into play all the latent faculties and powers that inhere in human nature. Only the individual whose purposes in life relate themselves to objectives that lie in the future can experience that sense of well-being and aliveness which comes when all our powers are enlisted in the pursuit of some desired end.

In the light of all that, *salvation must be conceived mainly as an objective of human action, not as a psychic compensation for human suffering.* Though it is absurd to charge religion as such with being an opiate, the truth is that other-worldly religion did function as an opiate. But this fact by itself does not count even against other-worldly religion. In the two thousand years preceding the Enlightenment, religion had to function as an opiate, for so acutely aware had man become of evil which seemed to him irremediable that he might have been driven into despair, had he not been able to hope for salvation in the hereafter. By preserving the ideal of salvation, so to speak, in heaven, man could bring that ideal down to earth as soon as he learned enough about himself and the world he lived in to be able to improve both. But religion owes a genuine debt to those who have called attention to the danger in our own day of drugging the human with the opiate of other-worldliness. The effect of such an opiate at the present time is to keep us from the attainment of salvation on earth. This is equally true whether we think in terms of personal salvation or of social salvation.

In regard to personal salvation, the habit of conceiving it as coming from the grace of God has made men seek salvation by a withdrawal from the world and the flesh, and by resort to prayer, meditation and ascetic self-mortification. In the light of modern science, however, such measures defeat their own purpose. Man has a physical organism not unlike that of the lower animals, and the healthy functioning of that organism is a prerequisite to mental and spiritual hygiene. The effort to suppress any natural instinct is more likely to lead to a dangerous psychosis than to that serene, tranquil and happy state which we associate with salvation. Withdrawal from the world must result in an intense introversion and exaggerated egocentricity which inhibit those impulses to fellowship, friendship and love that for most of us express what we feel to be best and truest in our natures. Excessive prayer, too, often represents the verbalization of interests that should express themselves in deeds, not in words. Preoccupation with the sense of sin may result in such self-contempt as to emphasize rather than heal the breach between the crude appetites of men and their deeper, more stable and more significant social emotions. The masochism of self-mortification leads inevitably to the sadism of fanaticism.

We cannot hate human nature in ourselves and love it in others. "Be not righteous over-much," [39] and "Be not wicked in thine own esteem" [40] are injunctions, the significance of which other-worldly religion has too frequently overlooked. The self-righteousness which makes us withdraw in holy horror from contact with the wicked world, and the self-contempt which believes personal salvation impossible except by the intervention of some miracle of grace, are alike dangers inherent in the other-worldly viewpoint. The religion of the future will, therefore, turn from most of these practices and avail itself of such guidance as the science of psychology affords for the training of character, with personal salvation as its goal.

With respect to social salvation, other-worldliness has been, if that is possible, an even greater obstacle to its attainment. Indeed, it is the obvious failure of religion in this respect that is responsible for its condemnation by the class-conscious laboring masses. Other-worldly religion, by regarding patient resignation to social evil as a method of achieving merit and ultimate salvation in the world to come, definitely aligned religion with the forces of social reaction. To bear one's yoke was considered more virtuous than to rebel. [41] Revolution against the social order, no matter how tyrannical and oppressive that order might be, was condemned. This played so directly into the hands of ruling powers that these tended further to corrupt religion by State subsidies and special privileges. The State made itself the secular arm for enforcing Church discipline, and the Church made itself the religious arm for inculcating loyalty to the status quo. Although the multiplication of religious sects

[39] Ecc. 7:16.   [40] *Abot.* II, 13.   [41] *Cf.* Cant. *R.* on 2:7.

since the Protestant Reformation has in a measure pried loose this unholy alliance, nevertheless the role played by the churches during the World War shows that, on the whole, organized religion is still counted upon to defend the status quo against attack.

That religion may be a force for revolution or social reconstruction is best evidenced by the prophetic movement in Israel. Because the Prophets conceived of the scene of the Kingdom of God as on this earth, because they meant by it the manifestation of God's government of Israel through the establishment of righteousness and justice, they were almost always antagonistic to the existing regime. Contrast the attitude of Hosea expressed in the words: "I give thee a king in mine anger and I take him away in My wrath," [11] with the medieval doctrine of the divine right of kings. Religion must no longer betray the hopes of men for the abolition of poverty, oppression and war on this earth by regarding these evils as mere "trials and tribulations" or "chastisements of love," for which we shall be compensated in another world. It must cease waiting for an act of miraculous intervention to remove these evils "in the end of days." It must encourage men with faith and hope to apply human intelligence and good-will to the removal of these evils in the achievement of the social salvation of mankind.

3
Why the Sabbath should serve as the symbol of this-worldly salvation

The change in point of view from the other-worldliness of the past to the modern outlook with its emphasis on this-worldliness need not then lessen the significance of the Sabbath as a symbol. It expresses for the modern Jew as it did for his forefathers the thought that the world is so consti-

[11] Hos. 13:11.

tuted that man can achieve salvation if, by adhering to valid ideals, he puts himself in contact with the creative forces that shape human life and make it worth living. Since we identify God with that aspect of reality which gives to life its supreme value or holiness, this is but another way of saying in more traditional language that the Sabbath expresses for us the faith that man can achieve salvation by cleaving to God, the Source of salvation.

But the Sabbath is not only a symbol of the salvation to be achieved by communion with God. It is itself an instrument that we may employ to advantage in our pursuit of salvation. We need perhaps more than ever before to terminate each week with a day that shall stimulate our thirst for salvation and keep us faithful to the ideals that lead to its attainment. Otherwise our mere preoccupation with the business of "making a living," that is, of securing the conditions indispensable to life, tends to absorb all our attention and life itself becomes empty and meaningless. We work to keep alive that we may work to keep alive, until our powers are spent in this weary treadmill, and death brings surcease of labor. If life is to be lived zestfully and to employ all those human faculties the full exercise of which calls forth true joy in being alive, we dare not permit life to sink to such a level of mere preoccupation with the problem of survival. The Sabbath, with its insistence on interrupting the routine of our daily business and concerning ourselves with spiritual values, helps to save us from such a fate.

But that is not all. Modern man is seldom preoccupied solely with the business of survival. With the aid of machinery, modern man is able to produce much more than he needs for survival, although a stupid and wasteful economic order still permits want where plenty would be possible. But even in the pursuit of other aims we frequently become so absorbed in the means as to lose sight of the goal. Our preoccupation with the details of the processes by which we seek to attain desired ends obscures our perspective of more distant horizons. Here too the Sabbath comes to our aid. An artist cannot be continually wielding his brush. He must stop at times in his painting to freshen his vision of the object, the meaning of which he wishes to express on his canvas. Living is also an art. We dare not become absorbed in its technical processes and lose our consciousness of its general plan. Our ideal of the personality we would become, if we achieved salvation as here interpreted, is the object we are trying to paint; the Sabbath represents those moments when we pause in our brush-work to renew our vision of this object. Having done so we take ourselves to our painting with clarified vision and renewed energy. This applies alike to the individual and to the community. For the individual the Sabbath becomes thereby an instrument of personal salvation; for the community an instrument of social salvation.

In the public worship which is a characteristic feature of the traditional observance of the Sabbath, we have an expression of the urge to seek collectively the salvation for which each individual soul yearns, but which it can achieve only by identifying itself with the larger social entity of which it is a part. *The organized religions of mankind represent the determination of important historic groups to serve as the bearers of salvation to their people. This explains the place that religion holds in Jewish life. It represents the purposeful effort of the Jewish people to make the experience of Jewish group life in past and present and future an instrument of salvation.* The Jew was particularly aware of Judaism's functioning in this manner on the Sabbath. On this day he was liberated from the distracting cares of the week, and he participated in religious activities that renewed his faith in the ideals which gave worth and dignity to human life. He felt it good to be alive and good to be a Jew.

The sense of enhancement of personality which the Jew experienced on the Sabbath gave rise to the tradition of his acquiring on that day a *"neshamah yeterah,"* an additional soul.

What "additional soul" meant for the Jew is perhaps best set forth by Emerson in his essay on the "Oversoul." "There is a difference," says Emerson, "between one and another hour of life in their authority and subsequent effect. Our faith comes in moments; our vice is habitual. Yet there is a depth in those brief moments which constrains us to ascribe more reality to them than to all other experiences."

The foregoing discussion should suffice to make clear what is meant by speaking of the Sabbath as symbolizing the thought that God is the Power that makes for salvation. It has shown how the Sabbath implies an affirmation that the world is so constituted as to afford man the opportunity for salvation. But what is there in the world that gives us this assurance? In what aspects of life do we recognize the Power that makes for salvation? The answer to these questions is to be found in the three leading motifs enunciated in the Torah and developed by the Sages in their interpretation of the Sabbath. The first of these is the idea of creativity, for the Sabbath is associated in Jewish tradition with the completion of the task of creation, when God surveyed all that He had made and found it "very good." [**] The second is the idea of holiness. The reference to the Sabbath in the Decalogue bids us "Remember the Sabbath day to keep it holy," [**] and the prophetic passage from the book of Isaiah quoted at the beginning of this chapter calls the Sabbath "the holy of the Lord." [**] The third is the idea of covenantship, which regards the Sabbath as a sign of God's covenant with Israel. [**] These three leading ideas associated with the observance of the Sabbath play an important part in Jewish religion generally. [**] They therefore make the Sabbath the symbol

---

[**] Gen. 1:31.   [**] Exod. 20:8.   [**] Is. 58:13.   [**] Exod. 31:16, 17.
[**] These three ideas are implied in the following from the *Mekilta*: "'For it is holy unto you' (Exod. 31:14). This tells us that the Sabbath adds holiness to Israel. Why is the shop of so-and-so closed? Because he keeps the Sabbath. Why does so-and-so abstain from work? Because he keeps the Sabbath. He thus bears witness to Him, by Whose word the world came into being, that He created His world in six days and rested on the Seventh. And thus it says: 'Therefore ye are my witnesses, saith the Lord, and I am God.' (Is. 43:12)." (Tractate *Shabbata*).

of the most significant elements in the Jewish conception of
God.

4

God as the creative life of the universe the antithesis of irrevocable fate and absolute evil

The idea of creativity, which makes of the Sabbath a
zeker lema'aseh bereshit, "a memorial of the creation," has
functioned in Jewish life as an antidote to the pessimism
which experience with the evils of life tends to engender.
We are so accustomed to think of God as the creator of the
world that it is hard for us to associate the idea of godhood
with any being not conceived as endowed with superlative
powers of creation. It is, nevertheless, a fact that in primitive religion, and even in the more developed religions of
polytheism, the notion of godhood was seldom closely associated with the power to create. The psychological origin
of the belief in God as creator is undoubtedly wish-fulfill-
ment of man's desire to transform his environment when he
realized his own impotence to do so. The realization of that
impotence marks considerable progress in human development, and may be recognized by the rise of creation myths.

Before the age of philosophy, creation was always synonymous with transformation, or making over some pre-
existing substance. Even in the philosophies of Plato and
Aristotle, the existence of primeval matter is likewise assumed. That primeval matter was regarded as coeternal and
coexistent with the divine principle of creativity. The human
mind, as Kant has shown, cannot really solve the problem of
absolute beginnings, and identifying creativity with transformation marks the limit of its capacity. But the theologians who were intent upon maintaining the historicity of
the miracles recorded in the Bible felt that the power merely
to transform was not adequate for the performance of
miracles, for such power was limited by the inherent nature

of reality. Only the power to create out of nothing could comport with the performance of miracles. This line of reasoning made the belief in *creatio ex nihilo* the apple of discord among thinkers for centuries. To the modern way of thinking, its connection with spiritual life is remote, if not altogether irrelevant.

Only the moral aspect of that belief is nowadays of vital import. *The moral implication of the traditional teaching that God created the world is that creativity, or the continuous emergence of aspects of life not prepared for or determined by the past, constitutes the most divine phase of reality.* A modern equivalent of the notion of creativity, which tradition regarded as the very essence of godhood, would be the concept of the latent and potential elements in the universe as making for the increase in the quantity and quality of life. Since a spiritual conception of life is consistent only with a world-outlook which counts on the realization of much that is still in the womb of possibility, it implies the belief that both man and the universe are ever in a state of being created.

The Sabbath is regarded in Jewish tradition as celebrating the creation of the world. The modern equivalent of that interpretation of the day would be the use of it as a means of accentuating the fact that we must reckon with creation and self-renewal as a continuous process. The liturgy speaks of God as "renewing daily the works of creation." By becoming aware of that fact, we might gear our own lives to this creative urge in the universe and discover within ourselves unsuspected powers of the spirit.

The belief in God as creator, or its modern equivalent, the conception of the creative urge as the element of godhood in the world, is needed to fortify the yearning for spiritual self-regeneration. That yearning dies down unless it is backed by the conviction that there is something which answers to it in the very character of life as a whole. *There can hardly be*

any more important function for religion than to keep alive
this yearning for self-renewal and to press it into the service
of human progress. In doing that, religion will combat the
recurrent pessimism to which we yield whenever we mis-
judge the character of the evil in the world. It will teach us
to live without illusion and without despair about the future,
with clear recognition of the reality of evil and creative faith
in the possibility of the good.

We should not minimize in the least the pain, the agony,
the cruelty and the destruction that deface the world. But
we should not go to the extent to which the ancients and
moderns have gone when they interpreted all that evil as
inherent and eternal in the very constitution of the world.
Of what avail to strive to improve the conditions of life
when we know beforehand that life must ever remain the
same? Koheleth's conclusion "All is vanity" derives from
the premise, "There is nothing new under the sun." Religion
should indicate to us some way whereby we can transform
the evils of the world, if they are within our control, and
transcend them, if they are beyond our control. If we give
heed to the creative impulse within us which beats in rhythm
with the creative impulse of the cosmos, we can always find
some way of making our adjustment to evil productive of
good. It is not given to us, with our necessarily limited
vision and understanding, to know how the effects of this
creative adjustment can withstand the ravages of time. It is
enough that in the art of achieving such adjustment we experience self-fulfillment, as though that act were eternal and
an end in itself.

To effect an adjustment which shall partake of the nature
of faith and hope, it is essential to guard against the fatal
error into which men have always fallen with regard to the
place of evil in the scheme of things. We must avoid the
tendency to interpret our own despair as the collapse of the
moral order. The error has consisted mainly in personifying,

dramatizing or apotheosizing evil. Instead of being treated as mere negation, chance or accident which is inevitable only in the logical and passive sense that darkness is the inevitable concomitant of light, evil has been raised to the same level of intention and power as God. At times it has been represented as superior to God and whatever is associated with God; at other times as coordinate with God and as engaged in frustrating His purposes. This is not a question merely of metaphysics, but of world-outlook and attitude toward life. Misleading interpretations of evil have always dominated the human mind and found expression in the classic literatures, in the oracles of scientists, and even in the great religions of the past. Their unwholesome and paralyzing effects may be noted in the ordinary conversations and actions of the average man and woman of today. As a first step in affirming and eliciting the creativity, that latent and potential good in the world which spells God, it is necessary to identify for the purpose of deprecation the conceptions of evil which obstruct the realization of the good.

One interpretation of life, which western civilization has inherited from ancient Greek culture, is that human life is the inevitable working out of a dire doom from which there is no escape. Man may delude himself with the belief that he is free to make of his life what he will, but in actuality he is trapped by a destiny which is deaf to his most heart-rending appeals. The very antithesis of that is the version of life implied in the Jewish religion. According to that version, human life is part of the process of creation which God initiated, a process in which the future always somehow redeems the past, and man is always being tested as to how long he can hold out in awaiting that future.

The idea of Fate, or Necessity, which in one form or another is to be found in every civilization, became a veritable obsession with the Greeks. It attained a depth and pathos unknown to any other people. It is writ large on almost every page of their great literature. In a variety of ways unparalleled in any other language, the Greeks sounded the threnody of man's impotence in the face of "Ananke," "Moira," or "Ker." The idea of fate was the keynote of Greek tragedy. Euripides put it clearly in *Orestes:*

> "Ye tear-drowned toiling tribes
> Whose life is but a span,
> Behold how fate, or soon or late,
> Upsets the hopes of man!
> In sorrow still your changing state
> Must end as it began."

The pattern of the world as the ancient Greeks conceived it may be said to have been that of a huge spiderweb, at the center of which Fate, or Necessity, like a great spider, feeds on the victims caught in the filaments of the web. In his ignorance man worships these very filaments as gods, praying to them to help him in his struggle against Fate, forgetting that they themselves are nothing but the very ooze of Fate. "Ah me! if Fate, ordained of old, held not the will of gods, constrained, controlled," sings the Chorus in Æschylus' *Agamemnon.* "Pray not at all, since there is no release for mortals from predestined calamity," says the Chorus in Sophocles' *Antigone.*

Although western civilization has long repudiated the Greek mythology and the Greek religion, it is dominated by the Greek mood and has come under the spell of the Greek view of life. In spite of the western man's acceptance of the religion that came from the East, he is the western man still and cannot free himself of the habit of thinking in terms of cold, impersonal and iron law which is relentless and unchanging. At bottom, this is nothing more than a resurgence of the belief in Fate. The idea of nature and natural law is the empire of Fate, conceived as extending into the innermost depths of the human soul.

This fatalism with which the western mind has always been obsessed has acted like a canker which disintegrates the soul of every people it has attacked. In ancient Hellenic culture the dread of Fate at least begot great epic and dramatic art. The plays of the great tragedians elicited from Aristotle the observation that they had the effect of purifying and exalting the emotions. They helped to give man a sense of his own worth and dignity. Because Fate was conceived as external to man himself, a power operating upon him but not inherent in his makeup, his attempt to measure himself against Fate rendered him morally victorious. He remained, like Prometheus, a defiant Titan, chained to the rock but unsubdued. It is otherwise with the modern elaboration of fatalism into scientific law. All human values dissolve under the scrutiny of scientific self-analysis. When fatalism is thought out to its logical conclusion, and the human being is shown up to be nothing but a congeries of wild and uncontrollable hates and passions that inhere in the blood, then the last shred of human worth and dignity disappears, and all that is left is abject self-pity. This is always the swan song of art; this marks its decadence.

The reiteration of this decadent note in the serious literature of contemporary America has led some writers to question whether our whole American civilization with all its fierce energy and activity is characterized less by youthful verve and vigor, as optimists would have us believe, than by a pathological restlessness that suggests a dangerous maladjustment to life. In the tragedies of Eugene O'Neill, in the novels of Dreiser, Anderson and Lewis, the most poignant theme is the struggle of characters, preconditioned by circumstances against a healthy adjustment to life, falling slowly victims to the inevitable consequences of their conditioning. But this note is no more characteristic of America than it is of other nations of the western world. It cannot be considered, as has been suggested, to be due to some racial compulsion. Rather is it to be ascribed to an intellectual compulsion, to the compulsion that inheres in the assumption of the occidental mind. The incubus of curse and calamity, bred of the elemental fear expressed in the belief that some irrevocable Fate has set its seal upon the career of the universe, has lain altogether too long on the mind of the western man. It must be shaken off, if western civilization is to survive.

According to the version which the Jewish civilization at its best has always given to man's place in the world, life is conceived not as the working out of a doom but as the fulfillment of a blessing. The process of that fulfillment is continually interrupted by all manner of evil. Evil is an interference; it is not Fate. "The die is cast," says the occidental man; and Jewish religion retorts, "But the final issue is with God." For God is the creator, and that which seems impossible today He may bring to birth tomorrow.

Once we learn to regard evil as the chance invasion of sheer purposelessness, and learn to identify all meaningful factors in the world with good and blessing, we become adjusted to whatever befalls us, not in the spirit of desperate resignation, but of hopeful waiting. Thus, for example, the Jews have been taught to regard their national history in the light of the blessing which God had bestowed upon Abraham. Though every page of that history records unparalleled suffering and tragedy, the Jews as a people never for one moment surrendered their faith in the blessing. The suffering and the tragedy have always been viewed merely as interruptions which have postponed the fulfillment of the blessing. They were never thought of as the fulfillment of some irrevocable doom. It is only Christianity, which has assimilated a great deal of the Greek spirit, that has made the doctrine of original sin a fundamental teaching. Calvinism, with its crystallization of Jewish thought into the fixed molds of western logic, has gone so far as to make of God a cosmic monster who delights in the tortures of the eternally damned.

According to Jewish traditional teaching, man is not trapped but tested. His vicissitudes should serve as a challenge to his faith, and patience in the face of the retardation of that blessing which he has a right to expect with the gift of life. To deny the worth of life and to fall into despair because the promise is slow of fulfillment is to fail in the test. This is the main point in the cycle of Abraham stories, which culminates in the account of the test to which God put Abraham when He commanded him to offer up Isaac. At first sight, it appears that in the Jewish religion, too, the notion of some inexorable doom hanging over mankind is present; for what else is the meaning of the curse imposed upon Adam and Eve for their having eaten the forbidden fruit? But the fact is that from the standpoint of the Torah the curse inflicted on mankind is not treated as irrevocable. On the contrary, the assumption throughout Scriptures is that God has revealed to the descendants of Adam the means whereby they may nullify the effects of the original curse.

Yet it would be untrue to say that Jewish civilization has always managed to steer clear of the idea of Fate. Time and again some of the wisest in Israel fell under the influence of Greek thought, and were so thrilled by their newly acquired teachings that they prated of them with the glib cocksureness of converts. One such wise man was Koheleth. He states that the doctrine of Fate in the well-known verses: "Everything has its appointed time, and there is a time determined for every occurrence under the sun. There is a time appointed to be born, a time to die; there is a time appointed for planting and a time for uprooting." [**] The sons of men are snared in an evil time, when it falleth suddenly upon them." [**] No wonder life was nothing to him but a series of vanities. His

[**] Ecc. 3:1, 2.   [**] *Ibid.*, 9:12.

book was taken into the Bible only because it has been reinterpreted to harmonize with the traditional outlook of
Judaism. Note, for example, what the Rabbis did with the
verse, "There is no new thing under the sun," [40] which
evidently contradicts the religious faith in man's power of
self-renewal. "The Sages said to Solomon," we read in
Pirkē de R. Eliezer,[41] "the righteous and all their works will
be *renewed,* but the wicked will not be renewed, and 'no new
thing' shall be given to all who worship and trust *under* the
sun. Therefore it is said, 'There is no new thing under the
sun.' "

The present condition of western civilization, with its
failure of nerve, may be traced to the sense of frustration
which man now experiences. This frustration is the outcome
of man's failure to attain that happiness to which he had
looked forward by reason of his increased knowledge of
nature and his ability to manipulate its forces. He has discovered to his consternation that there are forces within him,
selfishness, greed and lust, which rage within his soul and
work with the same inevitability as the mechanical forces
about him, but which he finds himself unable to bring under
control. He feels himself more trapped than ever. Out of
this realization nothing good can come, only despair and disillusionment. There is an urgent need for a renewal of that
faith in life which Jewish religion proclaimed when it identified God with creation.

Jewish religion, in its conception of God as creator, is the
antithesis not only of ancient polytheism and modern atheism, with its tendency to put Fate in place of the gods or God
as the final arbiter of human destiny. It is the antithesis also of
dualistic religion. It has always combated the assumption that
the good life is essentially one of continual battling against
malignant forces within and without man. It emphasizes the

[40] *Ibid.,* 1:9.   [41] Ch. LI.

fact that the universe is at one with man's highest nature and ready to cooperate with man in his efforts to elicit the best that is in himself.

It is true that dualistic religion, in contrast with polytheism, also attempts to interpret life spiritually by giving due weight to man's moral strivings. The world-outlook of dualistic religion does, in fact, imply an appreciation of man's efforts to better himself spiritually. But, in according divinity to the forces which frustrate man's higher strivings, it robbed those strivings of sanction and hope.

Ancient Egypt developed dualistic religion early in its career. That religion interpreted life as a conflict between two hostile forces—light and darkness, health and sickness, calm and storm, abundance and want. The world was looked upon as torn between two sets of forces antagonistic to each other, each struggling to get control over man and to determine his destiny.

Dualistic religion reached its climax in the Zoroastrianism of the Persians. In Zoroastrianism the world is conceived as being the creation of two powers, one of which from the very beginning chose the good, and the other the evil. They are engaged in mortal combat which is to continue until the end of time. It was this dualistic type of religion that an anonymous Prophet found it necessary to deprecate when he declared that the God of Israel was the creator of both light and darkness, of both evil and good. By representing God as the creator of evil, tradition intended to convey that evil was not abiding and could be transformed into good.

Christianity adopted the dualistic conception of the world. It accorded to Satan, the successor of Ahriman, a status coordinate with that of God. It regarded Satan as God's antagonist, a being intrinsically evil and the author of all evil. In Christianity's scheme of salvation, it was necessary for God to descend to earth, become incarnate, and sacrifice Himself to overcome the machinations of Satan.

The Jewish religion has been unsparing in its condemnation of the dualistic conception of life. It took every possible precaution to discourage the belief that the world was a battlefield of two antagonistic forces. The Rabbis of old seemed to be constantly on their guard against any open or secret adherence to the doctrine of double divinity. They had to make provision against the attempt to smuggle into the established liturgy prayers that implied the acknowledgment of a dual deity.[42] In the Mishnah we read: "Man is bound to bless God for the evil, even as he blesses God for the good." [43] Commenting upon the verse, "Ye shall not make with me gods of silver," [44] R. Akiba adds: "Do not act toward me as other nations act toward their gods. The other nations, when they are prosperous, honor their gods, but when misfortune befalls them, curse their gods. But they who are of Israel should give thanks, whether I bring upon them prosperity or suffering." [45] Both the mishnaic dictum and Rabbi Akiba's interpretation of the verse in Exodus, no doubt, imply that God is the author of all the evil in the world as well as of all the good therein. That is in keeping with the teaching of the Scripture: "He formeth light and createth darkness; He maketh peace and createth evil." [46]

Similarly R. Isaac, commenting on the very first words of Genesis, stresses their assertion of the unity in contradistinction to the duality of God. Associating them with the words of the 119th Psalm, "The beginning of Thy word is truth and all Thy righteous judgments are for ever," he observes, "For every sentence which Thou decreest for Thy creatures, they justify the verdict and accept it faithfully, and no creature can say, 'Two authorities have created the world.'"[47]

If we declared the doctrine that God created evil as a fixed dogma in Jewish religion, we would commit Jewish religion

[42] *Berakot* 33b.   [43] Mishnah *Berakot* IX, 5.   [44] Exod. 20:30 (23).
[45] *Mekilta ad locum.*   [46] Is. 45:7.   [47] Gen. R. I, 7.

to what the modern man must of necessity regard as a paradoxical conception of God. For to ascribe anything that is evil, whether relative or absolute, to God is to violate the logical law of identity. None of the theodicies has ever proved convincing. The very idea of a God requiring justification is self-contradictory. The argument that whatever may appear evil to us may, from an objective standpoint, be good is just so much wasted breath, because to the extent that anything is evil, even if it be mistakenly regarded as such, it is evil and nothing else. That it is a means to the good, or that objectively considered it is no longer evil, in no way detracts from the fact that, according to the traditional theologies, it is necessary to conceive God as having to make use of means that are evil and of being the author of experiences that are subjectively not good.

Historically considered, however, rabbinic teaching on the subject of evil is to be viewed as intended primarily to counter the religions that affirmed a dualistic conception of reality. According to that conception, the evil in the world was not intended as a means to the good or as part of a unitary plan in which it was subservient to the good. The dualistic religions regarded evil as coordinate in power with the good, as being the manifestation of a principle no less divine than goodness. By proclaiming its God as the author of both good and evil, the Jewish religion did not solve the question of evil, but it took an important step in the direction of a truer conception of God whereby He is identified solely with the good. *The duty which Jewish religion imposes upon the Jew to bless God for the evil as well as for the good should be interpreted as implying that it is our duty so to deal with the evil in life as not to permit it to negate our belief in God.* We should so identify ourselves with the divine in the world as to greet in the evil an occasion for reaffirming the reality of the divine. *Evil is chaos still uninvaded by the creative energy, sheer chance unconquered by will and intelligence.* So far as our power permits, such an attitude toward evil would of necessity impel us to transform the situation in which it inheres, so that it be eliminated. And where such elimination is impossible, as is the case with the fact of death, we would be impelled to acquire the capacity of transcending it. But in no instance would we confront evil in a spirit either of terror or of desperation. To be sure, this is no theoretic solution of the problem of evil, but it is the only way in which the human being will ever learn to adjust himself to it *creatively.*

It must not be assumed that traditional Jewish religion presents us with consistent and unvarying patterns of its main teachings. This is scarcely the case with anything that has come down from the past. But it is in its dealing with the problem of evil that traditional Jewish religion has most often swerved from the line of consistency. This is illustrated by its occasional lapses into a kind of microcosmic dualism. Though the Jewish religion managed to suppress all dualistic conceptions of the macrocosm, it failed to do so in its interpretation of human nature. Instead of treating the natural instincts and impulses in man as in need of being controlled and coordinated, it hypostatized the desires and hungers of men as the Evil *Yezer,* as the tool through which Satan sought to undo the work of God. The serpent that tempted Eve attained the status of a demigod. In the Kabbalah, he is the great enemy. Life in accordance with the law of God is conceived as a struggle against a host of inner enemies that beset the soul. The passage in Deuteronomy which contains ordinances pertaining to war is reinterpreted as applying to the war against the Evil *Yezer.* Throughout the days of penitence the Jews read the twenty-seventh Psalm to avow their confidence in God, despite the hosts with which the enemy besieged them. Again "enemy" is a metaphor for the hostile forces that prevent man from attaining his purpose in life. The Evil *Yezer* became a sort of rival to God, contesting for the possession of the soul of man.[48]

Thus even the Jews have not yet realized the full implications of their own monotheistic teachings. It should be noted, however, that certain of the rabbinic dicta pertaining to the Evil *Yezer* show an awareness of the dualism implied in the concept, and seek to resolve the paradox of the dualism of man's nature by the thought that even those aspects of human character which are considered as the promptings of the Evil *Yezer* may be made to serve God. Such, for example, is the interpretation of the verse, "Thou shalt love the Lord thy God with all thy heart," [49] to mean "with thy two *Yezarim*, the Evil *Yezer* as well as the Good *Yezer*." [50] To appreciate the originality of this conception try to imagine a Christian theologian urging his people to serve the Lord with the "Old Adam" in them as well as with the Divine Grace. Whether the author of this Midrash perceived the implication of his teaching or not, it unquestionably points to the idea that even that aspect of human nature which is self-regarding rather than altruistic and which, consequently, is responsible for any anti-social behavior may, nevertheless, be turned to good, if given its proper place in an integrated personal and social ideal.

In general, however, the Jews in the past yielded to the dualistic tendency which has led religion to evolve the idea of other-worldliness; for, other-worldliness is based on the despair of, and contempt for, this world. This dualism has also bred in religion the contempt for, and despair of, human nature, so that men came to believe that only a miracle, only the manifestation of supernatural grace, could redeem their nature from the dangers to which it was exposed. Instead of aiming to achieve the harmonious functioning of all the powers with which man is endowed, he has been treated as

[48] The verse, "There shall no strange god be in thee," (Ps. 81:10) is interpreted as referring to the Evil *Yezer* (*Shabbat* 105b).
[49] Deut. 6:5.   [50] *Sifrê ad locum.*

the battlefield of contending forces. A strife-torn mind must needs breed intolerance, truculence and sadism.

It may appear that dualism in religion is no longer a vital issue. But we must remember that certain errors are so inbred as to take on a new guise each time there is a change in men's thinking. The modern version of ancient dualistic religion finds expression in the popular interpretation of the facts about the struggle for existence which have become common knowledge. "Ethical nature," wrote Thomas H. Huxley, "may count upon having to reckon with a tenacious and powerful enemy as long as the world lasts." [61] That enemy was to him cosmic nature. Cosmic nature is only a new name for the old Satan, and man considers himself once again in opposition to world forces that are bent upon his destruction. In reality, however, it is incorrect to assume that cosmic nature is "red in tooth and claw," and that the ethical strivings of man lie outside nature and constitute as it were a world by themselves. If there is any metaphysical significance to the doctrine of the unity of God, it is that the ethical and spiritual strivings should be considered as belonging to the same cosmos as the one in which there is so much that is evil and destructive of the good.

For purposes of religion, we need not undertake to account for the existence of evil and suffering by proving them in detail to be serving some good. All that religion calls upon us to believe is that the element of helpfulness, kindness and fair play is not limited to man alone but is diffused throughout the natural order. It asks us to obey the moral law in order that we may call to our aid those forces in the world which make for human life and its enhancement. We cannot claim to comprehend why evil should be necessary in the process of world making and development. *But in affirm-*

[61] *Cf.* Huxley, Thomas H.: *Evolution and Ethics and Other Essays.* N. Y. 1897, 85.

*ing the existence of God, we deny to evil the nature of abso-
luteness and finality.* The very tendency of life to overcome
and transcend that evil points to the relativity of evil. As life
progresses, the tendency is increasingly reinforced and organized, resulting in the growth of man's power to eliminate,
transform or negate the evil in the world. Even in regarding
God as the author of evil, the Rabbis realized that "the
divine attribute which confers goodness excels the attribute
which sends punishment." [52] But for anticipation of what
must needs be the modern conception of God, we have to
refer to the following less frequent type of dictum, "The
Holy One, blessed be He, does not associate His name with
evil, but only associates it with that which is good." [53]

The modern man cannot possibly view earthquakes and
volcanic eruptions, devastating storms and floods, famines
and plagues, noxious plants and animals, as "necessary" to
any preconceived plan or purpose. They are simply that
phase of the universe which has not yet been completely
penetrated by godhood. Of course, this involves a radical
change in the traditional conception of God. It conflicts with
that conception of God as infinite and perfect in His omniscience and omnipotence. But the fact is that God does not
have to mean to us an absolute being who has planned and
decreed every twinge of pain, every act of cruelty, every
human sin. *It is sufficient that God should mean to us the
sum of the animating, organizing forces and relationships
which are forever making a cosmos out of chaos. This is
what we understand by God as the creative life of the universe.* Religion is the endeavor to invoke these animating
and organizing forces and relationships and to get us to place
ourselves in rapport with them.

That the world has not reached finality, but is continually
being renewed by God and in need of improvement by man
if it is to serve his ends, is a familiar Jewish idea. [54] Like-

[52] *Yoma*: 46a.   [53] Gen. *R.* III. 6; *Cf.* Gen. *R.* LIII, 4.
[54] *Cf. Ps.* 104:30; *Hagigah* 12b; Gen. *R.* XI, 6.

wise is the idea that man also is, in a sense, a creator, and therefore a collaborator with God.** Thus according to the *Zohar*, "the word *'Ami'* in the verse 'to say to Zion, thou art *Ami'* ** (my people) may be read *'Imi'* (with me), meaning to be a collaborator with Me." ** But the significance of these two ideas and of their relation to each other is beginning to be grasped more fully as man unfolds the creative powers latent within him. Man can transform his environment and bring into being such combinations of existing elements that they may with justice be regarded as new creations. The artist is the human being as creator *par excellence*. Out of a block of stone with a chisel, out of some grains of colored earth with a brush, or out of a few disparate sounds, he can fashion an environment of culture and spiritual illumination. But the artist is not the only creator. The inventor who achieves some new device for manipulating the forces of nature, and the scientist who discovers some new formula wherewith to fathom the truth, are also creators. It is in creating, not in possessing, that man finds his truest happiness. It is in what a man creates that his personality finds its complete fulfillment.

The scope of the creative faculty in man is continually on the increase. The whole complex of industrial civilization offers an unlimited field for the exercise of man's creative powers. In more recent times the organization of human life has come within the range of the creative faculty, and the possibility of a social order based on freedom, righteousness and peace is eliciting new spiritual powers. The rabbinic dictum, "The judge who renders a just decision is as though he had collaborated with God in the work of creation," ** anticipated the growing comprehension of the truth that man's creative function must find its principal exercise in the establishment of a social order based on justice.

We should learn to behold the divine element of creativity

** *Shabbat* 10a; *Ibid.*, 119b.
** Is. 51:16.   ** *Zohar* I, 5a.   ** *Shabbat* 10a.

in the functioning of intelligence which enables man to protect himself against the inclemencies of nature, to avail himself of its bounties, and to improve on its works by resorting
to social cooperation and good will which make our planet a
more comfortable place of abode. The courage and moral
resilience of human nature or morale, whereby man is enabled to face suffering and overcome fear of death, is equally
an expression of divine creativity. God is experienced as
creator, every time our thought of Him furnishes us an
escape from the sense of frustration and supplies us with a
feeling of permanence in the midst of the universal flux.

If we were to detach ourselves from the preoccupation
with the events of the moment and view the history of
civilization as a whole, we could not fail to note that the
opportunities for creative life are more widely distributed
than ever, though far less than ever in proportion to the
demand for those opportunities. But the demand itself is a
mark of progress. The abolition of slavery, the enfranchise-
ment of the propertyless classes, the emancipation of women
—these portend the awakening of the creative powers in
man.

Jewish mysticism caught the true spirit of the kind of religion man needs. The keynote of its teaching is the truth
that man shares with God the power to create. In the
Zohar [**] we are told that every new truth one discovers
when studying the Torah gives rise to a new firmament.
And out of the combination of such newly discovered truths
will ultimately arise the new heaven and earth, the creation
of which the great anonymous Prophet foresaw. The kind
of truth to which the Zohar ascribes this creative quality is
evidently ethical truth. This creative power of ethical truth
is trenchantly set forth in the following by Nicolai Hart-
mann: "It is man's knowledge of good and evil which puts
him on a level with divinity; it is his ability and authority to
help in determining the course of events, to cooperate in the

[**] Cf. Zohar I, 4b-5a

workshop of reality. It is his training in his world-vocation, the demand upon him to be a colleague of the demi-urge in the creation of the world. For, the creation of the world is not completed so long as he has not fulfilled his creative function in it. But he procrastinates; he is not ready; he is not standing on the summit of his humanity. Humanity must first be fulfilled in him. The creative work which is incumbent upon him in the world terminates in self-creation, in the fulfillment of his ethos. The ethos of man includes both the chaotic and the creative. In the former lie his possibilities but also his danger; in the latter he finds his vocation. To fulfill is to be human." [**]

A universe that responds to man's creative powers cannot be one in which either Fate or Satan shares the mastery with God. Such a universe is entirely God's. In the measure that man learns to release its potentialities for good, he transforms and transcends evil and associates himself with the divine energies that inhere in the universe. This is implied in the following two legends:

When all the materials of tabernacle and its appurtenances had been got together, the Israelites tried in vain to set it up. They then asked Moses to set it up, but he was unable to do so. He then turned to God and said: "I do not know how to set it up." "Try again," God replied, "and before long you will find that the tabernacle will set itself up, as it were." [*1] This apparently is the Jewish version of what is referred to as the temple not made by human hands. The implication is that, in the last resort, the structure of the spirit is rendered possible through the invisible forces that help to sustain and develop it.

The other legend illustrates the thought that at the disposal of man are invisible forces ever ready to cooperate with him, provided he takes the initiative. It tells of Haninah ben Dosa, a saint, who lived not long before the destruc-

[**] *Ethics,* translated by Stanton Coit, N. Y., 1932, Vol. I, 31.
[*1] *Tanhuma* on Exod. 39:33.

tion of the Second Temple. Haninah was walking along the
road to Jerusalem when he saw the pilgrims on their way
to the Temple with the various offerings they were bringing
to it. He could not join them because he was poor and had
nothing to bring to the Temple. This made him very sad.
As he walked along, he caught sight of a stone lying on the
road. He hewed it, and polished it, until it became beautiful
enough to be used in the wall of an edifice. This was the
offering he wanted to bring to the Temple. But when he
tried to carry it, he found that it was beyond his strength.
He asked some laborers who were passing what they would
want for carrying the stone to the Temple, but he was too
poor to pay the price they asked. Suddenly, as if from nowhere, five men appeared who, seeing his predicament, offered
to take the stone to Jerusalem, provided that he lent a helping hand. Before he realized where he was, he found himself
within the precincts of the Temple, presenting the stone to
the priests in charge. When he wanted to give the men the
few coins he had, they had already gone. Haninah told the
priests what had happened to him, and they said that the
men must have been angels sent by God, to help him in his
need."

The ancient Jew kept up his courage in the face of evil
with the thought that he must never despair, since the Creator could at any time effect a miracle, if necessary, to remove
that evil. The modern Jew, even if his scientific view of the
world has led to his placing reliance on the orderly processes
of nature rather than on the possibility of their being suspended, can keep up his courage, in the faith that the persistent and patient application of human intelligence to life's
problems will release the creativity that will solve them.
Whatever ought to be can be, even though it is not at present
in existence.

Man can no more operate with a finite and limited con-

" Cant. R. on 1:1.

cept of life's spiritual possibilities in the quest for salvation than he can operate with a finite and limited system of numbers in the pursuit of mathematical knowledge. He must either abandon the quest, or act on faith in life's unlimited creative possibilities. The Jew has been too much committed to the quest ever to abandon it. Every achievement of the creative spirit filled him with the conviction of the essential goodness of life. As the biblical narrative imagined God, after the creation of the world, reviewing His work and pronouncing it good, so he too, after every evil that he either had removed or transcended by the hope of future triumph, pronounced his benediction on life. *Oneg shabbat* was on the Sabbath the emotional reaction of the Jew when, surveying the toils and efforts of the week in the light of his faith, "he saw all that he had made and behold! it was very good." There is no reason why the Sabbath cannot similarly function for the modern man, why he cannot devote one day out of every seven to evaluating the work of the week in the light of his highest personal and social ideals, profoundly grateful for what has been achieved and eagerly and hopefully expectant of future achievement.

5

God as manifest in life's holiness which pre-
supposes personality

As the Sabbath serves to save the Jewish people from pessimism by emphasizing the idea that God manifests Himself in creativity, so it serves to save them from cynicism by emphasizing the idea that God manifests Himself in holiness. It represents not only the affirmation that life is not evil, but also the affirmation that it is not vain or futile, but supremely worthwhile.

The term "holy" is not frequently on people's lips in modern times. But we must not leap to the hasty conclusion

that holiness represents a concept that has no valid meaning
for our day. Words are frequently subject to peculiar vicissitudes of fortune. In an earlier generation there was no
higher praise for a man than to be called holy; today the
expression is more likely to be used with a tinge of con-
temptuous sarcasm. That is doubtless due to the fact that
the term "holy" or "sacred" has so frequently been applied
by interested individuals or organizations to outworn institutions which they wished to protect from destructive criticism. But when a communist, even though he may belong to
the "League of the Godless," fights for the possession of the
red flag that to him is the symbol of revolution, he is in
effect declaring it to be holy. When he observes May Day
as a day to be devoted to the interests of the laboring classes,
he is in effect pronouncing it a holy day. When he observes
Lenin's birthday or pays a pilgrimage to his tomb, he is to
all intents and purposes making a saint of him.

If we consider all the various objects, institutions and persons that have been declared holy, not only by the Jewish religion but by any of the other religions, both those of antiquity
and of modern times, we find that they are the objects, institutions and persons that particular groups felt to be of supreme importance to them. Many of these objects may, from
our particular point of view, be unimportant, and the ascription of holiness to them may appear absurd. We cannot today
thrill to the worship of "sacred cows." Doubtless that is one
reason why the term "sacred" has fallen into disrepute. It has
been applied to too many objects that are not sacred to us
at all. But there are objects to which we react with that
same degree of reverence. The distinction between the holy
and the profane, the sacred and the secular, is essentially the
same as the distinction between the valuable and the worthless, the important and the trivial, the significant and the
meaningless. Holiness is that quality by virtue of which an
object is felt to be of transcendent importance to us. Every

civilization recognizes the existence of such *sancta,* or transcendently important objects. The Constitution of the United States, the Declaration of Independence, the Liberty Bell, the national cemetery at Arlington, the Stars and Stripes, are but a few of the *sancta* that have been hallowed by America in the course of its history. The *Sefer Torah,* the Sabbaths and Festivals, Zion, the Hebrew language are a few of the Jewish *sancta* that the history of Israel has hallowed.

But the value or sacredness of such holy objects is not inherent in them. The flag is but a piece of colored cloth, the *Sefer Torah* a piece of parchment with ink-marks on it. It is life or the relationship to those purposes that spell life's meaning for us, that gives value to these objects. Their holiness is derivative and depends on our faith in the supreme value of life itself, in the holiness of life. If life itself is worthless, no object on earth can have any value. When religion ascribes holiness to God, it is saying in effect that life as a whole, the life of the universe of which our lives are but a part, is the supreme value from which all others are derived. The criterion for the sacredness of any object is its contribution to the enhancement of life, to our sense of its worth and importance.

The destruction of the supernatural sanctions of otherworldly religion, combined with the insecurity and instability of the economic and social order, has led to a profound skepticism and pessimism. Many who have lost their faith in a salvation that is of the other-world have not found an alternative faith in the possibility of salvation on this earth. To them human nature seems a hopeless jumble of irreconcilable impulses, the inhibition of which means frustration, and the free expression of which means distraction and satiety. "The eye is not satisfied with seeing nor the ear filled with hearing." ** Reason, which was so exalted in the liberal thought of the eighteenth century, has been dethroned

** Ecc. 1 :8.

from its position of eminence. It is no longer regarded as the judge and arbiter between conflicting impulses within the individual, nor as the disinterested observer and reporter of what goes on in the world outside. It has been shown to be guilty of "rationalization," to be an advocate pleading in behalf of our favorite prejudices after we have already decided on our course of action, or, more accurately, after subconscious urges have decided the issue for us. With such a view of human nature, what can we expect of human society? The smug assumption of progress, based on the advances of science, which characterized the nineteenth century, has yielded in the twentieth to a feeling that social change is effected not by the advancement of knowledge, but by the accidental shiftings in the balance of power between various national, racial and economic groups. Religion and ethics, which were once regarded as the forces that would bring about the Kingdom of God on earth, are now held to be mere epiphenomena, mere incidental concomitants of man's desperate struggle with nature and his fellow men for the material needs of his existence and the gratification of his lust for power and dominance. From such a point of view life loses all holiness, and no object in life becomes worthy of reverence.

Against this frame of mind the spirit of Jewish tradition protests by continuing to affirm the holiness of life. It does not deny the evils that exist, any more than in past ages it could deny the injustice, persecution and oppression which fell to the lot of the Jewish people in full measure. But in the face of them all it reaffirms the sacredness of life and proclaims the hope of salvation. To the question: "Is salvation attainable?" the Jewish religion answers: "Seek it and find out." There is no other way to answer the question. It is not subject to argument, because the affirmation must come not from our reason alone but from our whole being. The quest for more abundant, more creative and more harmonious living is itself an expression of the will to live. Though it is directed to the achievement of remote objectives, it is a source of immediate satisfactions even when it involves what is called self-sacrifice, but actually is self-fulfillment. For this quest is a characteristic of spiritual health, and spiritual health like physical health is manifest in serenity. That is why the joyousness of the Sabbath has received such emphasis; why, for example, it was deemed inappropriate to fast or mourn on the Sabbath day, and why the Rabbis recommended that the day be not entirely devoted to serious religious devotion, but should be divided equally between religious consecration and enjoyment, for there is a definite relation between the *kedushat shabbat* and the *oneg shabbat*.**

Out of this deep conviction that human life, whether its circumstances be happy or unhappy, is never futile or meaningless arises one of the most significant ethical and religious ideas with which the Jewish religion has enriched the spiritual thought of mankind, the idea that man is created in the image of God. The concept of meaning and value is itself meaningless except as it relates itself to personality. Only as we become aware of desires and regard objects from the point of view of their ability to satisfy desire do we evaluate them. The consciousness of selfhood or personality comes with the recognition that we have wants, and have also resources within and outside us by which we may hope to satisfy these wants. These wants are not necessarily selfish in the sense of being related to the self-preservation of our individual organism. On the contrary, as pointed out in the discussion of the concept of salvation, they are no less directed to the preservation and enhancement of the lives of others

** *Cf. Pesik. R.* end of Ch. XXIII; festive meals, *Shabbat* 118b; change of garments, *Shabbat Jer. Peah* VIII, 8 (21b) ; the myrtle as decoration of the home on the Sabbath, *Shabbat* 33b; preparation for the Sabbath, *Ibid.;* 119a, *Bezah,* 16a.

than of ourselves. But they all require for their satisfaction a certain rallying of our powers to meet a situation, an assertion of the will to be effective, a sense of responsibility and importance of our contribution to life, out of which the ideal of selfhood or personality emerges.

This emergent personality is the distinguishing feature that differentiates man from all other forms of organic life. Some of the lower animals may also have wants, and many of these wants, as in the case of such social insects as the bees and ants or of the gregarious mammals, demand at times the sacrifice of the individual life for that of the community. But the response to the situation that creates these wants is instinctive and involves a minimum of conscious evaluation. In the case of man, however, owing to the memory and imagination with which he is endowed, each situation summons up the past and involves anticipations of the future. The faculty of speech allows him to rehearse, as it were, in his own mind various possible responses to situations that impend. Along with the awareness of limitations that oppose his realization of his aims, there comes the awareness of the possibility of transcending these limitations, for in the course of living he has done so again and again by the use of memory, imagination and reason. The faculty of language has not only made it possible for him to evaluate situations on the basis of his direct personal experience, but through its use as a medium of communication has enabled him to live vicariously through the experiences of others, even of other generations that have preceded him. Man's personality, therefore, expresses itself in the creation of a hierarchy of meanings and purposes, or of a kingdom of ideals. These ideals direct his will to be effective, which is only another name for the will to live, as it manifests itself in human beings.

It is the sense of man's dependence for the satisfaction of his wants on powers in the universe other than himself which gave rise to the God idea. It is the organization of these wants in terms of personal ideals that gave rise to the conception of a personal God. When the Bible tells us that "God created man in His image," it testifies to the modern historian that man created God in his image. But we must not minimize the significance of what is implied in that statement; it undoubtedly implies a sense of kinship between the human differentia and the divine. That this kinship was fully realized is evident from the following characterization of man: "Yet thou hast made him little lower than the angels (or more correctly gods) and hast crowned him with glory and honor." ** In response to an assertion by R. Akiba that one of the greatest principles of the Torah is "Thou shalt love thy neighbor as thyself," Ben Zoma declared, "An even greater principle is that expressed in the verse: 'This is the book of the generations of Man. In the day that God created man, in the likeness of God made He him.' " ** The medieval philosophers were at great pains to disabuse the Jews of their day of the notion that God had anthropomorphic attributes. The denial of these attributes is indeed one of the principal dogmas of the Maimonidean creed. But viewed in historic perspective, one of the greatest strides made by man in his religious development was when he advanced from an animistic fetishism to anthropomorphism.

So long as the wants which expressed men's sense of dependence on God were mainly of a material nature, the power on whom men depended could easily be conceived in the form of any natural object. Bull worship probably arose at a time when the bull, because of its use to a pastoral and agricultural people, was conceived of as supremely important. Since it meant so much to their food supply, and since their food supply was their dominant interest in life, the main want which their god had to satisfy, it seemed appropriate to conceive of him in the form of a bull, the father

** Ps. 8:7.   ** *Jer. Nedarim* IX, 4 (41c).

or archetype of the beings on whom their life depended. But as their civilization advanced and as their supreme wants assumed the forms of ideals, they demanded of God assistance in the realization of these ideals. He ceased to be primarily the bread-giver and became the law-giver. The holiness of God ceased to be based solely on His power, and came to be based on His righteousness.

Since such a conception as righteousness could be associated with no identifiable object in nature except a human being, God was conceived in human form. Later, in a more reflective and philosophic era, there was a tendency to analyze the human being into body and soul. Then, inasmuch as personality and ideals were associated only with the soul, the change in man's conception of man resulted in a change in his conception of God. He became pure soul, but He remained a person. In fact, the physical universe became a sort of unanthropomorphic body with which God invested Himself to effect His personal will.

Modern science has again reconstructed our picture of the universe and destroyed the dichotomy of body and soul, matter and spirit, physical and metaphysical, which characterized the Middle Ages. We cannot conceive of God any more as a sort of invisible superman, displaying the same psychological traits as man, but on a greater scale. We cannot think of him as loving, pitying, rewarding, punishing, etc. Many have therefore abandoned altogether the conception of a personal God, and prefer to think of ultimate reality in terms of force, energy and similar concepts.

Such an attitude, however, is erroneous. It violates completely our sense of the sacredness of life. It is irrelevant to human ideals and the quest for salvation. It partakes of the same error as primitive animism, for it associates God primarily with man's sense of dependence on powers other than his own for the satisfaction of his material wants, while leaving the thirst of his spirit unslaked. Whither shall we look for encouragement in our quest of the ideal? To apotheosize force or energy is contrary to that intuition of the Jewish spirit which, from the time that the Jewish religion may be said to have come into existence, always identified God as that power in the universe which sponsored the ideals that gave meaning to life.

We do not need to pretend to any knowledge of the ultimate purpose of the universe as a whole, as the theology of the past sometimes claimed for itself. But it is an undeniable fact that there is something in the nature of life which expresses itself in human personality, which evokes ideals, which sends men on the quest of personal and social salvation. By identifying that aspect of reality with God, we are carrying out in modern times the implications of the conception that man is created in God's image. For such an identification implies that *there is something divine in human personality, in that it is the instrument through which the creative life of the world effects the evolution of the human race.* The corollary of the thought of man's likeness to God has always been the sense of the sacredness of human personality, of its inherent worth.

It is this which justifies Ben Zoma's assertion of the paramount ethical significance of the doctrine that man is created in God's image. Even to love one's neighbor as oneself becomes meaningless to one who does not reverence personality in himself. The logic of the principle, "Love thy neighbor as thyself" implies that if we hate ourselves, if we look with contempt upon human nature in us, regarding it as on a level with the impersonal meaningless life of the lower animals, we shall then be logically justified in using other men as we use the lower animals, for the gratification of any passing lust. There is a kind of cynicism which might be said to teach the principle, "Hate thy neighbor as thyself." It was formulated long ago by Bernard de Mandeville [97]

[97] Mandeville, Bernard de: *A Search into the Nature of Society*, 1723.

when he wrote: "I flatter myself to have demonstrated that neither the friendly qualities and kind affections . . . are the foundations of society; but that what we call evil in this world, moral as well as natural, is the grand principle that makes us sociable creatures, the solid basis, the life and support of all trades and employments without exception: that there we must look for the true origin of all arts and sciences, and that the moment evil ceases, the society must be spoiled, if not totally dissolved."

If, however, we recognize that every human soul is sacred, that as we have a personal ideal which represents our vision of the meaning of life, so also has our neighbor, and that we cannot interfere with his striving for self-realization without doing violence to our own ideal, we know that we must love our neighbor as ourselves. Recognition of the sacredness of the personality of the individual, in his desire to be an effective cause in contributing to the enhancement of life's value, is a fundamental criterion for judging social institutions. All tyranny, all oppression, all exploitation that uses human beings as mere pawns in a game not only inflicts hurt on them but serves *lema'et et hademut,* to "diminish the divine likeness," to cheapen and profane life and weaken our perception of its potentialities for evoking and sustaining the ideals that make life meaningful and holy.

6

Commitment to Judaism a source of salvation to the Jew

In all that has been said, it is assumed that the Jew is committed to the quest of salvation, to the service of the Power in the world that, manifesting itself in life's creativity and holiness, makes it possible for him to fulfill the possibilities for good that are latent in his personality. But there are many today who question the validity of this or any other Jewish commitment. The question frequently takes a form somewhat like this: How can the fact that I was born a Jew impose any obligations upon me? It was a mere accident in regard to which I was not consulted. I accept responsibility for my own individual acts and will stand committed by any obligations I have voluntarily assumed. But I deny the right of my ancestors to assume obligations for me. My religion is a personal matter between me and my God; my ethics is a personal matter between me and the individuals with whom I have personal relations.

The Jewish answer to this attitude is the idea of covenant-ship. This is the third of those ideas which are associated by tradition with the Sabbath, and which enable it to function as a means of salvation. The Sabbath has always been regarded as a sign of God's covenant with Israel. On other days of the week the observant Jew, when he says his prayers, wears the *tefillin* as a "sign of the covenant," but not on the Sabbath. For the Sabbath itself is considered a sufficient token of the covenant to require no further visual reminder. In the liturgy of the day, the idea of the Sabbath as a symbol of the covenant finds frequent expression. Thus, in addition to the cosmic significance of the day as a "memorial of creation," the *Kiddush* which ushers in the Sabbath refers to it also as "a memorial of the exodus from Egypt," when God took our fathers, "a nation from the midst of a nation," to dedicate them to His service. The basis of this twofold explanation of the significance of the Sabbath is to be found in the Torah itself, for in the version of the Decalogue contained in Exodus, the reason for observing the Sabbath is associated with the creation,[**] while in the version contained in Deuteronomy it is associated with the exodus from Egypt.[**] From the point of view of the traditional theory of revelation, there is no particular significance to this fact, since God could attach as many meanings as He wished to any day He asked Israel to observe.

[**] Exod. 20:11.   [**] Deut. 5:15.

But when we view the institution of the Sabbath as of human origin, and reinterpret the texts as expressive of human reactions to the experience of observing the Sabbath, the juxtaposition of the two ideas becomes very meaningful.

What it means is that when the Jew experienced on the Sabbath a renewed faith in the creative possibilities of life and a heightened sense of its sacredness, he was aware that this enhancement of his personality, this *neshamah yeterah,* or "oversoul," came to him not as an individual but as a Jew. No individual is spiritually self-sufficient. The meanings and values that life has for him are a result of his relationship to the civilization in which he participates. The more that civilization functions as a way of salvation, the more intense will be the individual's sense of identification with it, and the realization of its worth, or its "holiness." For the Jew of old, Judaism, the civilization of the Jewish people, did function as a way of salvation. Hence the feeling which was universal among the Jews before the so-called Emancipation, that it was a privilege to be a Jew.

Persecution and oppression only confirmed this feeling, for he could not identify himself by any stretch of imagination with the civilization that expressed itself with reference to him in terms of massacres, expulsions and *autos da fé.* His revulsion against such a civilization convinced him all the more of the superiority of his own, of the divine sanction of its laws and institutions and of the divine providence that presided over its history. He never felt God-forsaken. On the contrary, he looked upon his very persecution as a mark of special favor. His sufferings were not evidences of disfavor but, on the contrary, *yesurim shel ahabah,* "chastisements of love," which would be compensated in the world to come.

With the characteristic faith that their life was the fulfillment of a blessing, not the consequence of a curse, and that they were being tested, not trapped, they looked forward to the time when Judaism would be vindicated and victorious, when Israel would return to its land and the God of Israel be acknowledged by all men. Therefore they could say at all times, in the words of the liturgy, "Happy are we! How good is our portion! How pleasant our lot! How beautiful our inheritance!" And they could bless God, "who chose us out of all the nations and gave us His Torah," "who gave us the true Torah and implanted life everlasting in our midst."

When we compare this attitude with that of most modern Jews, we are aware both of the need of some analogous doctrine to make Jewish life in the present other than a burden to the Jew, and of the inadequacy of the ancient conception of the choice of Israel to function in this manner. If ever there was a situation in which Jews might pardonably surrender to a feeling that they were trapped by fate, it is the situation in which many Jews find themselves today. Can Judaism give them a secure economic position? Can it give them an opportunity to pursue the arts and sciences in a culture medium with which they are familiar and at home? Can it make them forget that the whole world seems to mock and deride them? Can Judaism function for them as a source of salvation when they are aware that they are Jews not by choice, nor even by the mere accident of birth, but because all escape from Judaism is cut off, even escape by way of open apostasy, a door that was not closed in the religious persecutions of the Middle Ages?

The average Jew today is conscious of his Judaism as one is conscious of a diseased organ that gives notice of its existence by causing pain. If we take any Jewish paper and eliminate from its contents reference to, and discussions of, anti-Jewish discrimination and the like, we will find little left in the paper. The interest of most Jews in Judaism is quite definitely a reaction to anti-Semitism. Even those Jews, who respond with an intensified Jewish chauvinism that praises everything Jewish, give the impression of whistling to keep up their courage. They may speak of the Jews as the Chosen People, but one feels that this vaunt is but the typical self-assertion of the personality that is haunted by an inferiority complex. That doctrine does not have the same meaning as it had for our fathers. This is seen from the fact that it does not carry the same implications in terms of conduct. Our fathers were convinced that the Jews were the Chosen People, because their faith expressed itself in loyal obedience to the Torah, which was God's precious gift to Israel and Israel alone. To the modern Jew who boasts of the Jews being the Chosen People, this belief expresses itself, for the most part, in scanning every bit of news from the sport sheets to the financial columns for success stories of Jews, that might serve to bolster up his pride in the face of the sense of inferiority that his position as Jew imposes.

Why cannot the faith in God's choice of Israel function today as it did in the past? The reason is not far to seek. It is because the form that this doctrine took in the past is out of drawing with our modern conception of God and incompatible with our highest ethical ideals. To imagine that God loves the Jewish people more than others, we must in the first place conceive of God as a loving God, not merely in the sense of evoking love in man, but in the sense of actually experiencing desire as man does, exercising choice as preference in an anthropopsychic, if not anthropomorphic, manner. Nor can we, with our knowledge of history and comparative religion, accept the traditional version of an exclusive revelation, which the covenant implied for our fathers.

We cannot fail to recognize in the claim of Jewish superiority a kinship and resemblance to the similar claims of other national and racial groups which have been advanced to justify oppression and exploitation. Such claims have been used in defense of the imperialistic exploitation of the yellow and black races by the whites on the ground that they were "the white man's burden." They are the ground for the German persecution of Jewry, in accord with the Aryan clause of the Third Reich's fundamental law. They were in the past the grounds on which our own people rationalized their conquest and expropriation of the Canaanites. The highest ethical thought of our day views all such claims to superiority of one race, nation or caste as detrimental to the interests of humanity, and hence as essentially vicious.

How can we solve the problem presented by the obvious need on the part of the Jewish people for a faith that shall function for us today as the ancient faith in God's covenant with Israel functioned for our fathers, and the obvious inadequacy of that faith in its traditional form? The idea of covenantship can be interpreted in terms that will enable it to satisfy the need of the Jewish people for faith in its future, if we focus our interest not on the specific ideas implied in the covenant as it was understood by tradition, but rather on the experiences that gave rise to these ideas. If the Jew saw in the Sabbath, and in those Jewish ideals of which the observance of the Sabbath made him aware, evidence that God had singled out the Jewish people for salvation, it was because of the joy that he experienced in pursuing those ideals. The folkways of his people gave him such an orientation to life, such an opportunity for the expression of his personality and its purposive direction, that he felt himself and his people an instrument for the achievement of a destiny mapped out by God Himself. Moreover, he was aware that the laws and customs of other peoples with whom he came into contact could not afford him the same degree of satisfaction; he inferred from this that his own laws and customs were inherently better than those of others, and that, since God was their source and sanction, He must have favored the Jewish people with a revelation which had been vouchsafed to none other.

From the point of view of Judaism as a body of revealed

doctrine, it becomes impossible to reconcile the idea of the covenant and its implications with the scientific and ethical assumptions that govern our daily thinking and acting. But no such difficulty confronts us, if we regard Judaism as the civilization of the Jewish people. Then *covenantship becomes the sense of the creative possibilities of Jewish life.* These give value and meaning to the fact that we are heirs of the Jewish past. Consequently the garnered experiences of the Jewish people as stored up in its tradition, and in the institutions to which it has given rise, are so many resources available to us in our efforts to achieve personal and social salvation. We are then no less aware that we are ancestors than that we are descendants. It is not so much our duty to our fathers that makes it important for us to maintain the continuity of our tradition as it is our duty to our children. All human progress has been achieved by the fact that each generation begins its career where its predecessors left off, availing itself of the accumulated knowledge and wisdom of past ages. But we cannot expect the Chinese people, for example, to preserve the heritage of Hebrew literature and make it available for the world, any more than we are ready or able to assume responsibility for preserving the Chinese classics and elaborating their implications for our day.

This is the answer to those who object to any specific commitments by reason of their being Jews. Such commitments are inherent in the very structure of society and civilization. Mankind is not all of one piece and, in the task of preserving and developing the spiritual heritage of the human race, the various historic groups have to assume responsibility, each one for the maintenance of its own identity as a contributor to the sum of human knowledge and experience.

But we must not lightly dismiss the objection to commitment by tradition. There are limits to the extent to which loyalty to the past may commit us to any specific forms of thought or behavior. If there is an extensive revolt against commitment to tradition, it is largely because the role of tradition in human history has been commonly misunderstood.

The role of tradition in society is analogous to the role of memory in the individual. It has two aspects, one that of retaining experiences, and the other that of recalling them. At no time do we retain all our past experiences in mind. But memory recalls for us particular tracts of past experiences as they are needed to meet a present situation. Such experiences as we have no occasion for recalling are eventually completely forgotten. Also such experiences as are hurtful rather than helpful tend to be forgotten, a fact that is cited by psychologists as an explanation for certain forms of amnesia.

All this has important bearings on our attitude to tradition. Just as the individual recalls from the store of experience retained in his subconsciousness only those experiences that are relevant to present needs, so tradition must be continuously evaluated in terms of its relevancy to modern needs. Institutions that have lost relevancy for a long period of time tend to become obsolete, just as experiences, which it is not found necessary to recall, tend to be forgotten. And just as any new experience is always interpreted by reference to the past and associated with it, so the new experiences of each era fit themselves naturally into the pattern of tradition. They may change the pattern, but do not disturb its continuity or identity. Like the patterns in a fabric, so long as the loom works, the pattern grows. The particular social organism to which the tradition belongs is the loom that produces it. Only the destructive maladjustment of the organism itself can destroy the continuity of the pattern.

To leave figures of speech aside, it is important for us to realize that loyalty to Jewish tradition does not mean the closing of our minds to present experiences and of our hearts to present needs. It does not mean that our ancestors can tell us what we ought to think, or how we ought to act. They can tell us how they thought about similar problems, and how they acted in similar situations, but the responsibility for the decision is our own, and there can be no responsibility without freedom. Our responsibility to our forefathers is only to consult them, not to obey them. Our responsibility to our descendants is only to impart our most cherished experiences to them, but not to command them. These responsibilities, though limited, are real and important. Their whole-hearted acceptance is implicit in the ideal of covenantship, and suggests the method by which Judaism in our day may serve as a way of salvation to the modern Jew and make him feel his Judaism to be a privilege rather than a burden.

The sense of burden and maladjustment which the modern Jew experiences comes to him through the combined operation of two important factors. The first of these is the antipathy of the Gentile world, which makes the Jew feel that the best he can expect of Gentile society is to be treated as a tolerated guest in a Christian civilization. In times of strain and crisis, he tends to become an alien competitor and scapegoat for all the social evils. The second factor is that he finds loyalty to his own people an impossibility, because such loyalty has been associated with the acceptance of ideas and forms of behavior that he no longer feels to be valid or sacred. He thus remains a Jew to the Gentile, and yet finds himself in inner revolt against much that he has been taught to associate with Judaism. He wants to identify himself with the culture of the modern world, but feels frustrated in that the Gentiles look upon him as an interloper, and his fellow Jews look upon him as disloyal to Jewish tradition.

The suggested interpretation of what is involved in loyalty to tradition offers an escape from this dilemma, and the only escape. It enables the modern Jew to assimilate whatever he is capable of assimilating of the best of modern thought, provided he also seeks contact with Jewish culture and endeavors to enrich Jewish communal life with the fruit of his thinking. It enables him to be as critical of Jewish tradition as he may wish to be, provided he tries not only to criticize Jewish tradition but to correct it. There is one indulgence which he may not allow himself—the indulgence of aloofness. "Separate not thyself from the community," [10] is an implication of covenantship on which we must insist.

The flight from Judaism, the effort to seek an escape in alien cultures, began in the eighteenth century, when loyalty to Judaism as it was then conceived and the free pursuit of values to be found in the civilization of the western world were definite alternatives between which one had to choose. Now that the flight has been turned back, and the need of a choice between alternatives no longer exists, Jews have nothing to lose and everything to gain by whole-hearted identification with their people. If the Jewish people succeed in establishing a Jewish community life, committed to the maintenance of Jewish tradition in the sense here formulated, there is no reason why Jewish civilization cannot again function as a way of salvation.

If we respond to the present situation with that optimism which has expressed itself in the faith in the creative possibilities of life, we will not give up in despair the age-old struggle of the Jewish people for life, nor content ourselves with the death-in-life of mere survival. We will mobilize all the powers of intellect, feeling, and will that reside in our people to reshape the conditions of Jewish community life, so that they will give free play to Jewish personality in the service of the loftiest ideals to which Jewish experience past and present has given birth. If we react to the present situa-

[10] *Abot.* II, 4; IV, 5; *Cf. Mekilta* (Tractate *Pisḥa*) on Exod. 13:8.

tion with our traditional faith that life in any circumstances is sacred and capable of yielding meaning, we will not respond to the present situation with mere protest and lamentation. Recognizing the fact of the community of Jewish interests, we will do all in our power to effect the co-operation of Jews in mutual helpfulness and in common striving for the salvation not of the Jews alone but of the whole world. Such objectives will restore to Jewish life that sense of fulfilling an historic destiny, which is the essence of the idea of covenantship.

Such an interpretation of covenantship escapes the evil that inheres in the traditional notion of God's choice of Israel, in that it in no wise assumes the superiority of the Jewish people over others. The value of Judaism is in no wise dependent on its ability to demonstrate its superiority to other ways of life. So long as it serves as a way of salvation for the Jew, that is its own justification. Let the other civilizations each seek to fulfill their own destinies in the light of their own highest ideals; their success can only help, not hinder, Jewish development. For we need have no hesitancy about appropriating the best thought of others, whenever we can enrich our civilization by doing so, and we may well cherish the hope that our own civilization may enrich the thought of others. But neither their assimilating our thought, nor our assimilating theirs, will destroy either our identity or theirs. The personality of the individual is not impoverished but enriched by an interchange of ideas and experiences with other individuals. And the same is true of the collective soul of a people.

Nor does covenantship, thus understood, assume self-sufficiency on the part of Judaism. The charge has often been brought against Jewish nationalism that it means the withdrawal of the Jewish people and the segregation of their interests from those of the rest of the world. Humanity is one and human civilization is one; why set up the ideal of a specific Jewish civilization?

True it is that humanity is one and that human civilization must be one. This is in harmony with the traditional Jewish ideal of the covenant, in that it always insisted that the covenant relationship between God and Israel would issue in the eventual establishment of God's Kingdom over the whole earth, when the dominion of arbitrary power would be removed and all the nations would be one united band to serve God whole-heartedly. But the unity of the human race is an organic unity, not a mere conceptual one. One does not build humanity by organizing individual men. Nature has already organized them into collective groupings that have evolved specific civilizations with distinctive character. What is essential is that each of these groups feel a responsibility for collaborating with all others to promote the welfare of all, and that each recognize the sacredness of such collective personalities in itself and in others.

Exaggerated national claims have impeded the development of a unified, integrated human society. But not so the nationalism which views Judaism as a religious civilization. It is committed to the thought that Jewish civilization is the collective effort of the Jewish people to organize their community life so that it may yield the maximum of self-realization. But self-realization implies the recognition of the selfhood of the *alter* as well as of the *ego,* and this is true whether we speak in terms of individual egos or collective egos.

That is how the Jewish conception of God evolved from henotheism to monotheism. The God of Israel was originally conceived as the Power Who manifested Himself as king in Israel, by laying down the law of righteousness which was to govern the relationship of the Jew to his fellow Jews. When the perception grew that there were ethical relationships between the Jew and other peoples, the God idea had

to be widened to give sanction to these relationships as well.
Thenceforth Israel's covenant with God was no longer conceived as a contract between a national god and his people,
by which he promised protection and security in exchange
for worship and obedience. It was conceived as the consecration of the nation to universal ideals which, it was expected,
would ultimately issue in an integrated cooperative human
society.

If we regard God as the Life of the universe, the Power
that evokes personality in men and nations, then *the sense of
the nation's responsibility for contributing creatively to human welfare and progress in the light of its own best experience becomes the modern equivalent of the covenant idea.* In
it is implied that reciprocity between God and the nation
that the term covenant denotes. For the life of the nation
is not lived in a void but in the world. It is dependent on
and conditioned by its geographic and social environment.
It thus owes all the values which it develops to the fact that
God, the Life of the universe, is such as to call forth these
values. They can be realized only to the extent that the
nation conforms to the highest ethical standards of which it
is aware. At the same time the nation is an active agent in
developing these ethical standards that express God's will,
and not merely a passive instrument. In this sense, God still
governs the nation, and the nation still establishes His Kingdom, in collaboration, of course, with all other nations.

Such an ideal of Jewish nationhood fulfills the conception
of Israel as a holy people, without any pretensions to a mission to the world different from that to which any nation
that chooses to live its life on a high ethical plane may lay
claim, and without any assertion of superiority. At the same
time, if Jewish life were so conceived by the Jewish people,
and if it were so organized as to give effect to this concep-.
tion of the role of the Jewish people in the world, the feeling
of inferiority and self-hate which poisons the mind of the

Jew today would at once be eradicated, and he would begin immediately to experience something of what is meant by Judaism's functioning as a way of salvation.

If the Sabbath, which is still observed, at least to some extent, by great masses of Jews, were utilized to the full to emphasize the implications of the traditional ideals associated with it, it would contribute immeasurably to the achievement of this goal. If its ritual and all Jewish activities connected with it stressed the view that emphasizes the creative aspect of life as against the destructive, if it emphasized the holiness of life as against the view that life is meaningless and futile, if it thrilled us with an appreciation of the role Israel has played and will continue to play in the history of mankind, the Sabbath would unquestionably be experienced as an occasion for delight in the Lord. For through our observance of the Sabbath we shall come to know God as the source of salvation, of that state of being in which all our powers are harmoniously employed in the achievement of worthwhile aims.

III

GOD AS THE POWER THAT MAKES FOR
SOCIAL REGENERATION

THE foregoing chapter has shown how the Sabbath may be reinterpreted for the modern Jew. It can be made to symbolize the meaning of God as the Power that makes for salvation. An examination of the other sacred days of the Jewish calendar will show us other meanings of the God idea as it might function in Jewish life. Of these days none are more permeated with religious meaning for the Jew than Rosh ha-Shanah and Yom Kippur. Those are preeminently *Yamin Noraim,* "Solemn Days," when the thought of God dominates the spirit of the religious Jew more than at any other time. The fact that on these days great numbers of Jews, who otherwise seldom attend the synagogue, feel impelled to join in its worship testifies to the important place they occupy in the religious consciousness of the Jew. For, while the Sabbath is legally the most binding, these days are emotionally the most stirring. A study of the ideas associated with these days and expressed in their ritual should, therefore, be rewarding to any one who wants to know what God meant to the Jewish people in the past, and what God can mean to us today.

In view of the soul-stirring significance of Rosh ha-Shanah and Yom Kippur, we should expect to find not only frequent reference to them in the earliest records of our people, but also evidence that they were treated from the very beginning with great solemnity. But when we turn to the Bible to have our expectations verified, we are disappointed. In contrast with the three Pilgrimage Festivals, Pesaḥ, Shabuot

and Sukkot, which are given an important place in Deuteronomy as well as in the other legislative parts of the Pentateuch, Rosh ha-Shanah and Yom Kippur receive no men-
tion whatever in Deuteronomy, and even in the other books
are referred to mainly in terms of special rites to be accorded
them in the sanctuary. Outside the precept to abstain from
work, and, in the case of the Day of Atonement, to fast and
afflict one's soul, there is nothing to indicate that these holy
days played by any means as important a part in early Israel
as did the Pilgrimage Festivals. Moreover, when we turn
to the other books of the Bible, we come upon passages, as
in the case of Ezekiel (45:18–20), that point to the fact that
these holy days were not yet fully established in pre-exilic
times.

Jewish scholarship has thus far made little headway in
determining the origin of their observance, or the spirit in
which they were celebrated before the Maccabæan period.
Historical study has yielded but few suggestions of general
interest. One of them is that Rosh ha-Shanah, as the first
of the seventh month of the year, derived its sanctity from
the sacredness which the number seven had for the ancients.
Like the seventh day of the week, the seventh year, and the
completion of seven cycles of years, so the seventh month
was also signalized as holy. Accordingly, its inaugural day
was celebrated with more *éclat* than that of the other months.
The other interesting suggestion is that made by the late
Meir Friedmann [1] with regard to Yom Kippur. According to
him, that day served as a prelude to the Festival of Ingathering. At that time of the year the Jew was accustomed to give
himself over to whole-hearted rejoicing in the yield of the
fields and the orchards. The fear, however, of having committed sin might cast a cloud on his rejoicing. He therefore
observed Yom Kippur to purge himself of whatever sins he
might have committed during the preceding year. This cir-

[1] J. Q. R. Old Series, Vol I, 66 *et seq.*

cumstance has made of Yom Kippur the climax to the penitential season which begins on the first day of the seventh
month, or our present Rosh ha-Shanah.

It is to this association of Rosh ha-Shanah and Yom
Kippur with the idea of penitence that these days owe that
development which has given them their present importance.
The penitential character of the season is stressed in the
ritual of these days by our accenting the kingship of God.
In the *Amidah* liturgy of the day, the phrase "the Holy
King" is substituted for "the Holy God," and the keynote
of the entire ritual is the prayer that the God of Israel be
acknowledged by all the nations.[*] The reason for this
emphasis on the kingship of God is clear. Penitence meant
to the Jew *teshubah,* a "returning" to the God of Israel.
Since to stray from Him was to ignore His godhood and
His authority, the first step in repentance was to become
aware of His godhood and authority, to acclaim His sovereignty. If we are interested in a study of the Jewish holy
days for the light they cast on the meaning of God to the
Jew, Rosh ha-Shanah will interest us primarily as illustrat-
ing what the Jew meant by belief in the kingship of God,
and how that belief functioned in his life. An analysis of
this concept will show us the important implications that this
doctrine had for our fathers. But it will also do more. It
will reveal to us implications that only our modern experience has enabled us to discover, implications that make the
doctrine important for us as a help to our daily living.

I

*The change in the conception of God's sovereignty necessi-
tated by the modern emphasis upon God's immanence*

To speak of God as King is to employ a metaphor that
would not readily suggest itself to any modern person. When

[*] *Cf. Sifrē* on Num. 10:10, par. 77 and Ps. 47 which is recited before
the sounding of the *Shofar.*

we use it in our ritual, we are speaking, as it were, in the thought-idiom of an earlier age. But we would be hard put to it, if we were to try to replace all such familiar metaphors with other figures of speech or with more literal language. That makes it all the more important for us to be aware of the literal truths which those ancient metaphors should convey to us. This applies especially to the most conspicuous metaphorical epithet used in speaking of God, the epithet "King."

Throughout the variety of facts or teachings implied in the metaphor of the kingship or sovereignty of God, there is the basic implication that the status quo of human life constitutes an imperfect manifestation of godhood. We are asked to affirm the sovereignty of God precisely because the authority of the divine aspect of life has not been universally recognized or fully established. Thus the earliest conception of God's kingship carried with it the thought that this kingship was not perfectly manifest so long as other gods were also worshiped in Israel. The later conception of God's kingship as the universal recognition of Israel's God implied that so long as other nations did not worship the God of Israel, His kingship was still not fully recognized. When the idea of God's rule was identified with the faith in the coming of the millennium and the life of the world to come, it implied that the existing order as experienced by the Jewish people did not adequately manifest the sovereignty of God. The very conception of the God of Israel as king was thus enriched through the inference one was expected to draw from it, that the only time when His godhood could be manifest would be one in which superstition would disappear, righteousness prevail and salvation be universal.

Modern experience has revealed new meanings that are latent in the conception of God's sovereignty, meanings suggested by changes in the idea of sovereignty as a political concept. In the past, political sovereignty was conceived as inhering in the person of the ruler. To command was not only

his political function but his personal right. All legal authority emanated from him. He was the State, and the people
were his subjects whose sole political function was to yield
obedience to his will. But since even kings are mortal,
and kingship is an abiding necessity, the sovereignty of
kings was commonly conceived as being delegated to them by
an immortal divine overlord or King of Kings—God. The
king was God's anointed who ruled by divine right. No subject could call him to account; only God could do that. Inevitably, God, the invisible King, the true sovereign of the
State, and later of the world, was conceived of in terms
analogous to those in which the political sovereign was conceived. He was a person apart from the world that was
governed by His will. The moral law was whatever He
commanded, and men had no responsibility for that law
other than the responsibility of obedience. Since in the general ignorance of the origin of legal institutions all traditional standards were conceived to be of divine origin, man's
moral life consisted of obedience to God's Torah and *mizvot*.

The ascription of kingship to God is by no means limited
to Jewish religion and the religions that derive from it. It is
rather inherent in the development of the God idea. For the
conception of a deity is fundamentally the hypostasis of the
interests vital to the life of the group, tribe, clan or nation.
The people feel the need of superhuman support and sanction for their wars, their laws and their routine transactions;
and since these activities are commonly administered by a
personal ruler, the superhuman aid invoked is similarly conceived as coming from a personal Ruler. But in Jewish religious development the effect of monotheism upon the notion
of God's kingship has been to accentuate the primacy of a
just social order. Under the guidance of the Prophets, Israel
had been taught to recognize "the holy God sanctified by
righteousness," the Source and Sponsor of the moral law, as
the sole God and King.

But God could be King only as men obeyed His law.
Hence the affirmation of God's kingship involved subscrib-
ing to the highest ethical standards of the nation, as reflected
in its interpretation of Torah. It also proclaimed the advent
of the Day of YHWH (ultimately to develop into a conception of the world to come) when God would assert His
kingship by destroying all who defied His authority, and by
establishing a new social order in the world. The Prophets
thus identified the sovereignty of God with His manifestation as the Power that makes for social regeneration. The
Psalmists, too, caught this prophetic spirit and hailed the
day when God would assert His sovereignty and authority:
"He cometh to judge the earth. He will judge the world
with righteousness and the peoples with His faithful-
ness." [*]

But this identification of God as the Power that makes for
social regeneration was in ancient times prevented from exercising its full effect as a stimulus to social reconstruction,
by reason of limitations inherent in the ancient conception
of sovereignty. Just as in political life responsibility for
the welfare of the State did not reside with the subject, except to the extent that obedience was demanded from him,
but with the sovereign, so the welfare of society in general
was not regarded as dependent mainly upon human beings,
except to the extent that they were required to conform to
the traditional Torah and *mizvot,* but upon God as the King.
He in His own day and of His own will, by a direct and
miraculous intervention in the natural order of society,
would establish the Kingdom of Heaven on earth. Man's
task was to wait, to obey and never to lose faith in ultimate
divine salvation.

*What is needed in modern life is a conception of God's
sovereignty that can function as an aid to the regeneration
of society by direct human agency, without reliance on an*

[*] Ps. 96:13.

illusory hope of miraculous intervention. This can be achieved, if we reconstruct our conception of the sovereignty of God to conform with our changed conception of political sovereignty.

In modern political theory, sovereignty is not considered as residing in some royal personage to whom the people is subject. It is not, as in absolutist hereditary monarchies, a personal prerogative that the monarch can convey to his heirs. Sovereignty resides in the people. It is recognized that the king of England reigns but does not rule, that he is but a symbol of British sovereignty rather than himself a sovereign. In other countries where the king may have more power, he is nevertheless regarded as the executive head of the nation performing important governmental functions in its behalf. He is little more than a minister of State. He exists for the nation, and not the nation for him. Sovereignty does not reside in him, but in the State or nation. Where there is a republican form of government, the fundamental law clearly implies, if it does not explicitly state, that "governments derive their just powers from the consent of the governed." Yet in all these countries sovereign political power exists and operates. But it operates not as the manifestation of the will of any one person. It results from the interaction of the personalities of all the individuals of the State in their relation to one another and to the political institutions of their social heritage.

Similarly, in our religious life we must identify the sovereignty of God not with the expression of the will of a superhuman, immortal and infallible individual personality, but with that Power on which we rely for the regeneration of society and which operates through individual human beings and social institutions. Faith in the sovereignty of God comes then to mean faith that in mankind there is manifest a Power which, in full harmony with the nature of the physical universe, operates for the regeneration of human

society. God does not stand apart from men and issue commands to them. His presence is evidenced in those qualities
of the human personality and of society by which the evils
of life are overcome, and latent good brought to realization.
By ascribing primacy to these qualities we acclaim the sovereignty of God.

The change in the conception of the sovereignty of God,
from one based on its analogy to the discarded idea of sovereignty as residing in a royal person, to one based on its analogy to the current conception of sovereignty as immanent in
the nation itself, implies a change in what we are to regard
as the spiritual interests of men. With the modern conception
of God's sovereignty as immanent, the antithesis between the
spiritual and the material interests of men falls to the ground.
Under the old theology, whatever was enjoined by divine
revelation as being the fulfillment of the will of God was
spiritual, and all other interests of men were merely practical
and of an entirely different and inferior order. From the
point of view of a truly modern theology, all the interests
of men are a response to practical life situations. Men seek
to employ to best advantage the physical, intellectual and
emotional powers with which they are endowed in securing
human life and rendering it more abundant. This involves
the subordination of certain human interests and impulses to
others, in accordance with their relative importance to human
life. *The spiritual interests of men are those which are so
important to human life as to demand the subordination of
the lesser interests, but they are not essentially of a different
order.*

From this point of view, the traditional religious objective of *"perfecting the world under the Kingdom of the Almighty" must mean the establishment of a social order that
combines the maximum of individual self-realization with
the maximum of social cooperation.* The most salient characteristic of the human animal as distinguished from other

biological species is that his whole evolution has been determined by the effort to harmonize and develop simultaneously
two contrasting types of interest, the individual and the
social. In no animal species are individuals as differentiated
from one another in behavior as among men, and in no animal species are individuals more dependent on mutual aid
and collaboration than among men.

2

*The revaluation of the concept of God's sovereignty in terms
of individual responsibility*

Every individual must be for himself. A parasitic dependence on others is allowed only to the immature, the insane, the physically handicapped and those criminals whom
society has not the heart to destroy but cannot trust as co-
operating members. Although in modern times the "Social
Contract" theory of government is no longer regarded as
descriptive of the process by which governments came into
being, its implications as to the rights of the individual retain most of their validity. According to that theory, all
government rests on a delegation of authority from the individual for effecting purposes which demand cooperation
with other individuals, with a reservation of the right to free
individual initiative in all other matters. For, basically, every
individual looks upon the world as his world. No matter
how circumscribed by social regulation and regimentation his
life may be, he still feels that he is shaping his own life by
day-to-day responses to the situations in which he finds himself. He works at his job, he spends his money, he bestows
his friendship and affection, he talks or is silent, he has opin-
ions and tastes in accordance with reactions that are dis-
tinctly his own. They are influenced by all the world about
him, but that does not make them less his own, for nobody
else can have these identical reactions. Each individual is

unique and irreplaceable, an effective cause influencing however minutely his social and natural environment as he is influenced by it. If God's Kingdom is established on earth, it must be established by individuals.

It is the perception of this truth that has given rise in religion to the idea of the soul, the divine spark in man that makes him a responsible moral agent accountable to God for the use he makes of his personal endowment. To be sure, our conception of the soul cannot be that which our fathers held in the past. It too must undergo a change similar to the change in our conception of God. We can no longer look upon the soul as a sort of invisible inner man that inhabits and animates the human body. The soul is nothing other than the human being as a person or self. But this in nowise changes the implication of sacredness that attaches to the soul, for God as the Power that makes for social regeneration can act only through the souls of men. His sovereignty is therefore dependent on them. Just as the sovereignty of the nation resides in the citizens and their relation to the State, so the sovereignty of God resides in the souls of men and their relation to society. It is no accident, therefore, that Rosh ha-Shanah, which is preeminently dedicated to the thought of the sovereignty of God, is also the *Yom ha-Zikaron,* the day dedicated to the conception of the importance of every individual soul to God. Thus we read in the liturgy of the day:

"For the remembrance of every creature cometh before Thee, each man's deeds and destiny, his works and ways, his thoughts and schemes, his imaginings and achievements."

For, though man is likened to a fragile potsherd, a fleeting shadow, a scudding cloud and a fugitive dream, we are not to infer from this that man's life is worthless and insignificant, a "vanity of vanities." Its true significance is expressed in another simile, one that runs like a refrain through our High Holyday ritual. It is that which compares life to a book into which we pray to be inscribed.

It is an ancient simile. We are told that when God was about to destroy Israel after the worship of the Golden Calf, Moses interceded in their behalf and pleaded that, if God would not forgive them, God should blot him out of His book that He had written.[4] The Psalmist uses the same figure of speech:

> "Thine eyes did see mine unformed substance,
> And in Thy book they were all written—
> Even the days that were fashioned,
> When as yet there was none of them."[5]

The comparison of human life to a book is significant, because it solves the paradox of religion's evaluation of man, now as a creature whose days are but "travail and nothingness," and again as an immortal soul who lacks little to being a god. For a book is composed of letters of which each letter by itself conveys not even an infinitesimal fraction of the meaning of the book. Viewed as a disparate entity, apart from his relations to his fellow men and to the society of which he is a member, the individual is a thing of naught. This is expressed in Hillel's dictum, "When I am for myself, what am I?"[6] All that we call character, personality, soul or spirit in the individual is utterly inconceivable except in terms of his relationship to other persons and objects. But if we view the individual in the light of his relations, as a single vital cell in the social organism of the human race, we must acknowledge that the whole life of society is lived in and through the individuals that constitute the present generation of men and women. Apart from them there is no society, no Kingdom of God.

If we recognize the sovereignty of God in the creative and regenerative forces at work in human society, it follows that

[4] Exod. 32 :32.   [5] Ps. 139 :16.   [6] *Abot.* I, 14.

that society most clearly manifests God's sovereignty in which human personality has the fullest opportunity for self-realization. This means, in the first place, that every individual should have whatever is needed for the normal functioning of his physical organism: adequate nourishment, healthful living conditions, a proper balance between work and rest, protection from disease, etc. It means that he should have economic security, lest he be inhibited by fears and anxieties from the full exercise of his physical and mental powers in the satisfaction of his personal wants. It means that no natural instinct of his should ever be totally suppressed and, more specifically, that he have the opportunity to exercise his procreative powers to the maximum personal satisfaction consistent with the interests of society and of the other individuals involved. It means allowing free play in every individual to intellectual curiosity, esthetic enjoyment and creativity, and initiative and responsibility in the improvement of the society in which he lives.

Such self-realization has nothing in common with egoism or selfishness, for it is based on a recognition that the ego can fulfill itself only by being an efficient unit of a social organism. We can enhance the value of our own life only by bringing into play all our human instincts, including those which have reference to the interests of the society in which we live. To live a self-centered life is not to fulfill one's function as a human being, not to live according to nature. It is to lead a stunted, thwarted existence, to be a separate letter of the alphabet torn out of its context in the book of life, to be a lost soul. Sooner or later, the self-centered human being comes to be "fed up" on what he considers life, whether it is pleasure or power. Egocentricity acts like alcohol or opium, transporting one for a time into paradise and then thrusting one into the hell of black despair. Suicide thrives where individualism prospers.

For there is something in the human being that craves

giving itself to others in selfless devotion, some objective to live for beyond one's self, whereby one's life becomes integrated into the context of universal human life. The suppression of this phase of human nature is more truly the cause of the sense of frustration and unhappiness than the suppression of one's physical hungers. Hence, if we do not want life to appear useless and fatuous, we must live for some goal which is linked with the good of humanity, some objective which can fit into the kind of human existence that makes sense, that has meaning, that possesses continuity, pattern, design, beauty, that points to progress in that it moves in the direction in which the stream of history can be shown to flow. The scientist who lives for the discovery of truth, the inventor who widens the social consciousness of masses of the people by bringing new experiences within their reach, the physician who labors to bring healing to his fellow men, the artist who opens our eyes to the beauty that is all about us—each of these finds a zest in life through his whole-hearted devotion to his chosen objective.

All these men are interested in something outside themselves that contributes to human welfare and progress. They find their personal enlargement and satisfaction in what they stand for. We cannot all be scientists, physicians and artists, but we can all make life more livable for ourselves and give it more worth and dignity by identifying ourselves with some social cause or movement. True, there are causes which may take us out of ourselves and yet work evil and rob life of meaning, such as the imperialistic ambitions of chauvinistic nations. Our choice of objectives must be governed by our devotion to the Kingdom of God, to a social order in which universal peace, justice and enlightenment make possible the maximum development of every individual's personality. But, having chosen our objective, we should identify ourselves with them in the spirit of *kiddush ha-shem*. This phrase, which denotes the sanctification of

God's name, has in the Hebrew language acquired the meaning of martyrdom. It signifies that no price is too great to pay for the privilege of devotion to God. For human dignity rests on the basis of human responsibility. Take away from human nature the sense of social responsibility, which is one of the deepest intuitions of the religious attitude to life, and it is indeed true that "the superiority of man over the beast is naught, for all is vanity."[7]

The note of moral responsibility which is implied in the conception of Rosh ha-Shanah as a Day of Divine Judgment is nowhere more impressively sounded than in the *u-netanneh tokef* hymn, the origin of which is significantly ascribed to an act of marytrdom. R. Amnon, who submitted to torture rather than accept Christianity, is said to have composed that hymn while dying from the torments inflicted upon him.

In the act of martyrdom, the power and grandeur of religion are brought to a focus. By dying for an ideal, the martyr makes death itself affirm the value of life and its power to cast off the evils that make life in the present intolerable under the yoke of oppression and persecution. By defying death, the martyr deprives evil of its deadliest weapon, the power of intimidation. Let none compare the suicide with the martyr.[8] The suicide welcomes death because he hates the world and cannot find God in it; the martyr because he loves the world and finds complete self-fulfillment in carrying out the will of God, though it involves his own destruction as an individual. To the suicide, death means a bankrupt's exemption from the discharge of life's responsibilities when these appear overwhelming; but to the martyr, death is a payment in full with all the resources that he commands.

The role of the martyr in history is significant from yet

[7] Ecc. 3:19.
[8] *Cf.* Gen. *R.* LXXII, 8; *Aboda Zarah* 18a (the answer of R. Hanina b. Teradion to his disciples); *Baba Kama* 61a (the comment on II Sam. 23:16).

another angle. Not only does it represent the sanctification of life in defiance of death, but it also points to the assertion of individual faith against social pressure. The martyr comes into conflict with the collective will of his contemporary society as expressed in its authoritative institutions because he views those institutions as *memshelet zadon,* as the dominion of arbitrary power which must vanish like smoke before the advent of the Kingdom of God. As a devotee of those ideals which he feels *should* be authoritative, he is a subject of that Kingdom. The etymology of the term "martyr" is significant. It is derived from a Greek word meaning "witness." The martyr is one who feels that his whole life must bear testimony to the supreme value of his ideal and that, if he surrendered his principles under pressure, his conduct would be a *hillul ha-shem,* a profanation of the name of God and a betrayal of His Kingdom. The Jew's crowning distinction is to be a witness to God. "Ye are My witnesses, saith the Lord, and I am God." [9] "If you act as My witnesses, I am God," says the Midrash, "but if you do not act as My witnesses, I am not, so to speak, God." [10]

The sounding of the *Shofar,* the most ancient rite in the observance of Rosh ha-Shanah, has been interpreted as a summons to the soul to present itself before the judgment seat of God. It has also been construed as the *teruat melek,* the salute to the Sovereign, with all its implications of fealty and allegiance. It has functioned, and should still function, in the life of the Jewish people as an invitation to the individual Jew to renew his oath of unqualified allegiance and loyalty to those ideals, the realization of which would convert human society into a Kingdom of God. He must not seek these ideals in any law or revelation external to himself, to which his whole personality, the result of his own unique experience, does not give full consent. He must recognize as authoritative his own best vision of his capacity for ren-

[9] Is. 43:12.   [10] *Sifrē,* Deut. 346.

dering service to the cause of humanity and helping to bring it under the yoke of God's kingdom. For, God exercises His sovereignty through us, and to delegate to others alive or dead the responsibility for our own ethical decisions is to refuse to contribute our share to establishing God's Kingdom; to act thus is to act irresponsibly and disloyally. Obedience to a code, no matter how ancient and sanctified it may be, is not enough. This is the clear implication of faith in the kingship of God, when we give to that metaphor the only meaning that it can have in the light of our modern attitude to kingship.

3

The revaluation of the concept of God's sovereignty
in terms of social reconstruction

There is another equally far-reaching implication to be derived from the conception of the sovereignty of God as immanent in human nature, in addition to that of individual initiative and responsibility in living an ethical life. As has been shown, belief in the coming of God's Kingdom always implied a discontent with the existing order as not in conformity with the divine. But so long as the sovereignty of God was conceived as external to the human souls which in their mutual relationships constitute society, the responsibility for bringing about the better order was conceived as belonging to the Divine Ruler, since the sole obligation of His subjects was to obey the clearly defined terms of His revealed Law. On the other hand, *from the point of view of the sovereignty of God as immanent in human society, the responsibility for ushering in the Kingdom of God on earth rests squarely with mankind.*

This change in point of view is not wholly to be accounted for on the basis of our changed conception of political sovereignty. The attitude of passive waiting charac-

teristic of past ages had deeper roots. Such passivity of man
with regard to the advent of the millennium, or of the world
to come, was engendered by the growing sense of deficit,
helplessness and frustration in the face of overwhelming
odds. In recent centuries, as man has learned to apply his
intelligence to the manipulation of natural forces, he has
become impatient of passive waiting. It is now recognized
that a better future cannot emerge out of the mode of life
that we at present lead, without human striving and initiative. A better future will come about as a result of our recognizing, appreciating and utilizing to the utmost the elements of the better life present in our everyday existence.
In comment of the verse, "The Lord will reign for ever and
ever," [11] R. José the Galilean adds: "If the Israelites at the
Red Sea had said, 'The Lord *reigneth* for ever and ever,' no
nation in the world would have exercised dominion over
them. Instead, however, they said, 'The Lord *will* reign for
ever and ever,' thus postponing His sovereignty for the
future.[12] R. José apparently considered it a mistake to post-
pone the realization of God's Kingdom to the future. That
Kingdom is essentially of the present. This does not mean
that we can afford to eliminate from our reckoning the
future beyond our individual life on earth. There will always be evils which man will be unable to transform. These
he will have to learn to transcend by making the better
future of the human race an integral part of his guiding and
satisfying idea of himself.

The main inference to be drawn from the "sovereignty of
God" must henceforth be the duty which that sovereignty
imposes upon man to transform the conditions of life so as
to make the world livable physically, socially, and spiritually.
This inference is in keeping with that growth of the conception of God which has led to the emphasis upon divine immanence in human life. *The tendency is now to view man's*

[11] Exod. 15:18.   [12] *Mekilta ad loc.*

initiative and active striving in transforming the conditions under which he lives as the way in which God manifests Himself or becomes sovereign in human life. The more recent conception of God's sovereignty is, in a sense, a return to the mood of earlier prophecy, when the dominant stress was upon righteousness as a means of immediate salvation rather than of salvation at some remote future.

Initiative and active striving presuppose a definite goal. The traditional notion of the world to come as unimaginably glorious will get us nowhere. After the bitter experiences which mankind has passed through, it is possible to state quite specifically what sort of a world would deserve to be called one in which God is sovereign. As already stated, it would be one in which the polarity of man's nature—individuality and sociality—could be fulfilled. In all our relations and dealings with one another the criterion should be: to what extent do they further the conservation and enrichment of individual personality and the ever-increasing measure of cooperation among individuals and groups? To synthesize these two objectives, which are apparently mutually exclusive, must become the dominant aim of all education and the passionate purpose of all social reform. Our urge to self-expression must seek satisfaction in ways that recognize and encourage the urge to expression in other selves. The recognition of our need for the collaboration of others in supplying our wants must assert itself in a truly voluntary exchange of services and goods to mutual advantage, and not in attempts at exploitation and forced labor. This is the inescapable ethical inference from the biological nature of man as a social animal, dependent for the satisfaction of his wants both on individual initiative and responsibility and on collective and cooperative action.

There is a disposition in our day to scoff at utopias, at imaginative reconstructions of the social order. In the name of realism such visions of a possible world to come are regarded as mere fantasies tending to divert men's minds from the sordid realities of the present. Utopias, as the term itself implies, always exist in the nowhere, never in the here; what relevancy can they have to practical life? Moreover, long before we change conditions to conform to our ideals, these ideals themselves change and we seem to be pursuing a will-o'-the-wisp. Where there is no fixed goal, can progress be anything but illusion?

Reasoning of this sort is characteristic of an age of transition and doubt such as ours. Old objects of our loyalties, institutions that we have invested with the sanction of religion, hoping to find in them our salvation, have cheated our expectations. How can we summon faith to reconstruct the ideal of progress, which was so rudely shattered for us by the experiences of the World War and the economic debacle? The mid-Victorian optimism which interpreted evolution to mean inevitable progress toward "that one far-off divine event to which the whole creation moves" has yielded in large measure to a pessimism that regards evolutionary changes as the mere shifting of patterns in a meaningless conflict of forces.

Progress cannot mean for us today a definite approach to a static final goal. But there is still a sense in which we can speak of progress. It lies in the perception that evolution has direction. Movements that conform to this direction are progressive; those that obstruct it are reactionary. Although that progress is not always in a straight line, the course of human history shows that the human race is moving in the direction of enhanced personality and enhanced sociality. Where people once identified society with a small family, tribe, or clan, we are beginning to think in terms of a world-society. Where at one time every detailed act of the individual in the pursuit of his work or his leisure was hedged about by traditional taboos of the tribe and had to conform to ancestral habits, men are demanding and obtaining more and more of autonomous direction in the development and expression of their personalities. Personality and sociality are not static goals. They can never be reached and passed. But their pursuit gives meaning and value to human life, and renders it inherently worthwhile.

With such a conception of human progress, we are in a better position to understand the significance of such religious concepts as the "Kingdom of Heaven" or "the world to come." Man is not merely affected by evolutionary change; he participates in the process. His ability to do so depends on his capacity for imagining situations that do not as yet exist, evaluating these possibilities and endeavoring to realize those which give promise of more abundant living. "Without vision a people perisheth." [11] Utopias are the effort of society to project its own future. *But our utopias must be conceived as projects; they must not be regarded as forecasts of an inevitable future. Their sole value lies in their serving as criteria for the evaluation of the institutions of our present social order and as indices of progress.*

It is in its failure to realize this function of the prophetic vision that other-worldly religion has made its fatal mistake. Other-worldly religion felt intuitively that human life was moving in a direction that suggested as its destiny a social order characterized by justice and peace. But it did not perceive that this destiny was mankind's projection of its own future, and hence was realizable only through human participation in its realization. Lacking the psychological and sociological approach to an understanding of human nature, the generations of the past thought that the vision of the millennium was imparted to man by God as a promise of ineffable bliss that He had prepared for His loyal servants. As long as men obeyed His revealed Law, they thought that they would have a share in the life of this future world. For our day such a casting of our burdens on the Lord is not

[11] Prov. 29:18.

justified. We cannot consider ourselves loyal servants of the Divine King, unless we take upon ourselves the task "to perfect the world under the Kingdom of the Almighty." We must strive to reconstruct the social order in ways that would give evidence of our allegiance to the creative spirit in human life, that spirit which makes for personal self-realization and social communion.

The conditions of our own day cry for such reconstruction. Our economic order has been well-summed up as one in which "they who reap harvests have to stand in the bread line; they who build houses have not a roof over their heads; they who sew expensive clothes have to go about in rags." The progressive concentration of wealth in the hands of the few, the increasing proletarianization and impoverishment of the middle classes, the increasing helplessness of the workers, these are actualities which are rendering the world unlivable. That millions of persons should be subject to the fear of the morrow and the consequent disintegration of personality at a time when plants for the abundant production of necessary goods and commodities are lying idle is criminal stupidity. This need not be. In such a situation the vision of the justice and tranquillity which could prevail, if men only knew how to live, should give us no rest.

The contemporary political scene is marked by the dismal failure of the various efforts that have been made to put an end to war. Democracy, on which men pinned their hopes, has proved inadequate. Having been made the stalking horse of a corrupt economic system, it has failed to produce governments that express the will of the people. But the ideal of democracy has not lost its validity, and a defeatist attitude toward it has no justification. We should not give up the hope of achieving an adequately representative government integrally related to a righteous economic order and to an internationalism without which there can never be universal peace.

Our educational system has failed us. The high hopes men entertained concerning the effectiveness of universal education have been dashed. There is no real correlation between higher education and character. Our academic training has not made better people of us. But the last word in education has not been said. We can still aspire to a system of education in which the individuality of the child, as the embodiment of the future, will be fully respected, and in which the welfare of humanity free from war and exploitation, will be the supreme objective.

In asserting the belief that the evils of our social order need not be, we take issue with the traditional interpretation of history, which prevailed throughout the Middle Ages, and which still influences the religious attitude of great numbers of men in our day. Tradition taught the paradox that human society was irredeemable, that no amount of human effort to improve it was of any avail. The world—that is, all collective endeavor—was natured in sin. This is the meaning of medieval asceticism. It was not alone the body individual that was the seat of Satan, but also the body politic. The only way to save one's soul was to flee society. The asceticism of the monastics and of the Protestant sectaries—the Anabaptists, Mennonites, Quakers—is the expression of those in the Church who took that doctrine seriously.

The Jews took a similar attitude. They had their ascetic groups who renounced all worldly occupations and were enabled by their families or the community to devote themselves wholly to the study of Torah, religious meditation and prayer. The remainder of the community, while it did not renounce the world altogether, made a virtue of passive resignation to its inherent evils. Even messianic movements were frequently frowned upon as attempts *lidehot et ha-kez,* "to precipitate prematurely the ultimate divine goal," before God had willed its attainment. Such opposition as the Zionist movement originally encountered from Orthodox quarters resulted mainly from this conviction that all human effort at social improvement was bound to be futile. In the past there was no such thing as faith in the growing goodness of men. Only the grace of God was the source of hope.

4

The ethical versus the communist conception of social reconstruction as the alternative to the traditional one

The expectation of social reconstruction by miraculous intervention in human affairs is today discredited, but the lack of faith in human nature and men's capacity for ethical behavior still persists and has influenced the philosophy of men who are at the very opposite pole from medieval religion. In communist circles the philosophy prevails that social change is effected not by the projection and realization of ideals but by the conflict of social forces struggling for economic advantage. If masses of men are oppressed and exploited, let them not put their trust in a general ethical advance, for even moral concepts are devices of the ruling class in society to maintain the advantages they possess under the status quo, but let them become class-conscious, become aware of their own interests and united in their determination to satisfy these interests. To be sure, communists have their own utopia of a classless society which is somehow to come about after the proletariat of the world has taken possession of all natural resources and machinery. But their strategy is to deprecate the possibility of an appeal to ethics and religion and to rely rather on an appeal to envy and resentment. Such an appeal puts the whole responsibility for effecting a better order on the oppressed and degraded classes, and not only exempts but excludes all other classes from participation in social improvement.

There is no gainsaying the reality of the conflict between

the possessing classes, on the one hand, and the propertyless workers, on the other. Nor need it be denied that the rationalization of the interests of the comfortable classes can be detected in much that passes for the expression of moral sentiment. We must likewise concede the right of the oppressed to combat their oppressors in trying to secure for themselves a just share of the world's goods. But with all these concessions to the philosophy of class-consciousness. one must still regard that philosophy as inadequate to effect its own purpose, and incomparably inferior to the point of view of ethical religion.

Moreover, class-consciousness always assumes that the status quo is satisfactory to the possessing classes and unsatisfactory only to the dispossessed. This is far from being universally true. People lose their appetite for food when hungry faces watch them at their meals. A class that finds its life dependent on the exploitation of others is frequently haunted by a sense of insecurity, as though they lived on the side of a volcano that is in danger of eruption. Particularly the more far-seeing and imaginative often look forward to a change in the social order which would leave them with less prestige but with more security, freedom and social communion. The history of revolutions would show that they are usually projected by individuals of the upper classes rather than by those who are to benefit most by the revolution, since the latter commonly lack faith in the promised emancipation, "by reason of impatience of spirit and hard labor." Moses who liberated the Hebrews from Pharaoh's yoke was himself reared in the house of Pharaoh.

The truth which ethical religion stresses is that any social condition which denies the opportunity of self-fulfillment to any class of men is dangerous not to the men of that class alone but to all men. We do not consider that the proper way to check an epidemic is to ask those who have been smitten by the plague to organize for their own cure. We realize that the same conditions which are responsible for some being afflicted with the disease today will be responsible for others being stricken by it tomorrow. All social evil tends to be contagious. Unemployment of labor causes a loss of purchasing power that makes capital investment worthless and leads to the impoverishment of once wealthy people. Only a just social order can be a safe one. The real evil that the proletariat has to contend against does not inhere in the irredeemable wickedness or irreconcilable hostility of the possessing class. It lies in the inadequacy of our capitalistic economy to effect objectives that even most capitalists would regard as desirable. Our task, therefore, must be to make people not class-conscious but condition-conscious, to make them aware of the nature of those conditions that cause widespread personal frustration and endanger the cooperative peace of society.

There is a lesson that modern technology should have taught us, but that we have been slow to apply. It is that *men can improve their lives neither by accepting existing conditions as final nor by trying to change the essential nature of things, but by studying nature and, in entire conformity with natural law, selecting the means that are adapted to the desired ends.* Men have learned this lesson and applied it to the transformation of their physical environment, but they have not learned to apply it to changing the conditions that affect more intimately their personal and social life. The improvement of human life does not involve changing man's hereditary nature. It involves merely the intelligent manipulation of his psychic and social forces for the maximum of cooperation and individualization. An appreciation of the difference between the medieval and the modern approach to problems of human life can be seen by contrasting the manner in which a medieval priest and a modern psychiatrist would deal with a personality problem. The former would seek to direct the will of the sinner to changing his character by his own effort in renouncing the world, the flesh and the devil and returning to the law of God, or else, despairing of the human will, would pray to God to intervene to save a lost soul by an act of grace. The psychiatrist, on the other hand, would assume that the personality problem was the result of the individual's reaction to certain aspects of his environment that conditioned his personality, would seek to discover the specific conditioning factors, and would find means of exposing his patient to new life situations that would recondition him for healthy living.

The establishment of God's Kingdom as defined by the foregoing discussion demands no revolutionary change in human nature itself and no miraculous saving act of Providence. It does demand specific changes in the factors that condition human life. It demands improvement in men's physical conditions. Better housing, better hygiene, better sanitation are immediate means to the end of a better human life. It demands improvement in the social conditions of men, changes in the institutions that determine our economic, political and domestic relations. Particularly must the institution of property be subjected to radical revision. It demands a change in the conditions of our mental life, a liberation from the unnecessary inhibitions that modern psychology has revealed as stifling the freedom necessary to the development of personality and from the self-deception which prevents us from facing the truth. It demands fostering personal and social growth through the educational process of making available to every individual the elements of the cultural tradition of the race that he can best utilize to personal and social advantage.

This is modern religion's alternative to dependence on a miraculous act of divine grace, on the one hand, or on the issue of bitter class-warfare, on the other. It is based on the perception that the true nature of things, including the nature of man, is not revealed completely in life as we have known it. *Whatever ills mar life should not be regarded as inherent in its very nature; the character of life should not be judged by the actual but by the possible.* We cannot hope to get a true perspective of life, unless we think in terms of the creative urge that inheres in it. When Koheleth said, "There is nothing new under the sun," [14] he denied the basic truth that life is continually renewing itself, and that the power of self-renewal which the human being possesses to a greater degree than other living beings is man's great distinction. It was doubtless as a corrective to the doctrine preached by Koheleth that the Midrash declares that when the Torah says: "In six days God created the heavens and the earth," it has in mind also the "new heavens and the new earth" referred to by an anonymous Prophet [15] for, when God created the world, He created not only the actualities in it but also the latent possibilities of a better world. [16]

5

What constitutes the religious attitude toward social evil?

It is on the creative possibilities of life that we must rely in seeking to remove those evils that thwart the assertion of God's sovereignty. We must cultivate what may be termed the ethical type of sensitivity to the evils that infest our social relations. Most of us are in the habit of judging life by what befalls us as individuals. We join the great host of grumblers who, like those in the Wilderness, stood groaning and weeping, each at the door of his own tent. Before we know it, we fall into a mood of frustration, for there is hardly a person who is free from disappointment and disillusionment. Add to that the sense of defeat which comes with a crushing feeling of inferiority and inadequacy. To cap it all there is fear of the future. The failure of yesterday

[14] Ecc. 1 :9.   [15] Is. 66 :22.   [16] Gen. *R.* I, 13.

only deepens our anxiety for the morrow. Is it a wonder that the older we get, the sadder we become, the longer we live, the less worthwhile does life seem to be?

No less mistaken an attitude toward social evil is that which is popularly described as "taking life philosophically." We imagine we are unprejudiced and view life objectively, because we pass judgment not merely upon ourselves but upon life as a whole. This, however, does not mean that we are necessarily the wiser in our judgment. It is not the part of wisdom to settle the problem in the fashion of Koheleth, and with a shrug of the shoulders to say, "Well, this is life; this is how things are. There are many good things but many more bad things. The only sensible course is to resign ourselves to the inevitable, to accept the cruelties which men inflict upon one another as part of the nature of things. There is nothing to do but to submit to the welter of human wrongs." Accepting our apparent helplessness as final, we anesthetize ourselves into insensitivity to the evils of society. If there is something of the Stoic in us, we begin by hardening ourselves to our own ills, and we soon become hardened to the ills of others. The logical outcome of such an attitude is moral chaos, anarchy, and ultimately suicide, in a spiritual, if not a physical, sense. Such was the failure of nerve which laid prostrate the ancient civilizations of Greece and Rome.

In contrast with both foregoing ways of reacting to social evil is the religious way. That is not to be confused with the Pollyanna attitude of shallow optimism. People imagine wrongly that religion teaches us to blind ourselves to the facts, to minimize the extent to which our lives are tainted by moral evil. On the contrary, to take life religiously is to face the truth realistically and courageously.

A striking illustration of what constitutes the religious attitude toward moral corruption is recorded in the account of Isaiah's first experience as a prophet. Stated in the language of objective fact, that account pictures Isaiah as contemplat-

ing the universe in all its splendor. But in the language of
the inspired poet, it pictures Isaiah as beholding the ministering angels surrounding the throne of God, proclaiming Him
thrice holy and acclaiming His glory as filling all the earth.
He beheld, as it were, the holiness of life universally realized.
But against this resplendent background there thrusts itself
upon Isaiah's awareness the poignant sense of his own sins
and those of his generation. "Woe is me! for I am undone,"
exclaims the Prophet, "because I am a man of unclean lips,
and I dwell in the midst of a people of unclean lips." [17] But
he does not long remain in the mood of despair. He rises out
of it. This is represented as a call to action, to arouse his
contemporaries to the danger in which they find themselves.
"And I heard the voice of the Lord saying: 'Whom shall I
send and who will go for us?' Then I said: 'Here am I; send
me'." [18] In the light of this spiritual experience of Isaiah,
we are able to understand what he meant when he said:
"Verily mine eyes have beheld the King, the Lord of
Hosts." [19]

The experience of Isaiah may serve as a criterion of what
constitutes the religious state of mind, when we consider the
sins of men and the sufferings they inflict on one another.
It is a state of mind in which both idealism and realism are
equally represented. As in the prophetic vision, they follow
one upon the other like contrasting motifs in a musical composition to be resolved at last in the acceptance of a task to
improve the world.

In the liturgy of Rosh ha-Shanah, these same contrasting
themes, the ideal possibilities and the discouraging realities,
find expression, and it is only when we understand their significance and relation to each other that we can grasp the
true meaning of the traditional prayers. If we follow the
traditional service as a sort of religious symphony, we should
find no difficulty in recognizing as the main theme the

[17] Is. 6:5.   [18] *Ibid.*, 8.   [19] *Ibid.*, 5.

sovereignty and holiness of God, and as a contrasting theme the frailty and vanity of human life.

Note, for example, that stirring liturgical composition, *u-netanneh tokef*. The poet begins at once with the major theme of God's kingship as associated with the holy day: "We will celebrate the mighty holiness of this day, for it is one of awe and terror. Thereon is Thy dominion exalted and Thy throne is established in mercy and Thou sittest thereon in truth." But to make clear the bearing of the announcement that heralds God as King, the poet finds it necessary to introduce the contrasting theme of the short-lived, unsubstantial character of man and his works.

Taken by itself, human life, the poet tells us, is of no more consequence than "a fleeting shadow, a scudding cloud . . . a fugitive dream." But viewed as the object of God's care and judgment, it becomes illumined with a splendid glory, like the leaden clouds lit up by the golden rays of the setting sun. Thus, from the contrast between these two themes, we learn to understand the meaning of the word "God." Since human life is redeemed from its vanity and frailty through the kingship of God, then God can mean only one thing: namely, the totality of all those forces in life that render human life worthwhile. The term worthwhile, in modern parlance, is the equivalent of the more traditional term, holy.

Since the liturgy was formulated, however, something has happened which suggests material for an additional liturgic theme, one that would render the main theme both more necessary and more significant. In the past, it was necessary to stress the worthwhileness of human life, because it was known to be feeble, transient and inconsequential. Man was incapable of measuring himself against the immense forces of the world around him which were far beyond his control. Hence his sense of the worth of life was dependent on the conviction that these forces themselves somehow expressed the will of a just and benignant God.

In modern times there has come to the surface a far more devastating argument for the apparent worthlessness of the human being. It is the fact that, in addition to being impotent in the face of destructive forces beyond his control, he is making life intolerable for himself and his fellows by misusing the opportunities and powers within his control. It is not man's frailty so much as his power, not his helplessness but his cruelty that seems to justify disgust with human life. As a result of man's increasing ability to manipulate the forces of nature, the range of the preventable ills has increased a thousandfold. Yet, instead of using these newly won powers to eliminate those ills, man employs them to render life unlivable for millions of his kind. Looking at contemporary life by and large, it spells insecurity, frustration, nightmare. Far truer than in Thoreau's day is his saying: "Most men live lives of quiet desperation." Though few commit physical suicide, vast numbers commit spiritual suicide. If we are to go on living at all, and especially if we want life to be fruitful and creative, we must refuse to accept as final and irredeemable the man-created evil in the world. Such a refusal is possible, provided we hear the call of religion. *The triumphant note sounded by Rosh ha-Shanah in proclaiming the kingship of God is the affirmation of faith in humanity. What courage is in the face of danger, religion is in the face of world-chaos brought on by man's own doings.*

The man of courage is not reckless. He is not unaware of the danger that confronts him. His bravery consists in his being able to discover and avail himself of the element of safety in the very midst of the surrounding peril. He is the sort of man who, in a shipwreck, will neither hurl himself precipitately into the water nor stand on deck wringing his hands, but will calmly assist in the orderly launching of the boats, on which the safety of the passengers wholly depends. In battle, he will neither give way to a blind impulse to flee nor court death unnecessarily, but will take advantage of every possible situation that will contribute to the safety and victory of his side. If marooned on a desert island, he will not at once yield to despair and permit himself to die of starvation or exposure to the elements, but will pit his resourcefulness against the perils of the situation and try to keep alive in the hope of being able to signal a passing ship that may come to his rescue.

Similarly *the religious attitude is one which seeks and, having found, clings tenaciously to that in human life which holds promise of redeeming it from chaos.* It discovers in man with all his cruelty and viciousness the element of goodness which in the end will replace hatred and strife with reason and good will. *To attain this faith in man, in the latent possibilities of his nature, is to accept the kingship of God.*

6

How to cultivate faith in the possibilities for good in human life

To achieve and hold on to this faith, a first prerequisite is that we disabuse our minds of certain mistaken notions. Frequently we are disillusioned because we expect too much. "I tell you after all," Dean Swift wrote to Alexander Pope,[20] "that I do not hate mankind: it is *vous autres* who hate them, because you would have them reasonable animals and are angry for being disappointed." What we expect of man is often based on a misunderstanding of his origin. Until recent times it was assumed that the evils observable in man were evidence of his having degenerated from an earlier state of grace. They were looked upon as evidence that he was not what God had intended him to be, and consequently that he had fallen. That, however, is an inference not borne out by the facts. We know now that man has attained to such spiritual powers and graces as he possesses by a long

[20] Letter to Alexander Pope, Nov. 26, 1725.

and arduous ascent from the beast. The social instincts which are mainly responsible for man's success in maintaining his life on this planet came into play only in the later stages of his evolution, and have still to contend with atavistic passions that are an inheritance from his prehuman past. That part of human existence which is recorded in history and which marks the rise of what we call civilization is but a very short period, indeed, when compared with the time since man's first appearance as a distinct animal species. The evils that exist in human nature are therefore not to be looked upon as evidences of the fall of man. The fact that they are recognized as evil and that man aspires to their removal may be taken as evidence of the probable eventual rise of man to heights that today seem unattainable.

If we are to hold on to our faith in the possibilities of human life, we must moreover avoid the tendency of keeping our attention fixed on the evil in the world, while overlooking the good that coexists with it. Such a tendency gives us a distorted and dismal view of life. It is not true realism but a sort of macabre romanticism. We may disagree with Browning's declaration, "All's right with the world," but we do not have to agree with the cynic's counter-declaration, "All's riot with the world." However aware we may be of the violent clashes of interests in human society between nations, classes and individuals, we must not be unaware of the unprecedented measure of inter-relationship, mutual dependence and cooperation by which the resources of each part of the world have been made available, to some extent at least, in all other parts. Over vast areas of the world today the average man commands goods and services that were not available to princes in the past. What is more, the spiritual horizons of men have been widened, and the society with which they identify themselves is no longer limited to a small kinship group or to the people who live within a radius of a few days' journey on foot or horseback, but, in ever increasing measure, men identify themselves with the whole of humanity.

True, new problems have arisen in consequence of the growing interdependence of men and nations. The apparent shrinkage in the size of the world through the facilitation of travel, commerce and communication has made it a more crowded place to live in. Nations jostle one another, and the menace of war seems more constant and is certainly more appalling, for the nations who have not learned to get along with one another still cannot get along without one another. Nevertheless, although it may not invariably be true that "God provides the remedy before the hurt," we can discern forces at work which give promise of an eventual solution of all these problems.

To begin with, our age is the first to recognize the abolition of war as a problem. The Prophets were aware of the evil of war, but its abolition was reserved for "the end of days," when God would establish His Kingdom in spite of, rather than by means of, the activities of men. And the Prophets were exceptions in their deprecation of warfare. In general, war was glorified as the highest expression of patriotism and as a legitimate method of advancing a nation's interests. Although this attitude still persists, it is by no means unchallenged. The League of Nations may have proved a feeble and fumbling experiment at the internationalism which alone can insure peace, and the League may be wrecked by the strain of the pressures from national interests to which it has been subjected. But it is a significant augury, for it represents the embodiment of an idea that is indispensable to human society and that, should the League be destroyed, would find its reincarnation in some future international instrument of similar function.

Furthermore, though we may not be able to find God in the tempests, conflagrations and earthquakes of our era, we should not permit these to prevent our hearing Him in "the still small voice" in which the patiently creative and constructive forces of life find expression. The disinterested and painstaking labors of a host of little-known scientists are continually being employed in discovering new truth about the world we live in and about us who live in it. They are waging a quiet but heroic fight against superstition, disease, and all the ills that flow from the ignorance of ourselves and of the universe in which we live. They do not strut in uniforms, and the dangers to which they frequently expose themselves are taken as part of a professional routine, but in their quiet speech and behavior we recognize "the still small voice" of God.

The same may be said of the creative artist. His is the unflagging quest for the beauty which transfigures common things by giving them meaning. Even the ugly and the evil can be made to enhance the value of life for us, if we know how to view them in a significant pattern, so that the ugly and evil become the background and foil for the beautiful and the good. Our Sages taught that there was no place that was "empty of the Divine Presence,"[11] but it is the artist who perceives and reveals to us the beauty by which God makes His presence manifest to us. Not only has the creation of beauty by the artist continued uninterrupted in our day, but there is a growing tendency to make the products of art more accessible to the people than they were in the past. Art education in the public schools, public libraries, public museums, public concerts have added something of inestimable value to our social life. Above all, the motion pictures and the radio have contributed to the enrichment of life for the great mass of people. Although without question the commercial exploitation of art characteristic of the cinema and the radio have in great measure prevented them from yielding all the good that it is possible for them to

[11] *Pes. R. K. 2b.*

yield, it is folly not to appreciate the opportunity of highly esthetic experience which they afford to millions.

And just as we need have no difficulty in finding the pursuit of truth and beauty operative in modern life, notwithstanding the existence of much that is false and vulgar, so together with the cruelty that is manifest in modern life we can, if we seek it, find ample evidence of the prevalence in wide circles of a spirit of humanity and good will. Reference has already been made to the peace movement that expresses the aspiration of our age to better and more ethical international relations. Closely related to it is the movement for inter-racial and inter-religious good will which is growing in extent and clarifying its program. It is directed especially to overcoming the prejudices that poison people's minds and promote discord between various racial and religious groups.

But of far more vital and universal concern is that justice shall prevail in the give and take of goods and services. Upon such justice hangs the life of millions of human beings. For lack of it they are compelled to drag out a sort of death-in-life existence. Yet so insane with greed and so lustful for power are some of those who hold the key to the economic relations of men that they stop at nothing to achieve their ends, so long as they can manage to keep within the letter of the law in the framing of which theirs is the determining voice. The greater part of mankind is reduced to helplessness; some to the helplessness of actual want and misery, and the rest to the helplessness of having to look on without being able to come to the rescue. It is no wonder, therefore, that many a sensitive soul is tempted to echo the cry of Job:

> "From out of the populous city men groan,
>   And the soul of the wounded crieth out;
>   Yet God imputeth it not for unseemliness." [22]

[22] Job 24:12.

To try to prove by logical argument that this conclusion of Job is unwarranted would deservedly earn one the rebuke God meted out to Job's friends. It might even come under the category of wrongs condemned in rabbinic literature by the telling application of the verse: "Whoso mocketh the poor blasphemeth his Maker." [12] But if the very victim of the orderly violence that marks our economic system can testify to a growing sense of justice, then surely is Job proved wrong, and we have no right to feel God-forsaken. Here, then, is the testimony of such a victim: "To me," wrote Bartolomeo Vanzetti from the Dedham, Mass., Prison, "this universal insurgence against a wrong in behalf of two humblest men, is an apotheosy. . . . It should cheer every one of good-will." [14] And in a subsequent letter he wrote, "What has been done for us by the people of the world, the laborers (I mean workers) and the greatest minds and hearts proves beyond any possible doubt that a new conception of justice is plowing its way in the soul of mankind; a justice that centered on man as man. For, as I have already said . . . they are doing for us what once could only have been done for saints and kings. This is real progress." [15] So long as words like these could come from one who was cruelly done to death by the Juggernaut of our present economic order, life can proclaim for us the Kingdom of God.

7

Social crises an evidence of God's sovereignty

But our religious faith in the potentialities of human nature must be such that, even if we should be convinced that our age has turned its back on God, that its wars and woes are evidence of moral retrogression and impending

[12] Prov. 17:5.
[14] *The Letters of Sacco and Vanzetti*, edited by Frankfurter and Jackson. N. Y. 1928, 263.
[15] *Ibid.*, 278.

cataclysm, we would still derive hope out of the very circumstances that drive others to despair. For the spirit of
desperation, unrest and revolt in the social organism has a
function similar to that of pain in the physical organism. It
is a symptom of disease, a danger signal that the life of the
organism is threatened. If the signal is heeded in time and
the appropriate action is taken, even though that action
demand an operation or other radical treatment, the organism may be restored to healthy and joyous living. To the
extent that pain suggests to the physician the possible source
of danger, it is unquestionably a boon.

The religious attitude toward social crises finds an interesting illustration in the conception of our ancestors as to
the place of catastrophe in the scheme of human life. They
entertained the peculiar notion that world-salvation would be
ushered in by world-cataclysm. We find the beginnings of
that idea in the book of Ezekiel, which contains the description of the war of Gog and Magog.[16] The Prophet foresaw
an era of invasions, wars, slaughter and spoliation as marking the end of the old world and the beginning of the new.
Also in the book of Daniel, the period preceding the millennium is pictured as one of ruthless tyranny and oppression.[17]
In a similar vein did the Rabbis conceive the prelude to the
messianic era. They depicted it as being filled with wars and
rumors of wars, darkness and earthquakes, famine and
pestilence.[18]

What can be the meaning of this paradoxical belief that
the millennium must be presaged by a series of disasters?
Historically, it was by means of that belief that our ancestors
somehow managed to survive eras in human history when
calamity spread over the known world and wrought havoc
everywhere. Mankind passed through such a period when
the Persian empire was breaking up. The disintegration of

[16] Ezek. 38-39. *Cf.* also Zech. 14. [17] Dan. 12:1.
[18] *Sanhed.* 97a and b.

the Hellenic world that Alexander the Great had planned
brought in its train dire evils which seemed to presage the
end of the world. Likewise, when the Roman Empire was
disintegrating and the barbaric hordes were ravaging its
frontiers, both rulers and subjects frantically looked about
for some means of staving off the coming of the day of
wrath. There was no people that was exempt from the
tragedies that ensued upon the disorder and the anarchy to
which social cataclysm gave rise. But the greatest sufferers,
as in all such periods, were the Jews. What enabled the
Jewish people to survive these tremendous upheavals was the
ability to find meaning in them. They beheld the hand of
God in those world-wide calamities, the ultimate consequence
of man's violation of God's law, of man's oppression of his
fellow man.

The way in which the Jew derived from such cataclysms
the conviction that God would vindicate the cause of the
oppressed can be seen from the following *midrash:* [19] "We
find that when God judged the generation of the Flood, He
was seated, as it is said, 'The Lord sat at the Flood.' [20]
Of them it is written, 'And He destroyed all living substance.'
In Egypt He judged the people while he passed through the
land, as it is said, 'And I shall pass through the land of Egypt
and smite all the first-born.' [21] But in the future, God will
stand while judging the world, as it is said, 'And His feet
shall stand on that day,' [22] and again, 'Therefore wait for
Me, saith the Lord, for the day when I rise as a witness.' [23]
Men must therefore say to themselves, 'If when He judged
the generation of the Flood seated, He destroyed them, and
if when passing through Egypt, He destroyed their first-
born, when He rises to judge the world, who shall be able to
stand before Him?' Therefore it is written, 'What shall I
do when God riseth up?' [24] What is to be the occasion of

[19] Exod. *R.* XVII, 4. [20] Ps. 29:10. [21] Exod. 12:12.
[22] Zech. 14:4. [23] Zeph. 3:8. [24] Job 31:14.

His rising for the Great Judgment?—the outcry of the afflicted, as it is said, 'Because of the outcry of the afflicted, because of the groans of the poor, now will I arise, saith the Lord.' " **

The tendency to seek in disaster itself evidence of some law or meaning enables us to understand how Rosh ha-Shanah, by reason of its association with the idea of God as King, came also to be associated with the idea of God as Judge. The condemnation of the evils of the existing order is implicit in the assertion of the sovereignty of God, and the suffering involved in these evils acquires meaning when viewed as the penalty imposed on man for having tolerated them. "The Day of the Lord," which was to usher in the era when God's kingship was to be manifest to all people, was interpreted as synonymous with the Day of Judgment. "Behold I will send you Elijah the prophet before the coming of the great and terrible day of the Lord. And he shall turn the heart of the fathers to the children and the heart of the children to their fathers; lest I come and smite the land with utter destruction." ** Such is the note on which the prophetic canon closes. Whenever the Jew looked forward to the establishment of the Kingdom of God, he expected it to be preceded by a divine judgment, and he stood in awe of the verdict.

Rosh ha-Shanah was therefore regarded as having been ordained to qualify the Jewish people for a favorable verdict, by keeping them in mind of the tremendous issues which were at stake in the judgment. Would they deserve to participate in the regenerate life of the world to come, where God's kingship would manifest itself in the salvation of the individual and of society? From this it was but a step to conceiving Rosh ha-Shanah as itself the *Yom ha-Din*, the Judgment Day on a smaller scale, when men and nations pass before God in review, and their destiny for the coming

** Ps. 12:6.　　　　　　　　** Malachi 3:24.

year is apportioned according to their merit.[17] "On it," we read in the Liturgy, "judgment is pronounced upon the nations, which is destined for the sword and which for peace, which for famine and which for plenty, and mortals are called to mind upon it to sentence them to death or life. Who is not remembered on this day? For the remembrance of every creature cometh before Thee, each man's deeds and destiny, his works and his ways, his thoughts and his schemes, his imaginings and his achievements." Thus .what was originally a figure of speech came in the course of time to be taken quite literally. The days from Rosh ha-Shanah, when the divine court opened, to the end of Atonement Day, when the final verdict was sealed, became indeed *Yamin Noraim*, "Days of Dread" for the Jew who was convinced that they were decisive for his destiny throughout the year that they ushered in.

But for the modern Jew to whom the conception of Rosh ha-Shanah as a day of judgment is a poetic figure of speech, the meaning which that figure conveys is that *Rosh ha-Shanah should help us discern in the very suffering that proceeds from our shortcomings the evidence of a divine law which shows us the way to overcome them.* When there is a flaw in a bridge and it breaks under its own weight, the engineer learns to appreciate all the more keenly the law of gravitation upon which he must depend for the security of the bridge he wishes to build. However we may suffer from the evils that sweep over the world, we are at least safe from consternation and despair as long as we possess the kind of religion which teaches us to behold in these evils the negative demonstration of the laws of God, which if reckoned with can maintain the human world in security and happiness.

Thus the attitude of religion to the evils of social injustice is neither one of resignation nor of futile and sullen pessi-

[17] *Cf. Rosh ha-Shanah* 10b, 11a, 16a and b, 27a; Jer. *Rosh ha-Shanah* I, 3(57a); *Pesik. R.* 186b; *Pesik. R. K.* 149b-156b; *Abudarham, Tefilat Rosh ha-Shanah.*

mism. It reacts to social peril as to individual peril, not with yielding and surrender but with courageous protest and vigorous action inspired by faith in the ideal. The realization of the ideal may not come about in our day, but the religious attitude never looks upon life as confined to the brief span of the individual's existence. The religious man can find life itself and the zest of living in his very defiance of death as long as he feels that his life contributes to the ultimate victory of the ideal. In this sense it is unquestionably true, without any reference to a life after death, that "the reward of the righteous is in the future that is to be." [**] Their faith is well expressed in the words of the poet:

> "Others shall sing the song,
> Others shall right the wrong,
> Finish what I begin
> And all I fail of win.
>   What matter I or they,
>   Mine or another's day,
>   So the right word be said
>   And life the sweeter made?
> Sound, trumpets far-off blown!
> Your triumph is my own."

8

God fully manifest only in the maximum attainment
of individuality and cooperation

From all the foregoing discussion it is apparent that the religious outlook on life which is expressed in the conception of the sovereignty of God is an idealistic one affirming the power of men to transform human life in accordance with ideal objectives. Conversely, it would not be incorrect to say that all idealism implies a religious attitude to life. For disinterested loyalty to an ideal, and faith in the possibility of its attainment, are themselves an affirmation that life is

[**] *Abot.* II, 16.

worthwhile and holy, that it manifests the divine. But at this point there is great danger of our drawing from these truths an unwarranted and dangerous inference. We must not infer that, since idealism constitutes the substance of religion, any cause that evokes it is *ipso facto* worthy of acceptance. This would be equivalent to saying that any object which people worship is worthy of being considered divine. This is idolatry. Jewish religion has never accepted this assumption. On the contrary, it has always assumed the acceptance of the sovereignty of God to imply the repudiation of idolatry.

One of the characteristic prayers of *Rosh ha-Shanah,* the *'alenu leshabeah* (which by reason of its importance was subsequently incorporated in the daily services of the Synagogue) after expressing Israel's allegiance to God as King, voices the yearning for the establishment of His Kingdom through the abolition of idolatry. Let us not assume that this prayer is irrelevant to our day, because image worship is nowhere the vogue among peoples with whom we live. An idol is any false god, any inadequate conception of deity, any unsatisfactory religion. These false gods are also worshiped with loyalty, idealism and faith. *A thing may be false, harmful and dangerous not because there is no grain of truth and goodness in it, but because there is not enough of truth and goodness in it.* When Nurse Cavell uttered those memorable words before her death that are inscribed on her monument: "Patriotism is not enough," she stated for all times and for all causes the criterion that distinguishes falsity from truth—*not enough.*

We have seen that the sort of social order that would express for us all the implications of the metaphor of God's kingship is one that combines the maximum personal self-fulfillment with the maximum of social cooperation. Considerable space has been devoted to elucidating what was meant by personal self-fulfillment and by social cooperation, but it is important that the concluding note of this discussion stress the word "maximum" in the foregoing definition.

Nothing less than the maximum attainable is enough. Any kind of society will necessarily afford some measure of personal self-fulfillment, and every society will necessarily afford some opportunity for social cooperation. That is essential to the nature of society. But we cannot be content with the social order, if it does not afford the individual all the opportunities for self-development that are possible in the present state of man's knowledge and power. And we cannot be satisfied with our social order, unless it afford opportunity for cooperation commensurate with the expansion of our social horizons and with the development of facilities for human intercourse.

Whenever our appreciation of spiritual insights contained in our cultural heritage from the past blinds us to new insights based on broader experience, and our loyalty to tradition leads us to reject new truth, we are faithful to an idol, not to God. *In the history of religion, the truths of one age commonly become the idolatries of the next.* This should not shock us. It is one of the ways by which God, the Sovereign of the Universe, asserts His sovereignty by destroying the false gods that detract from His glory.

Similarly all partisan loyalties, if they obscure the loyalty we owe to the larger social unit of the nation, or to humanity itself, must be condemned as standing in the way of God's kingship. Nationalism itself, in the extreme chauvinistic form so common in our day, is a form of idolatry. When it conceives of national sovereignty as implying that the interests of the nation as interpreted by its government are paramount over the interests of the individual, on the one hand, and of humanity as a whole, on the other, it represents a recrudescence of ancient henotheism, the exclusive worship of a national god. Although Judaism in very ancient times passed through a henotheistic phase, it has long left henotheism behind it. Its monotheism implies that devotion to a national sovereignty is "not enough." Nations themselves must acknowledge the sovereignty of God and the obligation of contributing to the establishment of His Kingdom of righteousness and peace.

At the dawn of the New Year, the Jew is therefore encouraged not only to revaluate his own personality and the society of which he is a member in the light of accepted ideals. *He is also impelled by the message of the day which affirms the sovereignty of God, to bring his ideals themselves before the bar of judgment, and to examine them as to their adequacy in the light of whatever truth experience has revealed to him.*

IV

GOD AS THE POWER THAT MAKES FOR THE
REGENERATION OF HUMAN NATURE

THE theme of the Day of Atonement, as the name implies, revolves about the conception of sin and repentance. As sin alienates us from God, we are urged on this day to seek reconciliation,[1] through religious exercises that are to effect a change of heart. The influence of the day is intended to make man *beriah ha-dashah*,[2] a new creature, a regenerate personality.

The term "sin" is a word that for most people has been emptied of meaning. People speak of vices and crimes, of faults and failings of human nature, but not of sin. The very validity of the concept of sin is often called into question. It is considered an invention of theologians, like Satan or the Evil *Yezer*. It need then be no more reckoned with than any superstitious relic of an outworn theology. If sin has no meaning, there is no need for repentance, and the whole observance of the Day of Atonement becomes much ado about nothing.

The fact, however, that a word loses favor does not necessarily signify that it is without meaning. The fortunes of words are frequently determined by how pleasant or unpleasant is the context in which they are used. If the word has been associated with certain ideas that have become offensive

---

[1] That repentance renders man *at one* with God is stated clearly in the midrashic interpretation (Lev. *R.* III, 3) of *vi-yerahamehu* (and He will have compassion upon him) (Is. 55:7).

[2] *Cf.* Jer. *Rosh ha-Shanah* III, 8 (59c) and Lev. *R.* XXIX, 12.

to us, it tends to fall into disrepute, even though the particular connotations that have given it its bad name by no means exhaust its meaning, and even though no other word exists in the language which can express as well the concept for which it stands. Indeed, when a word has been fraught with meaning for generations and even for ages, it is absurd to abandon it as meaningless for our day, without at least analyzing those human experiences that gave it meaning in the past.

Let us then see what our fathers meant when they spoke of certain forms of behavior or attitudes of mind as sinful, why they felt a need for atonement, and why they sought atonement in the particular manner that has become traditional. We shall then be in a better position to ask whether subsequent experience has so transformed human nature or the world that concepts of sin and repentance have necessarily become inoperative.

I

The evolution of the sense of sin

In earliest times sin and repentance undoubtedly had a sacramental significance. They were part of the thought pattern in which holiness was conceived as the experience of a presence which called forth awe, terror, fascination, wonder and devotion. The imagination of men endowed impressive phenomena of nature, or objects that were of tremendous importance to their life, with a personality similar to their own. If helpful, these objects might be worshiped as deities; if harmful, propitiated as evil spirits. More often the same object might at times be helpful and at times harmful. A stream that supplied water for irrigation and was thus a source of life might become a flood that destroyed the life it had seemingly created. The fire, which was man's protection alike from the cold and from preying beasts, might turn on man in an angry conflagration. Such objects that at once inspired hope and fear, admiration and terror, were conceived as holy. They were either regarded as being superior to man who held profound sway over his destiny, or else they were conceived as the haunts of such beings and as the instruments by which they manifested their will to men. To keep these superior powers friendly was the chief preoccupation of the spiritual life of primitive man. They could be approached only in certain ways, and to approach them in other ways was fraught with danger. From generation to generation there grew by continual accretion a mass of law and precept defining which behavior was permissible and which prohibited in the presence of the holy object. To violate these laws and precepts was to offend the deity that was regarded as having enjoined them. That constituted sin.

Such sin severed the tie that bound the deity to use his awe-inspiring power for one's protection, and invited him to use it for one's punishment. The dread of sin became an actual fear of physical consequences that might result from having offended the deity. One might be guilty of such offense without deliberately intending to transgress the prescribed laws. Sins might be committed without the sinner being aware of them.* This haunting fear led to the attempt to propitiate the deity by various methods. One of these was by bringing him a gift or offering. Another was by afflicting oneself either through abstinence or more positive forms of self-torture, in order to appeal to his pity. Prayer and praise were also resorted to for similar reasons. Such practices had the psychological effect of exorcising the dread of the terrible consequences which might have followed from some involuntary or unconscious transgression.

In the Bible there are many evidences that originally our ancestors, too, conceived of sin in this manner. The concepts of holiness and of dangerous power were closely allied. The

* *Cf.* Ps. 19:13.

fact that YHWH was conceived of as "dwelling in the thick darkness," [*] and that He revealed himself on Mount Sinai amidst flash of lightning and roar of thunder has been variously interpreted as meaning that He was originally conceived as the God of the storm-cloud, or as the God that resided in a then active volcanic mountain, the Sinai of Scripture. Cloud and fire are frequently associated with holiness and with deity itself. "And the glory of the Lord abode upon Mount Sinai, and the cloud covered it six days; and the seventh day He called unto Moses out of the midst of the cloud. And the appearance of the glory of the Lord was like devouring fire on the top of the Mount in the eyes of the children of Israel." [*]

Because of the dangerous power wielded by YHWH, and because of the inscrutability of the ways in which that power manifested itself, His worship was hedged about with innumerable taboos. Only in a state of ritual purity might one approach the sanctuary, which was the *Mishkan,* or habitation, that the people had built in order to insure His Presence among them. "They shall make me a sanctuary, that I may dwell in their midst." [*] In the innermost shrine of the sanctuary where He was imagined as enthroned on the cherubim (probably personifications of the storm-cloud), none might come except the high priest. Even he was not permitted to enter the sanctuary at will, but only after having performed the prescribed ablutions and having donned the holy garments, on the occasion of his taking part in propitiatory rites; otherwise he courted death. [*]

But no matter what precautions the people might take, they were still afraid that they might have offended God in some unknown manner. Such offenses would tend to make the sanctuary itself "unclean," that is, disqualified for the presence of God. Though He might overlook one or two

---

[*] I. K. 8:12.   [*] Exod. 24:16, 17. *Cf. Ibid.,* 19:12, 13.
[*] *Ibid.,* 25:8.   [*] Lev. 16:2.

such offenses, the uncleanness would become intensified with each one, and might eventually cause the withdrawal of God's presence, or its wrathful manifestation. A day, therefore, was reserved each year for propitiatory rites, described in Leviticus XVI, which were conceived as having a cleansing effect on the sanctuary. "And he shall make atonement for the most holy place, and he shall make atonement for the tent of meeting, and for the altar; and he shall make atonement for the priests and for all the people of the assembly." * This was originally the main function of the Day of Atonement.

As an additional means of being absolved of those sins which were conceived as disqualifying the people for communion with God, they were on that day to "afflict their souls." Tradition has interpreted this to imply abstinence from food and drink and other forms of sensuous enjoyment. The sacramental character of the atonement, i.e., its potency to nullify the effect of Israel's sinfulness through the putative influence of its ritual acts on God rather than through their influence on Israel directly, is evidenced in the fact that the purification of the sanctuary and of those who minister to it is the immediate object of the Yom Kippur ritual. Only after this has been effected can its beneficent influence extend to the people themselves. In such a sacramental conception of sin and atonement there is little of ethical significance. Its value lay in the release it afforded men from the haunting fears which were an inherent part of their outlook on the world. When the laws governing the forces of nature were unknown and their operation as yet uncontrollable by man, such release was highly useful. Ritual acts were, by a process of wishful thinking, believed to effect such a control, and the influence of this belief on the spirits of the worshipers was very much the same as if those rites were actually effective.

* *Ibid.,* 16:33.

2

The gradual moralization of the sense of sin

But this sacramental attitude to sin and repentance belongs to those early stages in the historic development of our people, when its religion was hardly different in any significant aspect from that of the surrounding peoples. Presently the social problems that confronted the people of Israel led to important changes in their religious attitudes, including their attitude to sin and atonement. There was the need for establishing in the hearts of the people the supremacy of YHWH over the local *baalim*. There was also the need for defending the liberties characteristic of the simple life of the desert against the encroachments of the governing class which the exigencies of a country subject to invasion by great powers had brought to the front. Both these needs were met by the Prophets who sought to establish the supremacy of YHWH, by identifying Him as the source of the ideals of justice and righteousness of which they themselves were the spokesmen. They instilled the faith that YHWH would assert His sole godhood, first over Israel, then over the entire earth, by vindicating the cause of the wronged and oppressed.

The holiness of God now assumed a new meaning. It was no longer confined to certain particularly impressive phenomena of nature. The triumph of righteousness could be assured only by a God, of whom it might be said "the whole earth is full of His glory," [*] a God who was the creator and sustainer of the world.[10] He still had to be approached with dread, even with a greater measure of dread than before, when His power was compared with that of other deities, and limited and local in extent. But the old ritual taboos were no longer adequate expressions of the fear of the Lord, nor were mere ritual acts of propitiation adequate measures

[*] Is. 6:3.   [10] Amos 4:13.

of atonement. *The fear of offending God by transgressions of the moral law supplemented, and eventually tended to supersede, the fear of offending Him by transgressions of ritual taboos.* The sacramental ritual then came to be interpreted symbolically.

The process by which this transition came about may well be illustrated by the vision of Isaiah, to which reference was made in the previous chapter. The Prophet has a vision of himself in the presence of God in the Temple before His holy altar. There are the usual physical manifestations of holiness that were part of the cultural tradition which the Prophet's age inherited from more primitive times. There are the flaming seraphim, the smoking altar-fire, the quaking of the doorposts, when God speaks. And the Prophet, in his vision, reacts with the same fear of a disqualifying uncleanness, which is characteristic of the taboos that hedged about worship in the primitive stages of civilization. But what is this uncleanness? Not an uncleanness caused by contact with the dead, nor any of the forms of ritual uncleanness elaborated in the priestly legislation. "Behold I am a man of unclean lips, and I dwell in the midst of a people of unclean lips." The abuse of speech through the utterance of falsehood is what, to the Prophet, disqualifies the human being from receiving and communicating the word of the Lord, from true communion with Him. The physical manifestations of God's power are but symbols of His authority in the realm of the spirit; the physical disqualifications for communion with God are but symbols of the spiritual disqualifications, and the physical ritual of propitiation and atonement must become the symbol of a spiritual transformation that puts one in harmony with the divine will. Thus did ethical religion evolve out of sacramental religion.

From the time that the prophetic teaching had impressed upon the Jewish people the conception of a righteous Sovereign of the universe, sin had this deeper meaning of an offense against the divine law of righteousness. Throughout the period of the Second Commonwealth and thereafter down to the period of the Emancipation, the law of the Pentateuch and the system of jurisprudence which was based on it were regarded as the revealed will of God, and are so regarded to this day by the traditionally minded. From this point of view, any violation of these laws was regarded as sin. This applied to ritual as well as to moral laws. Nevertheless, although the sense of sin still attached to transgressions of a purely ritual character, these ritual laws did not have the same meaning as in earlier ages. They were frequently interpreted as symbols of ethical laws. They were to be obeyed because of the influence which their observance was expected to have on one's moral attitudes; the perfunctory performance of them, without an awareness of their moral meaning, was regarded as inadequate.

In accordance with these changes in attitude, the ritual of atonement acquired a deeper meaning. To be in harmony with God was inconsistent with an attitude of hostility toward one's fellow-men, which violated God's law of justice and peace. The full efficacy of the Yom Kippur ritual was limited to such sins as did not involve any social obligation. It extended only to religious duties in which our relations to our fellow-men were not involved. In the language of the Mishnah: [11] "Transgressions involving the relation of man to God are atoned for by the Day of Atonement. But those involving the relations of a man to his fellow are not atoned for by the Day of Atonement, until he has appeased his fellow." Moreover, the efficacy of the ritual was conditioned on its being accompanied by the sincere determination not to repeat the offense. The person who confesses his sin without abandoning it is compared by the Rabbis to one who takes the prescribed ritual bath of purification after contact with an unclean object, while still holding in his hand the reptile

[11] *Mishnah Yoma* VIII, 9.

that is the source of his uncleanness.[18] This very analogy may serve as an instance of how the rites that grew out of the sacramental conception of atonement were symbolically interpreted to yield a moral meaning.

We must not imagine, however, that the sacramental conception of atonement for sin was wholly superseded by the moral conception characteristic of the theocratic religion of the Second Commonwealth. Sacramental religion is deeply rooted in human nature, and should be sublimated rather than suppressed. There are occasions when a sense of human inadequacy emotionally akin to the experience of primitive man in the presence of some object of holy awe still overwhelms us. We may not think of God as dwelling in the Temple, or in the synagogue, in any spatial sense, yet we think of these edifices as houses of God, and we feel *as if* God dwelt there. In our insistence on beautifying the synagogue, and even more in our insistence that we put on festive garments when we worship in it, we are expressing a feeling similar to that which made primitive man regard uncleanness in association with worship as something repugnant and displeasing to God.

But all this does not necessarily impede our realization of the distinction between ritual and moral transgression, or between ritual purity and moral righteousness. Indeed, it may help to further moral aims. For, the transfer of the emotions of fear and love from the objects to which they were attached in primitive religion to those aspects of life which evoke them appropriately today energizes our moral aspiration. The fear of ritual uncleanness may be meaningless today; but if we can associate that emotion with the fear of actions that are offensive to our sense of moral decency, our chances of living a decent life are enhanced thereby. *If the desire for absolution and restored serenity which lay behind the rites of atonement can be keenly experienced by us and*

[18] *Taanit* 16a; *Cf. Tosefta Taanit* I, 8.

*symbolically expressed in a stirring ritual, it may function as
an impulse to reconstruct our lives in accordance with our
highest ideals.*

3

*The traditional conception of the Torah not conducive to the
complete moralization of the sense of sin*

But the attempt to superimpose moral meaning on what
was once a sacramental ritual is not without its dangers; so
natural is it to relapse into the sacramental attitude. Although the process of spiritualization and moralization of
the ritual was very active during what may be called the
theocratic phase of Jewish development, when the God idea
expressed itself in obedience to the Torah which was conceived as His revealed will, it did not wholly succeed. The
Temple, though no longer thought of as the actual abode of
deity, was regarded emotionally as if it were such, with the
result that in traditional Judaism its restoration is still the
theme of prayer and is regarded as integral to the messianic
redemption of Israel.

Moreover, we find, side by side with the effort to give
symbolic significance to rituals that probably originated in
primitive taboos, a contrary tendency to deprecate such interpretations as leading to the substitution of the spirit for the
letter, and eventually to disobedience of both. Thus the
tendency to find a reason for laws that appear on the surface
to be quite arbitrary is deprecated in the following Talmudic
aggadah: [18] R. Isaac said: "Why were the reasons of the
laws in the Torah not revealed? Because in two verses
reasons were revealed and they caused the greatest in the
world (Solomon) to stumble. Thus it is written: 'He shall
not multiply wives to himself,[14] whereon Solomon said, 'I
will multiply wives, yet not let my heart be turned away.'
Yet we read: 'When Solomon was old, his wives turned
away his heart.' [15] Again it is written: 'He shall not multi-

[18] *Sanhed.* 21b.   [14] Deut. 17:17.   [15] I Kings 11:4.

ply to himself horses'; [16] whereon Solomon said, 'I will multiply them, but will not cause Israel to return to Egypt. Yet we read: 'And a chariot came up and went out of Egypt.'" [17] Similarly, when R. Johanan ben Zakkai was asked by a Gentile to explain the ritual for the purification of those who have been defiled through contact with a dead body, and his answer did not satisfy his disciples, they asked him his own candid opinion. He could only answer; "(God said) 'I have established a statute; I have issued a decree; it is not for you to question it.'" [18]

This points to a limitation in the ethicizing of the conception of sin and atonement. That limitation is inherent in the traditional belief in revelation, and cannot be overcome by the process of symbolic interpretation. So long as we hold to the belief in a supernaturally revealed code, and conceive of God as a definite Being external to the world which He has created, sin means disobedience to His manifest will, which results in His disfavor, and atonement means the restoration to His favor. This can be effected only by a renewal of the will to obey. The first manifestation of this renewal is naturally the performance of those sacramental rituals of atonement, which are part of the revealed law. This gives a tremendous impulse to the performance of those rites of atonement, since the very performance expresses the intention to obey the will of God. They are thus raised to an even higher level of importance than those social laws which in themselves do not function as symbols of obedience to God's Law as a whole. The result is that, if we regard the ritual observances as based on a revealed code, they tend to function in a quasi-sacramental manner; their performance brings with it that easement of our sense of sin and restoration of our spiritual equilibrium, which in an earlier stage of religion was associated with the sacramental act.

The Sages seem to have been aware of the spiritual dangers to which this emphasis on the ritual of atonement led.

[16] Deut. 17:16.   [17] I Kings 10:29.   [18] *Pesik. R. K.* IV (40a).

It was probably this awareness which is responsible for their selecting for the *Haftarah* on the morning of the Day of Atonement a passage which stresses the inadequacy of the ritual of atonement as such. In response to the complaints of the people, "Wherefore have we fasted and Thou seest not? Wherefore have we afflicted our souls, and Thou takest no note thereof?", the Prophet tells them,

> "Behold, in the day of your fast ye pursue your business,
> And exact all your labours.
> Behold, ye fast for strife and contention,
> And to smite with the fist of wickedness;
> Ye fast not this day
> So as to make your voice to be heard on high.
> Is such the fast that I have chosen?
> The day for a man to afflict his soul?
> Is it to bow down his head as a bulrush,
> And to spread sackcloth and ashes under him?
> Wilt thou call this a fast,
> And an acceptable day to the Lord?
> Is not this the fast that I have chosen?
> To loose the fetters of wickedness,
> To undo the bands of the yoke,
> And to let the oppressed go free,
> And that ye break every yoke?
> Is it not to deal thy bread to the hungry,
> And that thou bring the poor that are cast out to thy house?
> When thou seest the naked, that thou cover him,
> And that thou hide not thyself from thine own flesh?" [19]

It remains true, nevertheless, that although the Rabbis perceived the danger of overemphasizing ritual acts of atonement, they could not remove that danger, for it is inherent in the conception of these acts as explicitly ordained by God.

4

The ethical revaluation of the traditional conception of sin

If, in keeping with the modern world-outlook, we have come to conceive of God as that aspect of reality to which

[19] Is. 58:3-7.

we react with a sense of life's unity, creativity and worth-whileness, we cannot see the will of God in any one specific code of laws. Only in the spiritual life of man as a whole, only in the complex of forces which impel men to think in terms of ideals and to seek to implement their ideals through laws as well as through other social institutions can we discern the will of God. Such an interpretation of the relation of God to human life may be described as ethical religion. It is obvious that, from the point of view of ethical religion, the terms "sin" and "atonement" cannot have the same meaning as from the point of view of revelational religion. Sin can no longer mean the provocation of God's wrath through disobedience to His revealed law, nor can atonement mean the restoration to His grace by a pledge of future obedience, however sincere. The incongruity of these traditional concepts of sin and atonement with the modern ethical and religious outlook is doubtless responsible for the tendency to ignore the concepts of "sin" and "atonement." This tendency, however, is unwarranted. When a scientific hypothesis is proved untenable, a true scientist will always search for an hypothesis which will explain the same phenomena more adequately. We should proceed in the same manner in our religious thinking. *These traditional concepts may have been wrong, but they were rationalizations of deep-seated human needs, and these needs still cry out for an expression which conforms to our present sense of reality.*

What meaning, then, from the point of view of ethical religion, may we attach to the concepts "sin" and "atonement"? In order to answer this question, since we must seek the manifestation of the divine in the evolution of human nature itself, it is necessary for us to note that evolution as reflected in the history of those concepts. Man, like all other animals, is endowed with the instinct of self-preservation. This instinct functions in a multiplicity of responses to stimuli of the external environment. In response to them he seeks food, protection from enemies and from the elements, and the gratification of sex desire. He differs from other animals, in that the latter respond in patterns that are much simpler and more precise but correspondingly much less variable and adaptable to changed conditions. In the behavior patterns of the so-called lower animals there is little evidence of the awareness of alternative responses and the weighing of possible consequences of such responses. We say that they do by instinct what, according to their organic needs, is the right thing for their preservation. These responses are so stable and so closely associated with the habitual functioning of the organs as to be easily transmissible, without appreciable change, from generation to generation. Only natural selection over a long period of time can affect any change in the evolution of animal instincts. A radical change in environmental conditions frequently results in entire species becoming extinct.

In the case of man, however, adaptability to a greater diversity of environmental conditions has been purchased at a cost of precision of instinctive responses. His life situations always involve a choice between alternative responses. He has to rehearse, as it were, in imagination the various possibilities of action and choose that which his experience suggests as best. Even in the simplest forms of human life we can see this principle at work. A man, in the stone age, has killed a beast after a long and wearisome hunt. What is he to do next? Shall he respond to the claims of fatigue and weariness and lie down to sleep, at the possible risk of losing his prey to some wild animal or to some other man? Shall he satisfy the claim of hunger, eat what he can, and, abandoning the rest, return home and summon his mate or his children to carry in what remains of the carcass? Or shall he, weary as he is, shoulder his game and bring it home to his family? The decision as to which course he should take will be determined by his expectation of satisfaction which would follow from the consequences of his choice, and these will be determined by his past experiences of pleasurable or painful results of similar actions.

This process leads every human being to build up certain habitual patterns of response to similar situations which distinguish his personal behavior and constitute his character or personality. Inherent in this process is the subordination of certain interests to others, as being of less importance, or conferring less permanent, though more intense, satisfaction. Our generalized expectation of how we should react to anticipated situations constitutes our personal ideal.

But we often depart from our ideal of ourselves. Circumstances may focus our attention to such an extent on one aspect of a situation that we lose track of others, and react in a manner contrary to our personal ideal. The satisfaction that a man may have repeatedly experienced from victory in combat may have set up an ideal of intrepid daring. His experience of mutual helpfulness and camaraderie with the members of his family and friends may have built up an ideal of kindness and consideration. Nevertheless, in a situation of panic, he may be so obsessed by fear of his life that these considerations are for the time forgotten, and he behaves in a manner both cowardly and brutal. The situation past, he is bitterly disappointed with himself. He has not lived up to the best that was in him, to what he feels to be his normal or true self. His conduct has hurt others, but it has ruined himself; for, he can no longer face the future with confidence. He had met the successive situations of his past life by anticipating the consequences of his behavior, but now he can no longer do so. His character, on which he depended to meet these situations, has gone to pieces. He has sinned. What is he to do about it?

So long as man lived in a primitive society he would seek a sacramental solution to his problem. His confidence in himself in the past was largely based on irrational hunches. He never performed any important act without a ritual based

on tribal taboos, with elaborations based on his own wishful
thinking. If he succeeded, he attributed his success to the
divine or demoniac powers he was able to conjure up by his
charms, incantations and magic. When things went wrong,
he was convinced that he must have somehow offended the
superhuman powers, on whom he depended, through some
form of behavior that rendered his magic inefficacious. To
make amends, he had recourse to more magic, to propitiatory
sacrifices, to ascetic self-punishment, to prayer and entreaty.
This done, his confidence was restored; he had atoned for
his sin.

On the plane, however, of theocratic religion or religion
as revealed law, and in a more developed state of society, the
sense of sin is otherwise apprehended. A man's personal
ideals come to him only in small measure through immediate
personal experience. From earliest childhood he is conditioned to regard certain forms of conduct as desirable and
to look forward to conforming to them, because in expressing the will of the Creator, they give meaning and purpose
of his own life. He is taught the very words in which the
Creator laid down these norms for his behavior, and the
divine sanctions by which they are to be enforced are impressed on him. If he disobeys, he will be punished by God;
if he conforms, he will be rewarded. His sin is therefore
apprehended as a personal offense against the Author of his
life, who, like a father, told him what was good for him, but
whose admonitions he rejected. He fears his Father's wrath
and is ashamed of his Father's disapprobation. But his
Father loves him; else why should He have created him?
There must therefore be a possibility of reconciliation. He
will confess his sin, seek forgiveness and try henceforth to
be more mindful of his Father's injunctions. Does not the
divine law itself prescribe the very method by which its
Author may be appeased, if any of its provisions has been
violated? Having arrived at this conclusion, the harmony

between man and God is restored and, being assured of God's forgiveness, he forgives himself as well, and thus is restored to moral poise and self-confidence.

From the point of view of ethical religion, however, the spiritual gap between one's ideal of oneself and one's character as manifested in action cannot be so easily bridged. The wound to one's self-respect, the sense of personal inadequacy and frustration, cannot be healed by mere ritual acts nor even by sincere repentance and prayer for forgiveness. For, the human attributes of mercy and forgiveness cannot in any literal sense be ascribed to Deity, as conceived in keeping with the world-outlook of modern man. Such sacramental acts as fasting and sacrifice may still be of value, if symbolically interpreted. Prayer and confession can be helpful as well, if they represent not merely formal acts, but the upheaval of one's soul. But these can no longer suffice to restore to the soul that spiritual self-confidence which it needs, if it is to take the best of its life. The sense of sin persists, for it is implicit in the whole problem of human living. In the past, it was exorcised at intervals by religion, and the result was encouragement and the renewal of spiritual power and purpose. Can religion do the same for the modern man? If it does, the experience of its effect will be the meaning that atonement has for him.

In all conceptions of sin and atonement described above, sin involves a disturbance in the relation between man and God, and atonement implies the poise, solace and encouragement that come with the sense of a restoration to a better relationship. From the point of view of ethical religion, the same remains true. *If we identify God with that aspect of reality which confers meaning and value on life and elicits from us those ideals that determine the course of human progress, then the failure to live up to the best that is in us means that our souls are not attuned to the divine, that we have betrayed God.*

That men arrive at truth by trial and error, that the experience of evil as well as the experience of good is the very source from which they derive those ideals that give dignity and importance to their lives, means that they are able to transcend their shortcomings and to rebuild their personalities on a higher synthesis than before, "to rise on the stepping stones of our dead selves to higher things." Herein lies the point of the rabbinic saying: "In the place occupied by the repentant sinner, not even the sinless are worthy to stand." [20] Or, to quote another rabbinic maxim, "Great is the power of repentance, for, by it deliberate sins are converted into positive virtues." [21] When we have arrived at such an understanding of our sin as to enable this understanding to contribute to a reintegration of our characters on a higher level of moral purpose, we have achieved atonement, we have put ourselves in rapport with that aspect of life which makes life holy to us, we are at one with God.

5

The ethical revaluation of the traditional conception of atonement as symbolized by the ritual of fasting and the 'Abodah

If we hold consistently to the modern conception of God, there is no danger of our permitting the performance of religious rites like those associated with the observance of Yom Kippur to do duty for the inner transformation that spells true moral atonement. For that very reason it is all the more important to observe those rites for their symbolic value.

Implied in the rite of fasting is the duty of controlling the natural hungers. Every personal and social ideal implies a hierarchy of values in which the appetites and desires that minister solely to the preservation of the individual organism must be subordinated to those that minister to the

[20] *Berakot* 34b.   [21] *Yoma* 86b.

preservation of the race. Moreover, inasmuch as these appetites relate themselves directly only to a part of our organism and not to the whole of it, the pleasure which accompanies their gratification may lead to an indulgence in them in excess of the needs, and even to the detriment of the organic life of the individual himself. Gluttony and drunkenness are good examples of the tendency of some of our appetites to lead to behavior that is injurious to the health and well-being of the organism as a whole. The unrestrained pursuit of sexual gratification is an example of conduct which, under the lead of an insistent appetite, results in some forms of behavior that are detrimental to the well-being of the social organism, inasmuch as they tend to disrupt family life and prevent it from performing its most useful service to society. Since the unrestrained indulgence of these appetites leads to a sacrifice of the whole to the part, it runs counter to that tendency which is implicit in all ideals.

Ideals are the expression of life's tendency to organize itself. Life seeks to make of every organism, whether individual or social, a perfect pattern in which every part contributes to perpetuate and enhance the whole, and in which the whole energizes every part. *This effort of life to achieve and express unity, harmony and integrity is what makes life holy; this is the evidence of the divine; whatever thwarts this tendency is sin.* The pleasure which accompanies the ·normal functioning of our organs, and the pain which is commonly associated with their failure so to function, are natural instrumentalities for informing the individual of how his organs are performing their duty, and what they need in order to enable them to continue to do so. When the pursuit of sensual pleasure, however, becomes an end in itself and is dissociated from its organic significance, it means that a particular organ is getting more attention than it is entitled to at the expense of the others. Sensual indulgence can never lead to happiness, because it is an abuse of the functional relationship of the senses to the whole of life.

This is a truth which was partially apprehended in the past, but wrongly interpreted. Inasmuch as the appetites had their seat in definite organs and manifested themselves in immediate physical activities, they were considered as belonging to the body. The tendencies, however, that minister to the integration of personality and of society, like the tendencies to self-control, loyalty and disinterested love, were considered as belonging to the soul. The reason for that is that they are not allocated, so to speak, to any specific organ as the particular medium of their expression, but rather require the service of any or all, in accord with particular situations. The perception of the danger of sensuality was thus construed to mean that the body was the source of all evil, and that the soul was the source of all good." This led to the conclusion that to torment the body was beneficial to the soul. All sorts of ascetic practices were indulged in for the purpose of suppressing the natural appetites. The unnecessary anguish that was involved in the effort at suppressing, and, as it were, extirpating the appetites from human nature is one of the most severe indictments that must be brought against the other-worldly religion of the Middle Ages.

In our own day, however, the danger is more from a pagan reaction against medieval asceticism. Psychological theories, pointing to the danger of suppressing the *libido* in its normal functioning, have been used as rationalizations for following the lead of the appetites, regardless of their functional significance. The need for subordinating sensual gratification to the realization of personal and social ideals was not born of the medieval dichotomy of body and soul, matter and spirit, or the earlier dichotomy of the Evil *Yezer* and the Good *Yezer*, but is founded in human nature itself.

Jewish religion, even in its other-worldly phase, never fol-

" Romans 7:14-25; 8:5-8.

lowed the tendency to asceticism to its logical limit. Doubtless this was due in great part to the fact that its fundamental institutions originated before other-worldliness had
come to dominate men's thoughts. Since the Torah, which
became the Jew's key to the world to come, came into being
before the concept of the world to come was known, it had
nothing to say about ascetic practices being indispensable to
other-worldly salvation. In fact, the Rabbis strongly deprecated the extreme manifestations of asceticism. This was
notably the case in connection with the observance of the
Day of Atonement. Although the law prescribes that on the
Day of Atonement "ye shall afflict your souls," the Rabbis
interpreted the law in a way that set definite limits to the sort
of self-imposed penance that this phrase might seem to impose. In Leviticus we are told, "It shall be unto you a statute
for ever: in the seventh month, on the tenth of the month
ye shall afflict your souls and shall do no manner of work." [22]
Commenting on this passage the Rabbis say: "From the
words, 'ye shall afflict your souls' one might possibly infer
that a man should expose himself to excesses of heat or cold
in order to torment himself; therefore, we are told in the
context, 'And ye shall do no manner of work.' Just as the
observance of the prohibition of work involves only a passive attitude, so the affliction of soul intended by the law
must be only a passive one." [24] Thus, while abstinence from
food and drink and other forms of bodily gratification on
the Day of Atonement is commanded, self-torture for the
purpose of mortifying the flesh is discountenanced.

When we refrain from indulging our physical appetites
for a limited period, in order to devote ourselves for a time
more exclusively to demands that rank higher in our hierarchy of values, we are not denying the physical appetites
their just place in life; we are merely recognizing the need
of putting them in their place. An ancient *midrash* [25] com-

[22] Lev. 16:29.   [24] *Yoma* 74b.
[25] *Pirkĕ De-R. Eliezer* XLVI.

pares the Jews on the Day of Atonement to God's ministering angels, and one of the points of similarity is that, like the
latter, they neither eat nor drink. This analogy frees the fast
completely from all association with self-imposed penance,
and associates it wholly with the concentration on the higher
values in life, in contrast with those organic functions that
merely keep the mechanism of the body going. For the Jew
today, this is putting the emphasis where it belongs. The
experience of fasting can be a most impressive symbol of the
need and the possibility of self-control, and the advantage
of subordinating the appetites to higher personal and social
interests. "Rabbi said: A human being is conquered by
anger, but God conquers anger." [**] That power of self-control which the human being sometimes exercises when prone
to anger is the divine in man. Equally divine is self-control,
when other passions than anger threaten to get the better of
one.

There is a similar need for the reinterpretation of the
ancient 'Abodah rites which form the theme of the Yom
Kippur reading from the Torah, and of the concluding portion of the Musaf service. The object of these rites in the
sacramental stage of Jewish religious development was to
cleanse the sanctuary from contamination by the sins of the
people, and thus qualify the sanctuary for God's Presence.
What symbolic significance can these rites yield from the
point of view of ethical religion?

Implied in the existence of the sanctuary is the functioning of the collective life as a means of the self-fulfillment of
the individual in his achievement of character or personality.
The sanctuary may, therefore, stand as the symbol not alone
of the synagogue but of all the social arrangements, customs
and institutions that function to this end. In the recognition
of the fact that the sanctuary itself tends to become "un-

[**] Gen. R. XLIX, 8.

clean," we may see the symbol of the tendency of all these
social institutions to become disqualified for the purpose of
serving God, that is to say, of contributing to the unity,
harmony and integrity of personal and social life, whereby
life becomes holy. *The sins of the individual corrupt the
social structure, and the corruption of the social institutions
spread the contagion among individuals.* The sensuality of
the individual leads to the prostitution of the arts; these,
when commercialized, further encourage sensuality and the
commercial exploitation of sex. Greed and acquisitiveness
lead individuals to shape the political institutions so as to
facilitate the despoiling of the weak by the strong. Religious
institutions are no exception to the rule. Where the ethical
will of the individual functions feebly or unintelligently,
he will seek divine sanction for wrong purposes, and employ
the potency of religion as an aid in wrongdoing. How many
human sacrifices have literally been offered to the gods!
What torrents of blood have been shed in holy wars! Just as
in the case of the individual organism there is danger of
yielding to the clamorous demands of some special organ to
the detriment of the well-being of the individual as a whole,
so, too, in the social organism.

Nations, for example, can contribute to the creative development of personal and social life, and do so contribute. But
when nationalism becomes so domineering as to insist on
the absolute sovereignty of the State, and completely to
ignore the paramount interests of humanity as a whole or
the rights and needs of the individual, such nationalism
becomes the sin of chauvinism.

Tradition is indispensable to the life of the social organism. Were it not for tradition each generation would have
to repeat the experiences of the past, and would not be able
to avail itself of the useful habits accumulated through the
ages, or to transmit the benefits of its own experience to
posterity. But when tradition becomes so clamorous as to

refuse to recognize change or to admit the need of innovation to meet changed conditions, it can only stifle and frustrate the life of society. It then becomes sin. A holy iconoclasm must be invoked to destroy such unholy idolatry.

It is thus apparent that the reconstruction of personality involves also the revaluation of those social institutions that contribute to the making of personality, and the effort to restore them to proper functioning, where they have failed. The criterion in every instance must be the religious conception of the striving to make life whole. This is what our fathers must have sought to express when they spoke of *yihud ha-shem,* the affirmation of God's unity. *Translated into action, the doctrine of the unity of God calls for the integration of all of life's purposes into a consistent pattern of thought and conduct.*

Religious teachers have been wont to classify sins in three categories as sins against oneself, sins against one's neighbors, and sins against God. This is all wrong. Every sin is at the same time a sin against ourselves, a sin against our neighbors, and a sin against God. Sins against the organic life of the individual prevent him from giving as efficient service to society as he might otherwise give, and, in frustrating the tendency of life to seek integration, they are sins against God. Similarly, it could be shown that every sin against one's neighbor is at the same time a sin against oneself and against God, and that every sin against God involves oneself and one's neighbor. Just as any malady which affects a single organ of the body affects its life as a whole and the functioning of every other organ, just so every sin of an individual is a sin against God and against all other individuals.

What the *'Abodah* rite should symbolize is that just as each individual Jew was to assume responsibility for the contamination of the sanctuary and for the elimination from it of God's Presence, so must everyone today recognize his individual responsibility for the corruption of our social institutions and their tendency to defeat the divine purpose of life, and seek by all the means at his command to atone for the evil they do. This implies the realization of what is involved in accepting the principle of individual responsibility and patterning one's life in accordance with such realization.

The sense of individual responsibility expresses itself as sensitiveness to the disparity between what is and what ought to be in the domain of the true, the good and the beautiful, and as a feeling of obligation to reduce that discrepancy to a minimum. We are continually being confronted with alternative courses of action. We instinctively begin to compare and to evaluate each possibility in the light of the consequences that come to mind. As moral agents, we are inwardly impelled to consider the consequences from the standpoint of their destroying or enhancing the value of life. The statement in the Torah, "I have set before thee life and death, the blessing and the curse; therefore, choose life, that thou mayst live, thou and thy seed," [11] voices the irrepressible consciousness of the power and the responsibility to choose the right in the face of temptation.

This may sound like evasion of the complicated problem of the freedom of the will. But the fact is that whether or not we succeed in proving logically or metaphysically the reality of human freedom, practically, a just and peaceful social order is inconceivable, unless we hold the normal mature person responsible, to some extent at least, for his actions, and even for his thoughts. To accept behaviorism in its extreme form is to eliminate not only all moral values but to render the very factor of consciousness superfluous. So long as we deem consciousness an efficient cause and a factor in determining results, we inevitably imply in the case of the

[11] Deut. 31:19.

human being an awareness of alternatives and the power to choose between them. This is tantamount to the recognition of moral freedom and responsibility.

The sensitiveness to the disparity between two courses of conduct is sharpened by the awareness of the consequences of our actions. Such awareness is part of man's growth in the knowledge of cause and effect relationships that obtain in the confused tangle of human affairs. To impart this knowledge, and to cultivate habits of action based on it, should be the main function of education for character. The failure of our educational systems has been due to their tendency to evade the discharge of this function. Those in control of our schools and colleges are afraid of having people's eyes opened to the actual connections that obtain among the various aspects of the social process, the economic, the political and the spiritual. The revelation of the truth might be upsetting to the self-complacency of those who are "at ease in Zion"; they might discover that their much heralded generosity is made possible at the expense of ruthless exploitation of workers in mines and mills. The truth about our social institutions might ultimately reach the exploited themselves and arouse them to throw off their yoke. Yet, so long as the truth about human relationships as expressed in our laws, institutions and habits is suppressed, there can be no such thing as education for character, and man will continue to give the lie to his being a free moral agent. For by rejecting or suppressing the knowledge of the consequences of his actions, he is undermining moral responsibility.[18]

Finally, accepting the principle of individual responsibility involves recognizing our indebtedness for the gift of life and personality and for all that we value most, not only to

[18] The following two rabbinic statements emphasize the awareness of consequences as a spur to the sense of individual responsibility. (a) "Every single person is obliged to say, 'The world was created for my sake'" (*Mishnah Sanhed.* IV, 5) implying that he involves the whole world in his moral guilt. (b) "A single meritorious deed or a single transgression determines the fate of the whole world" (*Kiddushin* 40b).

those from whose hands we have received these gifts but also to the totality of creative tendencies, relationships and agencies that spell God. This sense of indebtedness gives us no rest until we reciprocate in some measure at least by contributing our share to the sum of the forces in the world that make for personality. Hence, when there is a choice between being care-free and self-indulgent, on the one hand, and assuming tasks that entail effort, thought and sacrifice, on the other, a sense of responsibility leaves no doubt as to what our choice shall be. He, however, who accepts all his advantages as a matter of course and sees no reason for being thankful to man or God, is likely also to be the one who does not want to risk his personal freedom by attaching himself to any relationship that exacts loyalty and sacrifice, whether it be the assumption of family duties or of communal responsibilities.

In the larger concerns of life, this resistance to responsibility manifests itself in the tendency to look to organizations and specialists to do our thinking and planning and governing for us. Some social machinery or some recognized authority is expected to organize our lives for us. The truth is that no leader, however wise or expert, can be entrusted with the ordering of our lives. If we do not want our powers of mind and character to be atrophied, or our personality to remain stunted, we must not surrender the right and opportunity to make decisions regarding vital issues. It is true that division of labor is an indispensable method of human living; we are therefore compelled to delegate to others the power to act in our behalf. But we must ever be on the alert, ready to revoke such power, if it is abused. Scientific progress demands that the scientist reckon with having his claims closely scrutinized by fellow-scientists. Social progress is likewise possible only when those who exercise authority have to reckon with enlightened public opinion. Such public opinion presupposes on the part of the individual citizen the refusal to surrender to despot or dictator, however benevolent, the responsibility for his own actions.

Many are the alibis we employ nowadays to absolve ourselves of the sense of responsibility. Nor does it require over-much reflection to discover the fallacies that underlie them. The first that comes to mind is the insignificance of human life in comparison with the vast infinitude of the cosmos. But does not the very ability to think in cosmic terms render physical measurements and proportions irrelevant? It has been well said, that the only true values in our human drama are those which are independent of the size of the actors. Even the apparent inability of the average individual to make an impression on the life of society or a permanent contribution to its values is counterbalanced by the fact that the most humble has his sphere of influence, where his behavior counts.

Then there is the argument which would absolve us of responsibility by pointing to the determining influence of heredity and environment. But that, too, is offset by our ability to utilize the knowledge of that fact to transcend the fact itself. For that knowledge imposes upon us the task of so controlling both heredity [**] and environment as to direct them into channels of greatest good. In the same way as the knowledge of the laws of physical nature becomes in our hands an instrument of control, so the knowledge of the laws of human nature should be utilized as an instrument of control in the interests of the good life.

The new psychology, with its discovery that the subconscious constitutes the greater part of the mind-content and is beyond man's control, has in recent years been added to the alibis for irresponsibility. Reason, according to this most

[**] One of the reasons, according to the Rabbis (*Sanhed.* 38a), God created only one man is that the wicked might not say: "Ours is an evil heredity," implying that they have no power to resist temptation.

recent absolution, is little more than a mechanism driven by blind instincts. The "ought" is not the voice of God, but of instinctive desire. Behaviorism teaches that human actions are automatic responses to stimuli, and consciousness is an illusion. All this simply means that, insofar as this new psychology is true, it should increase our powers of control over ourselves. Psychology as such should have nothing to do with the validity of meanings and potency of values.

But the refutation of the alibis is not enough. We have to count on those urges in the human being which make for wisdom, cooperation and creativity. These too are hungers which are irrepressible, and which give man no rest until they are satisfied. Only the mentally unbalanced are lacking, for example, in such significant traits as loathing for that which is felt to be unwholesome to the body or mind; only the degenerate are without a sense of honor, of fair play, or a respect for sincerity. By means of these traits alone beneficent character could be formed, if we only made the effort to know how. The problem of cultivating the sense of responsibility is, therefore, not one of calling into being something that does not exist, but of developing something incipient and inchoate. "Men on the whole mean right, but let their lives be wrecked by petty things, egoisms, vanities and misunderstandings. Human nature is somehow better than our performance, a paradox the explanation of which lies in the fact that clear purpose and unified will are the late development of those primary tendencies which in their dim groping merely frustrate one another." [20] The main trouble with human life is that the sense of responsibility tends to operate within too narrow a scope and to confine itself to our own family, economic class, social clique, or limited political group. The narrowness of its scope often encourages irresponsibility to those who do not come within the particular group one is identified

[20] Hobhouse, L. T.: *Social Development.* N. Y., 1924, 337.

with. This is what happens when normality, loyalty, honor, truth, etc., are invoked to justify selfish ends.

If the conscience, the sense of duty or responsibility, is to attain its fullest development and widest scope, it must be commensurate with our conception of God. Since God represents the sum of all the forces that contribute to life's worthwhileness, any sense of duty or responsibility, to be justly numbered among such forces nowadays, must needs be based upon the right of every human being to experience it and exercise it to the fullest extent within his power. This is possible only in an atmosphere of freedom, freedom from oppression and insecurity. Only as the human being is permitted to achieve responsible personality does human life attain true dignity and worth.

6

Repentance as the remaking of human nature

These thoughts associated with the symbolic significance of the Day of Atonement cast light on what is involved in the idea of *teshubah,* or repentance. Repentance stands for nothing less than the continual remaking of human nature.[11] As with social regeneration, so with the regeneration of human nature in the individual, God alone was depended upon, in the past, to bring it about. The ancients despaired of man as capable of changing his social order, or of changing himself. "I will give you a heart of flesh," said Ezekiel.[12] This the Sages interpret to mean that the human heart will be so transformed by God that it will revolt at the thought of taking what belongs to some one else.[13] We have seen how at the present time all hope is centered on the human being. It is expected that he will utilize his intelligence and

[11] The frequent association of repentance with good deeds indicates that repentance is conceived as a permanent aspect of human life. *Cf. Abot.* IV, 17.
[12] Ezek. 36, 26.   [13] Gen. *R.* XXXIV, 15.

inherent desire for cooperation to achieve what in his best moments he visions as desirable. The same applies to his character. Human nature has both its personal and its social aspect, and has as well its cosmic aspect, that is to say, its relation to the world of nature in which it lives. To remold it effectively in the interest of unity, harmony and integrity one must apply both introspection and that objective knowledge of human behavior which constitutes the science of psychology. The one without the other is doomed to failure.

To resort to introspection without reference to psychology in order to find out what is wrong with our character, and how to right it, is like looking into a mirror to find the cause and remedy of physical illness. Our personality is not a self-sufficient unit, but a system of relationships. It includes our relationship to our family, our occupation, our neighbors, our religious affiliation, our economic status, our race, our nation and innumerable other factors. If anything is wrong with our personality, the trouble is never limited to our individual selves, but inheres in the whole complex of our responses to the stimuli of our environment. To improve our personality, these external factors must be taken into consideration, and mere introspection will not change them. In fact, the attempt to remedy spiritual ills, without reference to such conditioning factors, frequently only aggravates them.

A man, for example, finds that he is addicted to the use of a habit-forming drug. He knows by introspection that, although the drug gives him certain satisfaction, as the effect wears off he is debilitated and nervous and incapable of enjoying the more normal pleasures life affords. Gradually the powers, the exercise of which gave worth and meaning to his life, slip from him one by one. He knows he has sinned. He says to himself: "I must stop this." He may even impose penalties upon himself for every time he violates his pledge. But these resolutions do not relieve the misery which he experiences when he denies himself the drug. In fact, they increase his misery. He feels, therefore, all the more keenly the need for indulging his habit as the only escape open to him from its evil effects. His very remorse and shame impel him to further indulgence, since they are part of the nervous effect of the drug itself. He needs self-confidence, and his introspection can afford only self-contempt. Yet his case is not hopeless. If, instead of seeking a cure wholly within himself, he consults a physician and perhaps retires for a time to an institution where his habits can be regulated by others in accordance with his needs as understood by a scientific observer, his habit can be broken and his personality redeemed.

Many of our sins are due to an exaggerated egocentricity caused by the frustration of our social impulses. In such cases it must be obvious that introspection can result only in emphasizing the introvert bent of our minds. Herein lies one of the chief dangers of religious asceticism. Self-hate does not lead to love of our fellows, but to contempt and envy of them. "Be not wicked in thine own eyes" [44] is sound psychological as well as ethical advice. But to apply it means that we must sometimes cease worrying about our faults and try to interest ourselves in doing the things that are good, and forget about ourselves. Introspection may point out to us where we have made a mess of our lives; but a knowledge of the external factors which contribute to our failure and of the best methods by which these may be controlled so as to help restore our personality to its normal functioning is necessary to effect a genuine repentance, one that will truly make us *beriah hadashah,* a new creation, a regenerate personality.

Nevertheless, though introspection has its limitations, it is indispensable. A psychological understanding of oneself is not enough. Such an understanding is not necessarily

[44] *Abot.* II, 13.

normative. It is not concerned with what ought to be, but with what is. It can tell us how human nature is conditioned, but not whether the results of this conditioning are good or bad. Only our subjective experience as recorded in memory can tell us whether and in what respects our past life has been good or bad; only the subjective activity of the imagination can conceive the alternative possibilities of life and choose between them. When we know what we want, psychology is indispensable to showing us how we can obtain it. It has more to tell us about the processes of our mental behavior than has introspection, but it has nothing to say about its aims. The joint application, however, of introspective thought with our modern scientific knowledge of human nature puts us in a better position to achieve the ideal of repentance than were the generations that went before us.

That even they were aware that repentance meant more than a momentary change of heart seems to be implied in the following *midrash:* [**]

" 'Let the wicked forsake his way and the man of iniquity his thoughts!' [**]
R. Bibi, the son of Abaye, said: 'How shall a man confess his sins on the Day of Atonement? He should say, 'I acknowledge all the evil that I have done. I stood in an evil way and I shall never again do the like of what I have done. May it be acceptable before Thee, O Lord my God, to pardon all my iniquities and forgive all my transgressions and grant atonement for all my sins.' "

Note the emphasis on the "evil way" as in need of being definitely abandoned. The "evil way" is the complex of elements in human nature and environment which must be broken up, or reconditioned.

In accordance with this conception of repentance, it is apparent that repentance is not merely a sentiment to be experienced when the awareness of sin rouses us to remorse.

[**] Lev. *R.* III, 3.   [**] Is. 55:7,

Repentance is part of the normal functioning of our personality in its effort at progressive self-realization. This is in part implicit in the very dedication of one day each year to the idea of atonement. It is even more clearly implied by the inclusion in our daily liturgy of the prayer:

"Cause us to return, O our Father, unto Thy law; draw us near, O our King, unto Thy service, and bring us back in perfect repentance unto Thy presence. Blessed art Thou, O Lord, who delightest in repentance."

There are three types of failure which repentance should aim to remedy. The first of these is the failure to integrate our impulses, habits, social activities and institutions in harmony with those ethical ideals that make God manifest in the world. As has been pointed out in the discussion of the nature of sin, this failure leads to distrust of oneself and to the sense of frustration. When, through introspection and the application of our best knowledge of human nature, we succeed in bringing our impulses into harmony with one another and with the aspirations of our fellow-men to achieve similar integration of personality for themselves, we experience a sense of fulfillment, a renewal of the zest of life, a heightening of our appreciation of life's worth and holiness.

When Abraham interceded with God to save Sodom and Gomorrah from destruction, he used the expression, "Far be it from Thee." The Sages [17] caught the true spirit of that expression when they added in comment of it: "It means," they say, "that to act unjustly is alien to God." They thereby indicated that the character of God is necessarily conceived as inherently consistent, integrated. Transferring this attribute of God to human character, we should say that, *if human character is to reflect the divine, it must be integrated and self-consistent. This involves a working synthesis of*

[17] Gen. *R.* XLIX, 9.

individual self-expression and social cooperation. Such a synthesis is, therefore, evidence of atonement won and the fruit of effective repentance.

The second type of failure which should lead to repentance is the failure to keep on growing in character. The behavior patterns which we built up in the past may have been quit*:* adequate for our needs then. But, in the meantime, the conditions of our life have so changed as to impose new responsibilities upon us, for which our past experience has not prepared us. This leads to the form of sin for which modern psychology has coined the term "fixation."

For the young child in the home of his parents a trusting and affectionate obedience is a virtue. It is commendable for him to defer to his parents' judgment in all important matters rather than to his own untutored impulses. But when the boy grows to maturity and is called upon to make important choices that will commit him to definite responsibilities for the remainder of his life, if he lacks the initiative to make his own decisions and remains dependent on his parents, he is bound sooner or later to come to grief and to bring grief to others. If his choice of a career, for example, is determined for him by the prejudices of his parents and not by his own aptitudes and the economic situation in his own generation, his economic life will not bring him satisfaction or enable him to give of his best to society. If his devotion to his mother makes him indifferent to the promptings of nature to seek a mate and he remains a bachelor in consequence, he is denying himself opportunities for self-realization, which again prevent him from giving to the world all that it is in him to give. According to Jewish tradition, marriage and the begetting and rearing of children are definite moral obligations. Behavior patterns which, while commendable in a young child, tend to inhibit him in meeting these later responsibilities and thus check his normal spiritual growth are unquestionably wrong.

The normal development of the individual from dependent childhood to dependable maturity necessitates as part of the law of growth a repeated reorganization of one's habits in accordance with the growth of one's powers, the widening of one's social horizons and the acquisition of new responsibilities. Nor does this process cease with physical maturity. No man can continue into married life all the habits of thought and action that characterized him before marriage. The commitment to share one's most vital responsibilities and interests with one's mate in a manner which, while building up the collective personality of the family respects the individuality of every member in it, requires again a reconstruction of the pattern of one's behavior to correspond with the new relationships into which one has entered. The care of the children, their nurture and education, the need for sheltering and guiding them while they are dependent, and helping them to eventual independence, again require continual reconstruction of one's habits and character. Changes in economic status, and innumerable other experiences which cannot possibly be listed, call for growth and cry out against the sin of fixation, of permitting previous habits no longer appropriate to the new conditions to continue to govern our lives. *Whenever we recognize the inadequacy of our acquired personality to do justice to the demands of a new situation, and we try to overcome the obstacles that prevent our lives from manifesting the divine, we are practicing repentance, or the return to God.*

The third type of human failure which we must seek to surmount is the failure to realize to the fullest degree the potentialities inherent in our natures and in the situations in which we find ourselves. We all have latent powers for good, powers which we do not summon to active use. The fact is that, in times of common danger, people who were in the habit of quarreling with one another, or standing aloof from one another, find it possible to cooperate and experience a genuine comradeship in so doing. This is evidence that, even when there was no common danger, the possibility of such cooperation existed, although it lay dormant. When touched by the sight of suffering, the most hard-hearted are frequently wont to respond generously to the need for bringing relief. This is evidence that their lack of generosity in the past was probably the result of an inactive imagination which can be stimulated into activity by more knowledge of how others live. Men whose conduct has stamped them as criminals and enemies of society have been known to volunteer to have themselves exposed to the ravages of contagious disease for the sake of scientific experiments looking to the ultimate elimination of such diseases. This is evidence that, under different circumstances, they were capable of making a more creative use of their faculties, and might be still capable of doing so, if the social conditions that tempt them to crime were removed.

Modern educators in experimental schools have elicited from children creative activity in the arts with results at which adults marvel. Confronted with these results, people are wont to explain them by reference to the greater plasticity of the minds of children. This is an incorrect explanation. If it were true, children in schools of the conventional type would show the same powers; but they do not. The truth is that the schools, in which the children showed such amazing creativity, applied intelligence in surrounding the children with environmental conditions that elicited creative efforts. If similar intelligence were applied to conditioning the life of adults so as to elicit their creative activity, the results would probably be even more amazing.

"Fixation" is a form not only of individual but also of social sin. That is the form of sin which is committed whenever social usages and laws that have outlived their usefulness and work harm are permitted to survive. The fact that these institutions arose in response to the needs of a past age, and may even have expressed the highest social ideals of that age, does not preclude their being utterly out of place under changed conditions. Yet we accept the status quo uncritically, from force of habit, even when we are aware of the evils which reveal its inadequacy. People today almost universally deplore the evils of poverty, economic insecurity and unemployment, but are for the most part prone to shrug their shoulders at any suggestion of radical change of the social order that has produced them. They even resent any criticism that might lead to instituting the necessary changes. Such cynical acceptance of social evils admittedly recognized as such, on the assumption that what is must always be, is the sin of "fixation" on the social scale, a sin for which every individual should deem himself responsible.

Ethical religion is incompatible with an attitude of submission to social institutions that work injustice. It denies the indictment of human nature as inherently evil. The vast majority of people in business, for example, want to be honest and considerate but, under the prevailing conditions of a cut-throat competitive economic system, find it impossible without courting ruin. This fact is sufficient evidence that dishonesty and cruelty are neither essential nor necessary traits of human nature; they are only the inevitable by-products of a world grown too small for "rugged individualism." To accept complacently ways of life that hinder us from realizing the best that is in us, or even to resign ourselves to the assumption that they are intrinsically and unalterable, is sin, and calls for repentance. Such repentance must express itself in determined and persistent effort to reconstruct our social institutions with a view to human welfare as realized in the synthesis of maximum individuality and maximum cooperation. Nothing less than the prospect of mankind achieving such welfare will satisfy the modern man, if he is to accept life as supremely worthwhile and holy.

The Day of Atonement is one of the few occasions which still elicit a religious response from the Jew. But that response is too often empty of ethical content, because the ritual of the day is still performed in the spirit of sacramental or theocratic religion. If it is reinterpreted, however, in terms of ethical religion, and its liturgy developed so as to emphasize the ethical ideas implicit in its meaning, it can contribute immeasurably to the spiritual growth and creativity of Jewish religion. In describing the order of procedure on fast days, the Mishnah [38] states that the Elder would address the people in words of exhortation. According to the Talmud,[39] this is how he addressed them: "Brethren, it is neither sackcloth nor fasting that brings about God's favor, but it is repentance and good deeds, for thus we find that in the case of the people of Nineveh it is not said, 'And God saw their sackcloth and their fasting,' but, 'And God saw their works, that they turned from their evil way.' " [40] The sacramental efficacy of the ritual of atonement is nil, and its symbolic power of no value, unless the sense of sin leads us to seek the reconstruction of our personalities in accordance with highest ethical possibilities of human nature; only then can we experience *teshubah,* the sense of returning to God.

[38] *Mishnah, Taanit* II.   [39] *Taanit* 16a.   [40] Jonah 3:10.

V

GOD IN NATURE AND IN HISTORY

I

The consciousness of history as an ethical influence

THE distinctive achievement of the Jewish spirit lies neither in philosophy, music, letters, or the arts, although Jews have made their mark in all these fields. Its unique contribution consists in having enriched the most difficult and inclusive of arts, the art of living. Jews have not discovered new continents, nor explored unknown regions, but they have discovered unsuspected meanings and relationships in the human scene with the cosmos as its background, meanings and relationships which not only convert living into an art but also indicate how to become expert in it. The truth of this general observation is borne out by what the Jews did with the three Pilgrimage Fesivals: Pesaḥ, Shabuot, and Sukkot.

The observance of festivals was from earliest times among all peoples an expression of gratitude to the gods for granting them life and sustenance. There was no people which did not have its spring festival, which did not rejoice in the awakening of the fertility of the soil. But there was no nation of antiquity which celebrated any festival to commemorate an historic event. *By utilizing the nature festivals to recall historical experiences, the Jews directed the human mind to the consciousness of history as an ethical and spiritual influence in human life.* "I love history," wrote H.

Taine in one of his letters, "because it shows me the birth and progress of justice; and I find it all the more beautiful in that I see in it the ultimate development of human nature." The Jews loved history because it showed them the way God dealt with man, and the way men should deal with one another.

Man differs from the rest of living creation mainly in the possession of self-consciousness. Other creatures live from moment to moment. If they have memories, they are not aware that those are memories. If the future in any way determines their actions, they have no mental picture of that future. The consciousness of history is the consciousness of that larger self which one shares with one's fellow men. The individual person is centuries, if not millennia, older than his chronological age. But if he also has a historical consciousness, he actually feels that the life which he lives extends far beyond the actual life of his body. Conscious of the experiences of the past, attached by a kind of umbilical cord to the history, the culture, the civilization of centuries, his being becomes coextensive with the being of his people. He enjoys, as it were, an earthly immortality.

The self-consciousness of the human being, contrasted with the simple consciousness of the animal, brings in its train a whole series of purposes, ideas, values, which constitute the entire character of spiritual and ethical life. Self-consciousness gives rise to the idea of moral responsibility, and to the distinction between right and wrong. In envisaging the future, it enables man to readjust himself to life in ways that would otherwise be impossible to him. Through his sense of history, man enlarges his field of operation far beyond the range of the three generations of time with which his life is usually contemporaneous. By means of this sense, human life is lived on a larger scale. It gives to the human being a dignity and significance which he could not otherwise possess. The individual instead of remaining merely a point on the circumference of human existence, becomes, as it were, a large enough segment by which to measure the entire circumference. Literally speaking, he becomes the bearer of collective consciousness or individuality. This is how the human being has achieved an awareness of godhood, for it is only as a member of society that man comes to know God.

The Jews were the first people to achieve national history. This means that no people before the Jews molded its life by an awareness of its own past. Great rulers made it a point to record their achievements on stone or parchment. The records of the Egyptian kings and the Babylonian monarchs were considered part of their expression of gratitude to their respective deities for their victorious exploits. These records were part of the religious ritual expected of a ruler. The people, not being conscious of their share in these exploits, could be influenced by them but little in their outlook on life. There was in ancient times also such a thing as literary history, which was cultivated by the Greeks and the Romans. Thucydides, Xenophon, Tacitus, Livy, wrote history in the same way that fiction is now being written—as a high type of literary entertainment. But their history did not become a means of molding national consciousness.

The nearest approach to what may be described as a sense of history was the epic poetry of the nations: the Homeric epics, the Icelandic sagas, Beowulf, the Arthurian legends and cycles. These epic poems were originally sung or recited in the hearing of the people, who were greatly stirred by the deeds of adventure and heroism, and for the time being were fused into a living human mass that thrilled to the same names, events and emotions. As the beginning of tribal or national unity based on memories, the fusion marked also the beginning of a sense of history. But it was not carried far enough to become an ethical and spiritual influence.

A most remarkable phenomenon in the development of the

collective mind, and one to which little attention has hitherto been paid, is that the various peoples of the world repudiated their own past and adopted the past of the Jewish people. The Teutons, instead of continuing to glorify the deeds of their gods and heroes, adopted the God of Israel and came to regard themselves as the descendants of Abraham, Isaac and Jacob. To appreciate what this implies, we have to recall that before the thirties of the last century all Christian children studied the history not of their own nation but of the Jewish nation. The French child did not study about Charlemagne and Jeanne d'Arc; the English child did not study about the origins of England, about the coming of the Normans; the German child did not study its own history and mythology. The child studied the history and mythology of the Jews: how God called upon the descendants of Abraham to become His nation, the stories of the Patriarchs, the legends about Joseph. The English Puritans formulated their political problems in the very terms of biblical incidents and precedents. The literary allegories of these nations were based not upon facts of their own native experience but upon biblical incidents. The Jewish past constituted the historical consciousness of all the European nations. The Protestant movement represents the coming of age of the European nations. Having outgrown the state of tutelage to which they had been subjected for centuries, they began to develop a historical consciousness of their own, which matured only after the French Revolution. Modern nationalism is the product of the feeling for history, of that feeling which the world caught from the Jewish people.

In contributing to human consciousness the sense of history, the Jews have not only enriched human life but have also created new problems. Just as the consciousness of self, which is characteristic of the human being, brings with it responsibilities unknown to the simple consciousness of the animal, so the consciousness of history brings with it cares

and ills unknown to man before he was able to think in terms
of history. Chauvinism, fanaticism, the deification of the
State are some of those ills.

The Jews, however, should not regret their having given
to the world a sense of history. Every refinement of the
human organism, every added complexity, every function
which tends to increase man's power and sensitivity, is
fraught with danger. Self-consciousness, the religions which
grow out of it, the conception of God, the nature of society,
all these have their by-product of evil. Yet that is no reason
for eliminating them from human life. This, however, does
not lessen the Jew's responsibility for counteracting with all
his energy the evil which accompanies their contribution to
the human spirit. Jews must realize that in awakening in the
nations the power of historical consciousness, they have
assumed the responsibility of directing that power into channels of peace and good will.

2

The continuity of the Jewish religion due to its emphasis
upon the ethical conception of God

There is another aspect to the Pilgrimage Festivals as
reminders of the past. The patriarchal traditions, the story
of Israel's stay in and deliverance from Egypt, the story of
Israel's journey in the Wilderness, had, no doubt, the effect of
inculcating in the mind of the Israelite the truth that the God
who ruled the destiny of his ancestors before the conquest of
the Land was the same God as the one who guided the destiny of his people in his own days. The ability to think of the
same Deity as governing the destinies of two distinct types of
civilization, and as having manifested His power beyond the
borders of His people's land, was a radical departure from
the religious conceptions current among men in ancient
times. Without exception, each civilization was always wont

to have its own gods. Whenever a people moved from an old environment into a new one, it maintained its allegiance to the gods of the old environment for a time, but in the end its allegiance was transferred to the gods of the new environment. The people of Israel, however, by retaining their allegiance to YHWH, the God of the old environment, the Wilderness of Sinai and Paran, in the face of the most tempting reasons to transfer their allegiance to the gods of Canaan, their new environment, accomplished a most remarkable spiritual feat. They were the first to realize that a god can retain his godhood under changing civilizations. By means of this realization, they paved the way for the recognition that the God of Israel was the God of all civilizations. That enabled the God of Israel to displace, so to speak, the gods of all other nations and to be accepted as the God of the universe.

Why did Israel remain loyal to YHWH even after it had entered Canaan? It was because the Prophets and leaders of early Israel taught their people to associate YHWH with the ordering of the social forces and of the tendencies in man that govern human relationships. This was something entirely new, for all other peoples were taught to expect the display of godhood chiefly in the natural phenomena of land, sea and sky. Only secondarily, and on rare occasions, did they associate godhood with the moral forces of human life. Physical environment usually varies with locality, and may undergo radical transformation in measurable time. Not so the character of the human environment. The same desires, passions and ambitions bring about the same types of conflict. Hence the emphasis upon the ethical attributes associated with the character of YHWH led to His continuing to play the role of God in the new land to which they had come, and to His completely eclipsing the local deities they had found there. Ever after, whenever circumstances brought Jews in contact with new experiences and new civilizations, they found it easy to enlarge their conception of their God in conformity with their new needs.

The God-consciousness of a people is an index of what that people considers important. Outside Israel, the God-consciousness always came into play primarily as a phase of man's efforts to assure himself of sustenance, shelter, health and mating. These were considered as the things that principally mattered. The contribution of Israel to the progress of civilization consists in pushing the God-consciousness beyond the attainment of these physical necessities into those aspects of human life that distinguish that life from the sub-human, into the aspects of personality, righteousness and peace.

3

The ethical versus the utilitarian function of religion

It would be a mistake, however, to conclude that the Jews in their zeal for history relegated nature to a secondary position in the economy of the spiritual life. The Jewish calendar is deliberately so arranged as to make sure that Pesaḥ will always fall in the spring or as near it as possible. Counting the months, as the Jews do, by the circuits of the moon, the month of *Nisan* during which Pesaḥ comes due would shift from season to season in the course of a few years. This is prevented by the addition of an intercalary month, *Adar Sheni.* The reason it is important to have Pesaḥ in the spring season is that Pesaḥ is intended not only to commemorate the historic event of Israel's Exodus from Egypt, but also to celebrate the reaping of the first harvest of the year. This shows that in the Jewish festivals both nature and history are given their due share of recognition. *Both the creative powers in the physical world and the spiritual forces in the human world that make for personal and social redemption are treated as manifestations of the divine.*

Not only are both forms of energy thus accorded an equal degree of importance in the scheme of life, but they are by implication declared to be interdependent. We do not have a special festival to commemorate the Exodus and another one to celebrate the barley harvest, a special festival to remind us of the giving of the Torah and another one to signalize the wheat harvest, or one to recall Israel's journeyings in the Wilderness and an additional one for the purpose of thanking God for the vintage and the fruits which have been gathered in.

The twofold aspect of life is stressed in each of the three great Pilgrimage Festivals, as if to indicate that the normal manner of reckoning with God in the world is to realize that we should serve Him by making the benefits derived from the external world a means to the growth of the human spirit. That is to say, that the function of religion is to cultivate such appreciation of the material blessings that fall to our lot as would evoke from us a sense of moral responsibility for the use to which we put them. This function of religion Judaism was the first to announce to the world, though to this day it has not yet succeeded in having its own adherents fully conscious of all that is implied in such a conception of religion.

The avowal of this function of religion which Judaism accentuates in its Pilgrimage Festivals is a protest against a generally prevailing notion that religion is committed to being a means of bringing the physical environment under control. In its crude and undeveloped form, religion was universally practiced with the concrete end in view of obtaining food. Man worshiped the spirits that he believed animated the springs, the hills, the trees and the sky, because he expected them to clothe the earth with vegetation and to multiply his sheep and his cattle. Man did not come upon the idea of God through disinterested reflection on the beauty and order of the world. Rodin's "Thinker" pondering over the mystery of the universe is a myth. The first thinker was no low-browed, naked savage, just emerged from the wilds, but a much civilized and highly sophisticated dweller in some ancient city. The kind of god or gods that man originally believed in required no furrowing of the brow or painful thinking to be discovered. On the contrary, primitive religion is the product of man's mental feebleness. Being too immature to think out the connection between the various elements in nature and the part they play in making life possible and supplying his needs, he jumped to the conclusion that every object had a spirit of its own which was just as fitful and subject to whims as he was. Hence the elaborate systems of rituals and offerings, and prayers and dances, by which he believed he would cajole these spirits to give him rain, cause the sun to shine, the animals to multiply, and the earth to yield its vegetation.

The very way in which man approached his gods shows that primitive religion was not the product of mental activity. He resorted to actions by which he indicated what he wanted them to do. He enacted in dramatic form the passing of winter and the return of spring, as when he wept over the death and rejoiced in the rebirth of the god Adonis (Tammuz) in the hope that he would thereby hasten the arrival of the spring. He garbed himself in what purported to be leaves and flowers in order to precipitate the budding of the leaves and flowers on the trees. He poured libations of water in the sanctuary in order to induce the god of the sky to give him rain. This method of dramatic representation as a means of getting the gods to render abundant the yield of the earth led to all forms of licentiousness which were practiced as religious rites. These are only a few instances of the vast complex of rites repeated in every land and in every clime with the same practical purpose of getting control over the powers of nature.

So long as man depends upon the fulfillment of his elemental needs and he allows his imagination, instead of his reason, to serve him in discovering ways and means of meeting those needs, he is bound to think of religion chiefly as a purveyor of the physical necessities. Despite the progress made by science, such aberrations as Christian "Science," or for that matter Jewish "Science," will win numerus disciples even among so-called people of culture. The real significance of science has not yet been grasped by the multitudes. Hence for a long time to come people will use religion in the hope that through it they will be able to ward off illness and to secure prosperity and safety.

This utilitarian function, however, cannot but bring religion into disrepute, for ultimately man will not only acquire greater control over the forces of nature but also realize how inconsistent the scientific control of nature is with the resort to magic and superstition. That is already happening with thousands of the more enlightened. Never having learned that it is possible for religion to have other than a utilitarian function, they conclude that it is bound to disappear with the enlargement of man's sphere of control over his environment. Many believing themselves sufficiently intellectual, or wishing to be counted among the intellectuals, act out that conclusion.

That religion is as inevitable a part of human civilization as is science or art derives from the fact that, with the progress of civilization, religion ceases to be utilitarian and becomes ethical. This change of function is Judaism's contribution to the spiritual life of mankind. Jewish religion has taught the world that the business of religion is not to help us secure the things we need for our well-being, but to get us to use those things righteously once we have secured them. It is undoubtedly much more difficult to know how to utilize, than how to retain, our health. A far greater amount of effort is involved in the righteous use of power and influence than in winning them. The Sage who said it is more difficult to conquer one's spirit than to conquer a stronghold,[1] knew whereof he spoke. Alexander conquered the whole world except Alexander.

It is toward this self-conquest, this control not of the physical but of the human environment, that the Jewish civilization would have religion direct its efforts. When the Greek philosophers grew wise to the folly of employing religion as a means to the control of the physical elements of nature, they abandoned religion and turned to the cultivation of a religionless ethics to guide man in the art of living. When the Prophets denounced the utilitarian use of religion, they transformed and exalted it into a means of cultivating social responsibility.

It is interesting to note that the Prophets contrast Israel's relation to YHWH with its relation to the nature deities. The former is generally compared to a relationship of love, the latter to a relationship of lust. The significance of these comparisons is made clear when we realize the difference between lust and love. Lust is a physical appetite that is promiscuous in its expression. Love is a sex emotion which is selective and takes into account the personal and individual qualities of its object. By virtue of this emphasis upon personal values, great possibilities of spiritual development that would otherwise remain dormant are made available. Likewise, by being selective of certain traits in its God, which it held up for admiration and imitation, Israel raised religion in general to a higher moral and spiritual level. Among the means which it employed to raise religion to this higher level of ethical monotheism was its emphasis on the manifestation of God in history.

The interpretation of history, viewed as a function of religion, is not merely a didactic or contemplative affair. It is not meant as an object of quietist reflection for those who stand on the side-lines and watch the endless human struggle

[1] Prov. 16:32.

for existence and for the light. It is meant for those who are in the thick of the struggle, as a plan of the battle they must wage against all the forces of evil and darkness. It implies marching orders in the direction of that goal which, when achieved, will demonstrate that human history is after all the chief incontestable self-revelation of God.

4

The reason for retaining the nature aspect of the Pilgrimage Festivals

If the foregoing is true, why retain at all the nature aspect of the Festivals? Why should not Pesaḥ be confined to the celebration of the Exodus? Why be so particular about having Pesaḥ fall in the spring of the year? Since the main function of Sukkot is to recall Israel's journeying in the Wilderness, why insist upon having it come at the time of the year when the harvesting is over?

The answer is that the ethical emphasis in religion lends itself to a wrong inference concerning the place of man's material wants in his spiritual development. To prevent such wrong inference it is essential to keep alive the connection of Sukkot with the manifestation of God in nature. That inference is that the material wants of man must be regarded as a necessary evil; at worst, they are supposed to prevent his spiritual achievement; at best, they stand outside it. The wisest course, therefore, for man to pursue is to starve or suppress them. According to that inference, to live spiritually means to emancipate oneself as much as possible from the dependence upon the things of the world. Asceticism, though practiced by few, has until modern times been regarded as far more conducive to spirituality than the striving to get the most benefit and joy from the world, however much precaution we may exercise against yielding to its temptations. The mere contact with the world was considered as somehow defiling, as something that had to be lived down, if one wanted to be worthy of bliss in the hereafter. The good and saintly man was he who yielded grudgingly to the exactions of the physical nature of the human body and its environment.

Many thoughtful people, laboring under the impression that this attitude toward the physical aspect of life is inherent in a religion that emphasizes the primacy of the ethical and the spiritual, repudiate religion altogether. They regard human life as too deeply rooted in the physical realities to be able to negate nature, or to flee from it without suffering distortion or deterioration. They realize fully the temptations of the flesh, but to mortify it is to them like trying to live in a vacuum, when the air one breathes happens to be impure. It is therefore all the more essential to stress the truth that originally the Jewish religion did not draw from the ethical function of religion such an inference concerning man's physical wants. It did not ask man to breathe in a vacuum. What it sought was to purify the air which he lived on. Not to flee nature, but to utilize it to the full, in accordance with the will of God, is the only way to reckon with man's physical wants. "Everything ideal," says Santayana, "has its natural basis, and everything natural has its ideal fulfillment."

That is why, despite the emphasis upon the manifestation of God in history, Jewish religion would not have its adherents forget that He is also manifest in nature. Thus, in addition to Pesaḥ recalling the Exodus, it retains its character as a harvest festival, and Sukkot marks the final ingathering of the produce of the fields and the orchards, as well as Israel's journeying in the Wilderness. Giving thanks for the yield of the earth is not compatible with regarding things earthly as a necessary evil. The purpose of the nature aspect of the Pilgrimage Festivals is not to keep alive the magical attitude of primitive civilization, but to awaken in us a sense of gratitude for the material benefits which we enjoy through the bounty of nature. Such gratitude is bound to translate itself into a realization of the responsibility as to the manner in which we employ that bounty. It is only then that we are likely to become aware that the material blessings we enjoy are not so completely ours as to enable us to gratify with them some passing lust or fancy. "The earth and all that it contains belong to the Lord."

Thus, in place of the utilitarian function which paganism was accustomed to assign to religion and which still operates in the minds of those who are dominated by superstition, Jewish religion through its Pilgrimage Festivals reminds us that the purpose to be served by worshiping God is to align ourselves with Him in furthering His Kingdom of righteousness, of which the Exodus marks the initial event. And instead of looking for the establishment of that Kingdom to some other kind of world where we might not be hampered by the needs of the body, we are urged to lay its foundations in the earthly scene of changing seasons, of rivers and fields and cities taking on new life each year, with the returning sun.

In the ritual of grace after meals, we voice this conception of religion. First we thank God for having supplied us with the necessaries of life. Then we thank Him for the opportunities He has afforded us through delivering us from Egypt, and giving us a land and a Torah, to utilize that life to bring about the era of universal peace, when "God's Name will be blessed by the mouth of all living."

VI

GOD AS THE POWER THAT MAKES
FOR COOPERATION

OF the three Pilgrimage Festivals, Sukkot is the one which illustrates most strikingly the unique way in which the Jewish religion has conceived of God as manifesting Himself both through history and through nature. At first entirely an agricultural festival, Sukkot assumed by the beginning of the Second Jewish Commonwealth a national-historical significance, with the *Sukkah* as the chief symbol. Yet it also retained its connection with its ancient character as a nature or seasonal festival. The symbol of that connection was the Temple-libation of water.[1] In the festivities attendant upon that rite, the waving of the "four species of plans" including the palm branch (*Lulab*) figured prominently. Both symbol and festivities were an expression of thanksgiving for the yield of the year that had passed, and of petition for an abundant crop in the year to come.

Sukkot is known in the Bible also as the Festival of Ingathering,[2] because it marked the conclusion of the harvests in the fields and the ingathering of the fruits from the orchards and the grapes from the vineyards. It is also designated as the "Festival of YHWH"[3] and by the unqualified term "The Festival"[4] (regularly so in the Mishnah),[5] implying that it was at one time regarded as the festival *par excellence*. Originally, it appears, Sukkot was the only Pilgrimage Festival. On it the Israelites would leave their

---

[1] *Mishnah Sukkah* IV, 9. Cf. *Rosh ha-Shanah* 16a.
[2] Exod. 23:16 and 34:22.   [3] Lev. 23:39.
[4] I K. 8:2; Ezek. 45:23; II Chron. 7:8.
[5] Cf. *Bikkurim* I, 6; *Yoma* II, 5; *Sukkah* III, 13, etc.

homes and their local *bamot*, and repair to one of the larger sanctuaries like the one at Shiloh,[6] at Beth El,[7] or at Jerusalem, where large groups of people were gathered and helped to create a holiday atmosphere. The behest to rejoice on the festival[8] merely states what had been the practice since ancient days.[9] Indeed, the spirit of festivity seems to have been carried to a point where it broke out into orgies of hilarity and drunkenness, which became the special target of prophetic denunciation.[10] To Hosea the spirit of their celebration still bore a pagan or Baal character.[11] A radical change, however, in the observance of Sukkot took place when all sacrificial worship outside the Temple at Jerusalem was banned. From that time on Sukkot began to bear a national-historical character, and has had that character down to our own day. Whatever additional meanings the festival has retained or acquired, the principal one is that stated in Leviticus 23:42, 43: "Ye shall dwell in booths seven days; all that are home-born in Israel shall dwell in booths; *that your generations may know that I made the children of Israel to dwell in booths, when I brought them out of the land of Egypt: I am the Lord your God."*

In subsequent periods, when the interpretation of religious values yielded first place to those which were individual or other-worldly in their reference, the *Sukkah* came to be regarded as symbolic of teachings dealing with man's personal life. Thus, according to Maimonides,[12] the purpose in remembering the days that Israel spent in the Wilderness is "to teach men to remember his evil days in his days of prosperity. He will thereby be induced to thank God repeatedly, and to lead a modest and humble life." According to Isaac Aboab,[13] "The *Sukkah* is designed to warn us that a man is not to put his trust in the size or strength or beauty of his

[6] I Sam. 1:3.   [7] Amos 7:10.   [8] Deut. 16:14-15.
[9] Judg. 31:19-21.   [10] Amos 5:21-23; Is. 28:7, 8.
[11] Hosea 2:7.   [12] *Moreh Nebukim* III, 47.
[13] *Menorat Hamaor* III, 4, sec. 6.

house, though it be filled with all precious things; nor must he rely upon the help of any human being however powerful. But let him put his trust in the great God Whose word called the universe into being, for He alone is mighty, and His promises alone are sure."

The other rite which is still observed on Sukkot is that of waving the "four species of plants," including the palm branch (*Lulab*). That rite is a survival of the elaborate rites which were practiced in the Temple at Jerusalem. Those rites, in turn, date back to the purely naturalistic character which the festival had among the nations and in ancient Israel. Like the *Sukkah*, the "four species" received in time various allegorical and symbolical interpretations,[14] each one removing the rite one step further from its original association with the nature or seasonal aspect of the festival, though never severing it completely.

I

The original connotation of the Sukkah the basis of its significance for our day

To render the festival of Sukkot significant for our day, we have to go back of the interpretations it acquired during the rabbinic development of the Jewish religion, and retrieve the primacy of the significance given to the festival by the Torah, in the above quoted verse from Leviticus. The reason for this procedure is that most of the symbolic or allegorical meanings assigned in rabbinic lore to the Sukkot rites are either irrelevant to our way of thinking or are much more pointedly conveyed in other Jewish teachings and practices. On the other hand, the implications in the historical reference of the Sukkot ascribed to it by the Torah fit in aptly with our current understanding of what, in the main, is wrong with human life, and what is necessary to set it right. Like-

[14] *Cf. Lev. R.* XXX: 9-15.

wise the nature aspect of the festival, with its accent on "rejoicing before the Lord," has an equally far-reaching implication for our day. It may be interpreted as a symbol of the proper place of happiness in the scheme of human life. In the light of these implications, many of the rabbinic homilies concerning the *Sukkah* and the *Lulab*, which would otherwise remain dormant, assume significance. Moreover, since these implications are to be woven into the current pattern of Jewish religious thought they will serve as an index of what God means to the Jew of today.

Whatever the actual origin of the *Sukkah,*—and no archeologist so far has discovered a plausible explanation—there can be no question that when it was accepted as a specific festival rite, it functioned as a reminder to the Jews of the life which their ancestors led in the Wilderness before they came to the Promised Land. At the season of the year when the Jews were likely to feel most secure and contented, they were commanded, as the Talmud points out, "to leave their permanent abode and to make themselves a temporary abode."[18] It is evident that there was something in the experience of the Israelites in the Wilderness that the Torah wanted their descendants to keep alive.

To know what aspect of Israel's life in the Wilderness the Torah wanted the Jews to relive, we must familiarize ourselves with the context of ideas associated with that stage of Israel's history. In spite of the occasional lapses into sin and rebellion which marred that period, it was always looked back to with wistful longing as the golden age of Israel's religious career. According to tradition, it was in the Wilderness that Israel established its covenant with God and consented to live by His law. In contrast with the idolatrous tendencies of Israel in Canaan, the Wilderness period was regarded as, on the whole, one of loyalty to YHWH. It was viewed as Israel's honeymoon period when, in love and faith,

[18] *Sukkah* 2a.

the people followed the pillar of cloud and flame in which their God journeyed before them. "I remember for thee the affection of thy youth, the love of thine espousals; how thou wentest after Me in the wilderness, in a land that was not sown." [16] The Prophet Hosea, who witnessed the decline of the Northern Kingdom of Israel, saw the only hope for his people in their again being led forth into the Wilderness:

"I will visit upon her the days of the *baalim,*
Wherein she offered unto them,
And decked herself with her earrings and her jewels,
And went after her lovers,
And forgot Me, saith the Lord.
Therefore, behold, I will allure her,
And bring her into the wilderness,
And speak tenderly unto her . . .
And she shall respond there, as in the days of her youth,
And as in the day when she came up out of the land of
    Egypt." [17]

This idealization of Israel's career in the Wilderness became in the hands of the YHWH zealots, a means of counteracting the influence of the civilization which Israel had developed in Canaan. Just as there is a tendency in American life, for example, to idealize the frontiersman, and to set up the life of the frontier with its simplicity, independence, self-reliance and democratic freedom from class distinctions as a criterion of Americanism by which to judge and condemn the prevalent regimentation, mob-mindedness, submission to boss-rule and overvaluation of material prosperity, so in their day the Prophets made the virtues of the nomadic life of an earlier period a criterion of piety and obedience to God, on the basis of which they arraigned the vices and iniquities of their own generation.

We have seen, from the passage just quoted, how the Prophets' opposition to the worship of the agricultural deities

[16] Jer. 2:2.   [17] Hos. 2:15-17.

of Canaan was reenforced by reference to the single-hearted loyalty of the henotheistic religion of the nomadic period. But it was not merely in the matter of religious worship that they contrasted the virtues of the nomadic civilization with the vices of the agricultural civilization of their own day. Along with the settled life in Palestine came the usual evils that are incidental to the development of a more complex social and political economy, the development of classes, the oppression of the poor by the rich and luxury alongside of poverty. Such conditions made the more idealistic look back regretfully to the simple and egalitarian life of the nomadic state. Some went so far as to try to reproduce it for themselves on a small scale. The Prophet Jeremiah points out with praise the example set in this respect by the family of Jonadab, the son of Rechab, who were faithful to the following ordinance which their father had imposed upon them: "Ye shall drink no wine, neither ye, nor your sons, for ever; neither shall ye build house, nor sow seed, nor plant vineyard, nor have any; but all your days ye shall dwell in tents, that ye may live many days in the land wherein ye sojourn." [18]

The protest against the developing material civilization, which was voiced immediately after the settlement of Israel in Canaan, was not merely sporadic and limited to a few striking personalities among the Prophets. It constitutes the spirit of all the biblical writings. The Torah, for example, traces the development of material urban civilization to Cain and his descendants. [19] It regards the power, which that kind of civilization made possible, as the source of man's rebellion against God. This is implied in the story of the city and Tower of Babel. [20] In the book of Deuteronomy, Moses is represented as cautioning the people in God's name not to forget their Wilderness experience and become arrogant and rebellious, because of the prosperity they would enjoy in the

[18] Jer. 35:6, 7.   [19] Gen. 4:16-24.   [20] *Ibid.*, 11:1-9.

Promised Land."[1] The Prophet Isaiah in his day cherished
the hope that the desolation incident upon Sennacherib's invasion would, perforce, bring the people back to a simple
pastoral life.[2]

The same spirit of revolt against the agricultural and
urban civilization is implied in the glorification of the nomadic and shepherd life which we find in the cycle of
patriarchal narratives. The question is often asked, how it
came about that Israelites chose to tell the story of their
pastoral ancestors. As a rule, the agriculturists hold shepherds in contempt, and it would, therefore, seem more natural for the Israelites to have depicted their ancestors as
farmers notwithstanding the fact that the Israelite conquerors of Canaan had been bedouin of the desert. People
who conquer a settled territory with a higher stage of material civilization and assimilate with the native population
usually appropriate both the gods and ancestors of the conquered people. The reason that the Israelites were not
ashamed of their nomadic origin was that those who kept
alive the loyalty to YHWH were, at heart, fond of the
nomad and pastoral life as being more pure and more free
than the civilization of Canaan. They liked to think not only
of their common ancestors, the Patriarchs, but also of their
law-giver Moses and of their hero-king David as having been
shepherds.

From the foregoing circumstances it follows that having
the Israelites relive their Wilderness experience on the festival of Sukkot was bound to place them in a frame of mind
which enabled them to detach themselves from the order of
life which they had come to accept as normal and to view it
critically. This call of "Back to the wilderness!" was the
first articulation of that call which is familiar to us under the
slogan, "Back to nature!" It, too, was a call to self-emancipation from the artificialities and injustices of current civili-

[1] Deut. 8:11-18.   [2] Is. 7:21-25.

zation, and, like the latter, it assumed the character of a yearning for an idealized past.

Whether it be "Back to the wilderness!" or "Back to nature!" the important thing is to discover what it was, in their idealization of the past, that the Prophets and social reformers harked back to with regret. These ideals which their own age failed to realize and which they set up as the goal of their striving, still remain unfulfilled and may serve as objectives for our own social efforts. Viewed in this light, the *Sukkah* becomes the symbol of protest against the injustices and inequities of current civilization, and of the need of upholding the standards of righteousness which that civilization should seek to achieve.

Whenever we would evaluate the civilization under which we live, our attention focuses itself immediately on that aspect of civilization which is basic and determinative of all the rest, namely, the economic. The symbolism of the *Lulab* is significant of the part which the economic aspect of civilization should play in relation to life as a whole. It is the symbol of gratitude to God and rejoicing in His goodness for the bounty which He bestows in the form of harvested crops and gathered-in vintage. As such, it may serve to remind us that the criterion which the Jewish religion applies to the economic aspect of a civilization is: does it give all who live by that civilization a sense of life's creative possibilities, of life's interrelated unity and cooperation, and of life's worthwhileness—in brief, does it enable them to rejoice in God? If our economic system does not add to the zest of living, it is psychologically impossible for us to bless God because of it. The *Lulab* thus emphasizes the need of making our economic life such that it will contribute to our joy in God. Obviously this depends on moral factors at least as much as on the presence of natural resources. This is implied in the rabbinic comment which connects the symbolism of the *Lulab* with the words of the Psalmist: "Yea, let all the trees of the forest exult before the Lord, for He cometh; for He cometh to judge the earth." [**] After God has manifested Himself in the judgment on Rosh ha-Shanah and Yom Kippur, say the Rabbis, and Israel has, by its devotion, vindicated itself in the judgment, then and not before is Israel entitled to bear the palm of victory and rejoicing. [**] Then nature, as it were, participates in Israel's triumph and "all the trees of the forest exult before the Lord." Translated into literal fact, the thought implied in this Midrash is that *only when God's justice is manifest in our midst, can the gifts of nature be appreciated in a religious spirit.*

This is the message of the *Lulab,* and, as a sort of antiphonal reply, the *Sukkah,* as a memorial of the idealized life in the Wilderness, says: For a people to rejoice in God, it must so dispose of the income from the resources of nature as to make its economic life conform to the social relations that obtained when Israel had not yet been contaminated by the life in Canaan. In the idealized version of the Wilderness life, the social relations which obtained in Israel were marked by a spirit of fraternity and cooperation. There were no degrading distinctions of caste, no subjection of the weak to the strong and no limitations of personal liberty that were not applicable to all alike in the interest of the common good.

In contrast with such a social order, the heathen civilization of Canaan was founded on the exploitation of the poor by the rich. It was a social order that disregarded human rights and was marked by waste, parasitism and frustration. The same may be said of all modern civilizations. They are still in the predatory stage. Society is based on class distinctions. The western civilizations, in professing religion which derives from Judaism, have outwardly given allegiance to the foregoing criteria of social life. But, at heart, the European civilizations and their Asiatic imitators rebel against these

[**] Ps. 96:12.   [**] Lev. R. XXX, 4.

criteria. Machiavelli and Nietzsche are far more typical of European civilization than are Moses and the Prophets.

Machiavelli, taking early Rome as his model, saw in the State chiefly an instrument for upholding the power of the ruling class. According to him, men are moved exclusively by self-interest, and no public policy can afford to be based upon moral considerations. The military State, aiming at the expansion of its power and ultimately world dominion, was his ideal. Nietzsche regarded class distinctions, insecurity and war as the means which nature employed to evolve the superman and, therefore, as highly desirable—from the standpoint of the superman. "Democracy and freedom mean the awakening of the superfluous ones, the many too many." "Morality is the will to power of the powerless." The superman, according to Nietzsche, can thrive only at the expense of the underdog.

It is only by such criteria that the civilization of the western world can stand approved. By the criteria which the Jewish religion offers and which are symbolized by the *Sukkah,* it stands condemned. In the eschatology of Zechariah [15] the ultimate acceptance by the nations of the sovereignty of God is coupled with the celebration of the festival of Sukkot. The Rabbis elaborate on that conception by reading it into the second Psalm which they interpret as a description of the Day of Judgment. The nations, according to the Rabbis will be given a chance to redeem themselves by observing the ordinances of the *Sukkah.* As soon, however, as they find that it fails to protect them against the strong heat of the sun, they will overthrow the *Sukkah.* [16] These and similar symbolic statements voice what is unhappily still the truth, that the world continues pagan at heart and repudiates the ideals symbolized by the *Sukkah.* But "He that sitteth in heaven laugheth" [17] at the futility of man's revolt

[15] Zech. 14.
[16] *Abodah Zarah* 2b. *Cf.* also *Midrash Tanhuma* on Lev. 22:28.
[17] Ps. 2:4.

against His sovereignty which must ultimately be acknowledged, if humanity is to survive.

2

The sacredness of human rights

The Jewish religious evaluation of the experiences of
Israel in the Wilderness implies the recognition of the sacredness of human rights. That recognition is based on the
assumption that a kinship exists between God and man. In
human nature at its best Jewish religion has always seen the
clearest revelation of the divine. "Ye shall be holy; for I the
Lord your God am holy," [18] would be utterly without meaning for us, if it did not imply the potentiality of human
nature to rise to the height of those ethical ideals which evoke
our adoration and worship. But *the recognition of the
sacredness of personality carries with it the acknowledgment
of rights of personality.* Jewish religion acts on that implication when it ascribes to God numerous ordinances intended
to prevent a person from wronging his neighbor by depriving
him of his life, possessions or reputation. It has even gone
further and interpreted the evils which befall human society
as the punishment which God metes out for the violation of
these rights. [19]

But is the recognition of human rights in harmony with
the realities of human nature? An affirmative answer to this
question is the only correct one. Man is by nature a social
animal. The life-urge within him expresses itself not only in
forms of behavior designed to preserve the individual organism from death, but also and equally in forms of behavior
looking to the preservation of the race. Cooperation with
other individuals is indispensable to him. Human life can
be as little conceived without social cooperation as can the

[18] Lev. 19:2.
[19] Compare the reasons the Torah and the Rabbis give for the Flood.

life of a colony of ants. On the other hand, man cannot trust to unerring instinct to guide him in his social behavior. He must therefore depend on the conscious recognition of an organic social relationship in which all men are involved, and he must see in every man an organ of a common life. The health of the social organism depends on the healthy functioning of all its organic components, that is, of all individual men. If one man oppresses another and thus thwarts the growth and creativity of his personality, he is interfering with the healthy functioning of the organism as a whole, and in this impairment the welfare of the oppressor as well is involved, although he may not realize it. Such thoughts as these are but the rationalization—if one may use that term without any connotation of wishful thinking—of the social feelings of men which are part of their instinctive endowment and indispensable equipment for life.

It is therefore absurd to assume that the only forces operative in society are those which emanate from differences in physical strength or animal cunning. To assume that there is no right but might overlooks the fact that right itself is a sort of might, an overpowering impulse to behavior in the interest of ends that transcend the life of the individual. The sacredness of personality is implicit in our recognition of the sacredness of life, which is but another way of viewing the instinct of self-preservation. Thus the sacredness of human rights derives directly from the sacredness of personality.

This does not commit us to the theory of "natural rights," as developed in the philosophy of Rousseau and made the basis of his theory of the "social contract." According to that theory men are conceived as having been originally endowed by nature with unlimited freedom to do as they pleased, but as having surrendered voluntarily a certain number of liberties in the interest of the advantages to be derived from social cooperation. This philosophy which profoundly influenced the democratic movements of the eighteenth and early nineteenth centuries has since been discredited. The distinction between "natural man" and "social man" is itself unnatural. Even before our common ancestors had attained in the course of their evolution the characteristics which we recognize as belonging to the *genus homo*, they doubtless lived a gregarious and quasi-social life.

The philosophy with which, in the past, the champions of democracy sought to sanction their advocacy of human rights was not correct. But this must not prejudice us against recognition of human rights itself. The refutation of that philosophy must not be construed as an apology for human wrongs. The sacredness of human rights is not to be based on the nature of man as a self-sufficient individual being, for such he certainly is not. It is to be based on the nature of man as a social being. Personality derives its being from the need of reacting to the natural and the social environment. It comes into existence in response to those tendencies and relationships that augment the unity and value of life. It is therefore a part of the divine aspect of reality, an expression of the immanence of God. This religious sanction determines the sacredness of personality and the rights that inhere in it.

Those tendencies and relationships that augment the unity and value of life, and thus point to the reality of God, are mediated for man chiefly through the organized life of society. Society is the matrix in which the very substance of personality is formed and nurtured. Our ideals are never derived merely from our own individual experience. The very language in which we think our most intimate thoughts is a product of social life. Whatever rights inhere in personality are at the same time integral to the very function of society. It is not that we have rights as individuals, some of which we waive by an implied social contract. We have rights, because without them we cannot maintain our responsible share of the life of human society. This gives to those rights their ethical sanction.

Respect for the personalities of our fellow-men and the recognition of their rights are far better guides to ethical conduct than the appeal to the sense of duty or goodness in ourselves. It renders us more sensitive to moral wrong. What constitutes an infringement of our rights is an immediate and emotionalized experience, and capable of being projected into our neighbor, whereas the sense of duty is a derivative idea and considerably weaker in emotional tone. "R. Akiba said: 'Thou shalt love thy neighbor as thyself' is the greatest principle in the Torah." "Ben Azzai said: 'An even greater principle is implied in the verse [90] 'This is the book of the generations of man. On the day that God created man in the likeness of God made He him'." [91] That verse, in reminding us that God created man in His likeness, emphasizes the fact that man possesses inherent rights which derive from the divine principle in him and is, accordingly, a more efficacious guide to conduct than the behest to love our neighbors as *ourselves*.

3
The meaning of equality

The human rights which are conceived as sacred and inalienable are stated in the American Declaration of Independence to be the right to "life, liberty and the pursuit of happiness." This classification is a just one. Properly conceived, these rights are inevitable consequences of the sacredness of personality which expresses itself in creativity, in the disposition to ethical behavior, and in the enhancement of life's values.

Life is more than mere existence. Duration in time applies even to inanimate objects. But life, humanly speaking, im-

[90] Gen. 5:1.   [91] *Jer. Nedarim* IX, 4.

plies organic functioning for ends in which the individual is interested. The right to life must therefore mean the right to have one's energies fully employed. Insofar as society conceives itself as an agency for personality, it must recognize this claim of the individual. Even if we regard the individual's contribution to the life of society as so minute that it is almost infinitesimal, nevertheless we must not forget that the total energy of society resides exclusively in the living generation of the individuals that constitute it, just as the energy of the individual organism resides entirely in the cells of the living tissues that compose it. *Society, therefore, owes it to the individual, in its own interest as well as in his, to give him the opportunity for employing his powers and faculties to the full.* It not only owes him employment, but such employment as will evoke from him the best service that he is capable of rendering.

The right to liberty, when derived from the concept of the sacredness of personality, cannot be conceived merely as freedom from restraint. A right is a claim to something positive. An objection to restraint implies a desire to do something which such restraint would prevent. The validity of the objection is therefore contingent on the legitimacy of the desire. Liberty from all restraint would be destructive of society and hence of personality. It could not therefore be inferred from the sacredness of personality. If liberty is to be claimed as a right, it must be clearly distinguished from the licentiousness which is destructive of personality and must therefore be considered wrong. Viewed in this light, *the right to liberty must be conceived as the right to the opportunity of leading an ethical life.* Society denies this right whenever it makes it impossible for vast numbers of men and women to earn their livelihood, without compromising with their consciences.

If society assures the individual of the right to life and liberty, it inevitably contributes as well to his happiness.

But something more than work and ethical social relationships are needed for the complete self-realization of human personality. Man is endowed with energy far in excess of what he needs to maintain his physical existence. The joy which is associated with the healthy functioning of any vital activity makes him seek to expend this excess energy in articulating personal and social ideals, for the sake of the enhancement of life's value which such self-expression affords. This gives rise to the esthetic and religious activities of men; and the right to the pursuit of happiness implies the right to engage in these activities. *A society which deprives men of the opportunity to enjoy and create esthetic values, or which manages its affairs in such a way as to render men godless, bitter and hateful of life, stands self-condemned as denying men their inalienable right to the pursuit of happiness.*

These rights, emanating as they do from the very attributes of personality, belong to every human being as such. Therein all men are equal. The fact that not all men have the same capacity to render service, or the same sensitiveness to ethical, esthetic and religious values in nowise contradicts or invalidates the equality of all men in respect to these inalienable rights. Nor does the recognition of the equality of all men in the enjoyment of these rights give ground for the criticism which is so often directed against the principle of democracy to the effect that it makes for mediocrity. *The doctrine of equality does not imply that all men must have identical opportunities for education, employment and esthetic and religious self-expression, but that all have an equal claim to the opportunity to pursue these activities to the limits of their own varying capacities and in accordance with their own individual interests.*

If the discussion of human rights is not to remain formal and abstract, it must reckon with the fact that the element of personality from which they emanate is dependent on things outside of man, notably on food, clothing and shelter. The entire question of rights is inextricably bound up with man's relationship to things. Not only is it obvious that, if one denies a man access to food, his right to life becomes meaningless, but defects of diet have physical effects which through diseases of malnutrition may affect his entire life. A man's clothing is almost as much a part of his person as an animal's fur is part of the animal, or a bird's feathers part of a bird. Birds cannot propagate their species without a nest, nor man his without a home. Nor is the relation of human personality to property limited to the so-called necessities. The voice of a singer is part of his personality; is not the instrument of the violinist a similar part of his? Every human relationship is ambivalent. It refers to other human beings and to things which condition the life, character and happiness of those human beings. *Rights are therefore contentless, unless they are rights to things, or property rights. Those rights to property which emanate from the concept of personality and are indispensable to its fulfillment are sacred and inviolable.* But any claim to things that are unrelated to personal wants, or that involve depriving others of property indispensable to them, is not a property right but a property wrong, or as R. H. Tawney has designated it, "improperty."

4

How civilizations have destroyed equality

Civilization has always tended to destroy equality, because it has favored the gravitation of control over things toward the few who happen to be stronger and more cunning. Realizing the power that inheres in the idea of rights, civilization proceeds to crystallize that control by identifying it as the embodiment of the right. In this way property wrongs are mislabeled "property rights," until even the dispossessed assume them to be such. As soon as that takes place, society invites all the evils that come in the train of monopoly, privilege and class distinction. Poverty, disease, crime, ignorance, insecurity, fear and hate are inevitable concomitants of this condition. The Jewish religion was the first to perceive this relationship and to make its primary task the denunciation of the abuse of civilization through the infringement of human rights. It thereby became the pioneer influence in the remaking of civilizations.

The tendency of civilization to destroy equality is evident in the unbroken chain of consequences resulting from what may be called its original sin, which it re-enacted whenever one people would conquer another. The victor would take possession of the land, cattle and tools that belonged to the vanquished. There would begin at once the inequitable division of the income which those possessions yielded; the greater bulk of it would go to the few who were in control of the possessions, and only enough would be granted to those who worked, to enable them to continue working. In the words of Herbert Spencer: "Violence, fraud and the prerogative of force, the claims of superior cunning—these are the sources to which these titles may be traced. The original deeds were written with the sword rather than with the pen; not lawyers but soldiers were the conquerors; blows were the current coin given in payment; and for seals blood was used in preference to wax." [22]

When civilization began to be urbanized, and trade and commerce presented to those in power new opportunities to augment their wealth, the distinction between classes grew apace, and inequality was further accentuated. The small freeholders who had somehow managed to retain a degree of independence, in the old agricultural order, soon found themselves in debt to the large landowners and merchants and at their mercy—a condition which is equivalent to the

[22] Spencer, Herbert: *Social Statics,* ch. ix.

forfeiture of the inherent rights of personality. Such forfeiture was accomplished by means of the influence brought
to bear by those in power upon the lawmakers and law ad-
ministrators. It is their protest against such practices that
made the Prophets preeminently the "tribunes of the people,"
against the aggressions of the ruling class.

"The Lord will enter into judgment
  With the elders of His people and the princes thereof:
  'It is ye that have eaten up the vineyard;
  The spoil of the poor is in your houses;
  What mean ye that ye crush My people,
  And grind the face of the poor?'
  Saith the Lord, the Lord of hosts." [88]

"Woe unto them that join house to house,
  That lay field to field,
  Till there be no room, and ye be made to dwell
  Alone in the midst of the land!" [84]

"Proclaim it upon the palaces at Ashdod,
  And upon the palaces in the land of Egypt,
  And say: 'Assemble yourselves upon the mountains of Samaria,
  And behold the great confusions therein
  And the oppressions in the midst thereof!
  For they know not to do right, saith the Lord,
  Who store up violence and robbery in their palaces." [88]

"Because ye trample upon the poor,
  And take from him exactions of wheat;
  Ye have built houses of hewn stone,
  But ye shall not dwell in them,
  Ye have planted pleasant vineyards,
  But ye shall not drink the wine thereof,
  For I know how manifold are your transgressions,
  And how mighty are your sins;
  Ye that afflict the just, that take a ransom,
  And that turn aside the needy in the gate." [88]

[88] Is. 3:14, 15.
[88] Amos 3:9, 10.
[84] Ibid., 5:8.
[88] Amos 5:10-12.

The protests of the Prophets, and of such religious leaders as fell heir to their spirit, did not, however, succeed in effecting a redistribution of wealth and power on the basis of the equal rights inherent in human personality. Inequality persisted. Before civilization could be sufficiently aroused to remedy the evils of inequality which had developed in human society, it became implicated in the industrial revolution. Although this revolution was contemporaneous with the rise of democracy and the espousal of "liberty, equality, fraternity," its effect was to increase rather than to diminish inequality. Under the feudal regime which preceded it, there was always the possibility, in spite of the power exercised by those in control, for large numbers of people to get beyond the reach of that power. The artisan could always manage to eke out his livelihood. If he earned enough to buy the tools he needed, and they usually did not involve any heavy outlay, he could ply his trade wherever he found conditions most favorable. Besides, there was always the choice of migrating to foreign parts. So long as that was the case, although there was less wealth in the world before man's productivity was enhanced by the use of machines, what wealth there was was not so unevenly distributed as to concentrate in the hands of a moneyed oligarchy the power over the lives, character and happiness of others.

All this has changed with the advent of the machine. The machine is a complicated and expensive tool, becoming ever more complicated and more expensive. It can produce goods far more cheaply than the simple tools of the artisan. Far fewer people can afford to own machines than could own artisans' tools. The owner of the machine can dictate the terms on which he will permit the worker to use it. He is in a position to exact "pure profits," that is, the surplus left after he has paid for raw material, wages of labor, interest upon the cost of the machine, wear and tear, wages of management and insurance of risks. To increase these profits, he keeps the wages of labor as low as possible, production is increased without regard to need, and the mad struggle and competition to dispose of the production results in wastage, wreckage, unemployment, and war as the inevitable sequence.

With the growth of industry and of the complexity of machinery needed to produce goods and withstand competition, individual owners are replaced by stock companies. Ownership becomes entirely separated from management and becomes tantamount to a private tax imposed on those who work the machines. The owners invest no thought or labor in the enterprise and have no pride in the quality of its product, the technical efficiency of its processes or the value of its services to the community. Their sole interest is in drawing as large a dividend on their investment as possible. This dividend management must produce, no matter at what sacrifice of ethical principle, human sympathy, or scientific interest in efficiency. Nor does the corporate form of ownership necessarily mean, as would at first seem to be the case, a wider participation in the income derived from the machines. For, the stockholders themselves are subject to manipulators who speculate on the profits of industry and buy stocks not for investment but for trade. By manipulating the market, they can give to stocks a fictitious value in accordance with artificially created supply and demand that has no relation to the actual value of the plant in which the stock is invested or the income it yields. They keep on bringing capital together into ever new combinations, taking a disproportionally large rake-off in profits for themselves every time such a new combination is formed and leaving it to the workers and shareholders to fight out among themselves how much of the residue they shall get.

From the standpoint of equality, the most deplorable aspect of the present social and economic order is the inordinate striving to seize as much control as the law permits. And the law, being based on complete ignorance or disregard

of the changed conditions which jeopardize the sacredness
of human rights, is such as to sanction the deprivation of
those rights. For such deprivation is inevitable when control
of the sources of wealth is in the hands of the few, with no
voice for those who labor to produce it. "As functionless
property grows, it undermines the creative energy which
produced property and which in earlier ages it protected. It
cannot unite men, for what unites them is the bond of service to a common purpose, and that bond it repudiates since
its very essence is the maintenance of rights irrespective of
service." [17]

Such being the case, it is clear that to change the social
order so that it shall conform to the ethical demand for
human equality involves nothing short of revolution. To
urge merely evolutionary changes evades the issue. The new
order cannot be an outgrowth of the very principles that
have produced the old. Any change in the direction of equality involves a transfer of power from the possessing class to
the masses which it now controls. The effecting of such a
transfer of power and of the wealth on which it is based
cannot be considered a further evolution of a capitalistic
economy. But by whatever means it is to be accomplished,
it is revolution. We should not permit an entirely praise-
worthy desire for peace and tranquillity to obscure the clar-
ity of our insight into the radical character of the change
that is demanded. The issue is not evolution vs. revolution,
but peaceful revolution vs. bloody revolution. The conflict
for human rights is now being waged. These rights are conceived realistically in terms of property; for, human rights,
without a secure economic foundation, are merely the right
to starve. In such a situation the desire to effect the necessary social changes with a minimum of disturbance to peace
and tranquillity is a worthy aim; but to offer the desirability
of peace as an argument against the radical revision of our

[17] Tawney, R. H., *The Acquisitive Society*. N. Y. 1920, 81.

economic situation is to "cry 'Peace! Peace!' when there is no peace."

If we are to look at the future through the eyes of the past, we find little reason for optimism. If there is to be no break in our tradition of violence, if a bold and realistic program of education is not forthcoming, we can anticipate only a struggle of increasing bitterness terminating in revolution and disaster. And yet, as regards the question of property, its present situation has no historic parallel. For the first time in history we are able to produce all the goods and services that people can consume. The justification, or at least the rational basis, of the age-long struggle for property has been removed. This situation gives to teachers an opportunity and a responsibility unique in the annals of education.

In an economy of scarcity, where the population always tends to outstrip the food supply, any attempt to change radically the rules of the game must inevitably lead to trial by the sword. But in an economy of potential plenty, which the growth of technology has made entirely possible, the conditions are fundamentally altered. It is natural and understandable for men to fight when there is scarcity, whether it be over air, water, food or women. For them to fight over material goods of life today is sheer insanity. Through the courageous and intelligent reconstruction of their economic institutions, they could all obtain not only physical security, but also the luxuries of life, and as much leisure as men could ever learn to enjoy.

The first essential to the achievement of human rights and human betterment is a conception of property, which is not "improperty." The energies for good latent in property can be realized only when the control of it is so socialized as to enable it to make for a maximum of creativity, character and happiness. This aim is in keeping with the Prophet's conception of the millennium in the verse: "And they shall

build houses and inhabit them; and they shall plant vineyards
and eat the fruit of them. They shall not build and another
inhabit; they shall not plant and another eat." **

5

The dispensing of happiness as the norm of a civilization

The festival of Sukkot is designated in the liturgy as "the
season of our rejoicing." Although all of the festivals were
observed as happy occasions, Sukkot was considered as preeminently such. The Mishnah describes the festive page-
antry that accompanied the drawing of water for the liba-
tion upon the altar, which was a feature of the Sukkot ritual
when the Temple was still standing. "Whoever did not witness the festivity of the drawing of water, never saw festivity in his life," exclaims the Mishnah.** *This emphasis on
rejoicing calls attention to the place that the pursuit of happiness is meant to occupy in our spiritual life, and to the importance of treating its attainment as the norm of true civilization.*

In Jewish tradition, happiness is regarded as a prerequisite
to entering into conscious relationship with God. "The
Divine Presence is not made manifest to man through mel-
ancholy . . . but through religious joy." ** The Rabbis
thus interpret the verse, "the spirit of Jacob their father
revived," ** to mean that as long as Jacob brooded despair-
ingly over the loss of Joseph, the Divine Presence kept far
from him, but when he was convinced that Joseph was still
alive and again experienced joy, the Divine Presence rested
upon him.** This is another way of saying that we identify
life's worthwhileness with the divine aspect of reality. For,
*we may define happiness as the state of mind dominated by
the feeling that life is worthwhile.* Without such feeling we

** Is. 65:21-22. ** *Sukkah* 51a. ** *Shabbat* 30b.
** Gen. 45:27. ** *Cf. Rashi ad locum.*

should have no experience of godhood; the Divine Presence would be hidden from us.

From the psychological standpoint, happiness is experienced whenever the entire personality, i.e., the human being in all his relationships, participates in the fulfillment of some specific need or needs, and there is no inner conflict of the type which might lead to the disintegration of personality. The gratification of a physical desire is attended with pleasure, but this does not necessarily mean that it results in happiness. If, for example, it takes place at the expense of the desire to be respected or held in esteem, it precludes happiness.

In whole-souled gratitude to God, the condition of happiness is completely fulfilled. This does not apply to the primitive man's conception of life as dominated by a multiplicity of gods, in which each god was the putative source of some particular good. An ancient Greek who was grateful to Dionysos for the gift of the grape, but who, in his gratitude, imbibed sufficient wine to make him forget the wisdom which was his gift from Athene, might derive pleasure from his worship of Dionysos, but not happiness. Nor is whole-souled gratitude to God compatible with the naïve conception of Deity, which is a vestigial survival of henotheistic religion in modern times, the conception of God as the apotheosis of the special interests of a particular historic group. The German people may be grateful to their Aryan god for the courage and valor to fight Germany's enemies with which his worship inspires them, but they cannot attain happiness through such worship, since it involves a maladjustment of Germany to the rest of the world. Whole-souled gratitude presupposes that we conceive of God as the apotheosis of the interrelated unity of all reality; for, it is only such unity that is compatible with life's worthwhileness. Hence, *to be grateful to God is to experience the sense of being in rapport with all the forces and relationships of life that make for the realization of its worth.* This presupposes taking into account the whole of one's personality. Gratitude to God is, therefore, the climax of happiness. "In the millennium," say the Rabbis, "all other sacrifices will be abolished, but the thank-offering will not be abolished; all other prayers will be abolished, but not the prayer of thanksgiving." [48] The Rabbis could conceive of a situation in which all propitiatory prayer and sacrifice would become superfluous and meaningless, but *the spirit of grateful appreciation is of the essence of religion, and can never be dispensed with. It represents the highest aspiration of the human soul for experiencing the goodness or godliness of life.*

In displacing polytheism and attaining to monotheism, Jewish religion has helped to transform religious gratitude from an expression of obligation to one deity or another, in order to be sure of further favors, into a spiritual attitude of deeper ethical significance. It has enabled gratitude to serve as a means of making man aware of the setting in which any particular good or enjoyment must be placed in order to yield him not merely pleasure but complete happiness. Erotic pleasure in ways detrimental to family life might be consistent with gratitude to Eros; but gratitude to "the Holy One, blessed be He" demands that man's sexual energy be channelized into forms of expression consistent with the recognition of the importance and holiness of all our social relationships. The same is true with regard to all other pleasures that do not engage the whole of our personality in harmony with its unitary purpose. The distinction between such pleasures and true happiness is implied in the Talmudic reconciliation of the apparently contradictory estimates of the value of joy which are found in Ecclesiastes. In one passage Koheleth declares: "I said of laughter, 'It is mad,' and of joy, 'What doth it accomplish?'" [49] In another he says: "So I commend joy." [50] The Rabbis reconcile the two state-

[48] Lev. *R.* IX, 7. [49] Ecc. 2:2. [50] *Ibid.,* 8:15.

ments by interpreting the commendation of joy to refer to the happiness associated with the fulfillment of a religious obligation, while its condemnation is said to refer to the sort of pleasure which has no such association.[44] Translated into modern terminology, we should say that pleasures which do not contribute to our appreciation of the sacredness and worth of life as a whole are but vanity, while those that do so contribute point the way to true happiness.

The benedictions and hymnologies which are used in Jewish worship are expressions of thanksgiving. They thus bring to the eye of the imagination the interplay of factors in man's world, to which man owes whatever good he enjoys. The articulation of such thanksgiving is an avowal of bliss, and an earnest intention to cooperate with the interplay of factors and forces that spell God.

6

Cooperation the chief source of happiness; competition its principal menace

Those who lived in the past may have scarcely realized the implications of the manifold expressions of gratitude they indulged in, but it must be conceded that gratitude to God was then a genuine experience much more frequent than it is in our day. No doubt the benedictions and hymnologies were for the most part recited in a spirit of theurgy, or as mechanical routine. But a great deal of true spiritual sentiment did accompany worship and rendered it vital; otherwise worship would not have survived. But if such sentiment did accompany the ritual expression of thanksgiving and praise to God, then we have an answer to the oft mooted question of whether men were happier in the past than they are now. Judging by the greater prevalence of gratitude to God, we must conclude that they were.

[44] *Shabbat*, 30b.

It therefore appears that man's progress in civilization, instead of being accompanied by a growth in happiness, as we might reasonably expect, has been accompanied by a greater measure of unhappiness. It is significant that those who suffer most from the inequities and deprivations that have shadowed civilization are not commonly the most unhappy. The latter are found very often among those who enjoy advantages and privileges that are the outcome of civilization. More nervous breakdowns and suicides result from disillusionment in the pursuit of pleasure, or the disappointments of a frustrated egotism, than from physical suffering or economic hardship. Ennui and world weariness are symptoms of a blasé sophistication which is characteristic of people who, like Koheleth, had the leisure and opportunity of experimenting with life for the purpose of some abiding pleasure.[41] That is why they are almost unknown among manual workers. This does not mean that the poor do not suffer, and suffer intensely. But their suffering is associated with specific circumstances, and does not usually result in a despair of the value of life as a whole. Hunger may mean acute pain, but it implies the goodness of food, and the value of the effort to obtain it. Injustice may issue in an aching sense of resentment, but it also results in a class loyalty and devotion that give meaning and purpose to life. The very experience of wrongs leads to the affirmation of rights and an assertion of the dignity of personality. "A man's a man for a' that."

The situation appears less anomalous when we consider how civilization has come into being. Civilization is the product of the application of intelligence and adventure to difficulties formerly regarded as insuperable. Natural resources are exploited, an infinite number of devices are invented, the barriers of space and time in the way of communication are eliminated, the labors of men are specialized,

[41] Ecc. 2:1-10.

the range of human interests is enlarged, old wants are supplied and new wants created. All this involves, to be sure, the upsetting of the inner equilibrium which, with the limited wants and narrow range of interests of the ancients, should have been comparatively easy of attainment. But unless civilization is a disease or a calamity, the loss of equilibrium or the unhappiness which is its by-product cannot be regarded as final. *The Sukkot festival, with its emphasis on joyous gratitude or happiness, is a protest not against civilization, but against its tendency to be a destroyer of happiness.*

What in civilization is responsible for this tendency? Civilization is motivated principally by the competitive impulse in man, and that motivation vitiates all his achievements. But in addition to the competitive impulse, man has also an impulse to cooperate. Though the latter is the weaker of the two, it is always active to some degree; for society could not exist without it. "Men have a pathetic instinct toward the adventure of living and struggling together," says John Dewey. Even chauvinisic nationalism is an evidence of the universal urge to find some outlet for genuine cooperativeness that extends far beyond the limits of family, or of face-to-face groups.

But instead of finding ways and means of strengthening the cooperative impulse and subordinating the competitive impulse to it, civilization has always adopted the easier course, and has furthered the reverse process. It has permitted the egoism and selfishness of the few to exploit the ideals of loyalty and solidarity which the many cherish. It has appealed to and rewarded generously the pursuit of private profit and personal aggrandizement, regardless of the evils in their train, and has disdained to address itself to social welfare and universal happiness as incentives to conduct. It insists upon allowing free scope to those who possess more than usual initiative and energy "to exercise their fighting instincts to triumph over their competitors and to appropriate the prizes of hazard and adventure, the spoils attesting personal force and prowess."

Civilization has helped to corrupt human nature not merely by goading man to compete with his fellows for indispensable commodities, but by accustoming him to cherish the power over others, which successful rivalry brings with it, as his highest goal and self-fulfillment. Thus *civilization has become synonymous with the progressive emergence of individuals and groups engaged in eternal contest for the control over one another.*

This ambition for power is recognized in the Bible as the curse of civilization and is made the target of its denunciations directly in the utterances of Prophet and Psalmist, and indirectly in its philosophy of history. Conversely, meekness, which is the antithesis of the lust to power and domination, is constantly emphasized in association with biblical heroes. Abraham refuses to contest with Lot the possession of the best pasturage; Isaac refuses to contest with Abimelek possession of the wells; Jacob does contest the blessing and the birthright with Esau, but the consequences which follow from his act are not indicative of its approval by the biblical author; for Jacob is subjected to one vicissitude after another, and finally dies an exile in Egypt, with the attainment of the birthright a mere hope that he passes on to his progeny. Moses, whose dominant place in Jewish tradition earned him the title *Mosheh Rabbenu,* 'Our master Moses,' is described in the Torah as "very meek, more than any other man on the face of the earth." [48] In response to the officious zeal of his disciple Joshua, who wants him to restrain Eldad and Medad from prophesying, his reply is: "Would that all the people of the Lord were prophets!" [49] When Saul, the first king of Israel, is chosen to rule, he is found hiding among the baggage. [50] David is commended

[48] Num. 12:3.   [49] Num. 11:29.   [50] I Sam. 10:22.

for forgetting his royal dignity in dancing before the ark."[1] When the exercise of royal power did arouse in him the lust for domination, and led to his sin against Uriah, he is rebuked by the Prophet Nathan and is moved to sincere contrition and repentance, which is reflected in the spirit in which he submits to humiliation, when pursued by his son Absalom. But why multiply examples? The lust for power and domination is throughout the Bible felt to be the very antithesis of the religious spirit, an arrogant rebellion of men who would usurp the place of God. This is beautifully expressed in the tenth Psalm (including the last two verses of the preceding Psalm which properly belong with it):

"Arise, O Lord, let not man prevail;
Let the nations be judged in thy sight.
Set terror over them, O Lord;
Let the nations know they are but men.

.   .   .   .   .

For the wicked boasteth of his heart's desire,
And the covetous vaunteth himself, though he contemn the
        Lord.
The wicked in the pride of his countenance saith: 'He will
        not require';
All his thoughts are: 'There is no God.'

He saith in his heart: 'I shall not be moved,
I who to all generations shall not be in adversity!

He doth catch the poor, when he draweth him up in his net,
He croucheth, he boweth down,
And the helpless fall into his mighty claws.
He hath said in his heart: 'God hath forgotten;
He hideth His face; He will never see.'

Lord, thou hast heard the desire of the humble;
Thou wilt direct their heart, Thou wilt cause thine ear to
        attend;
To right the fatherless and the oppressed,
That man who is of the earth may be terrible no more."

[1] II Sam. 6:21.

So long as civilization is dominated by the motive of competition, man will either indulge in gratified pride in the hour of success, or break down in complete hopelessness in the hour of failure. There is justification for the Psalmist's identification of the domineering competitive spirit with godlessness; for one who is governed by this spirit feels that he has no one to thank but himself for the attainment of his goal, and no one to look to for help when frustrated. *Though civilization has made for the emergence of the individual and the increase of wealth and of opportunities for enjoyment, it has deprived man of the capacity for thankfulness.* It has isolated his individual interests from the interest of humanity as a whole, and thus violated his human disposition to cooperation. It has put him out of rapport with those forces that represent the unity, interrelatedness and creativity of life. It has alienated him from God. Little wonder that he feels God-forsaken and unhappy.

Let us examine in somewhat greater detail the ways in which the competitive impulse, as fostered by our civilization, undermines happiness. In the first place, the overstimulation of the competitive, profit-seeking motive in our economic order deprives the vast multitudes of that minimum of security which is indispensable to happiness. There is hardly a person for whom life is not worry and struggle. Millions of men desirous of working are recurrently out of employment, due to the periodic overproduction of commodities, i.e., overproduction in the light of the limited purchasing power—a limitation created by unjust distribution of "surplus value." The overwhelming majority live in a state of fear of losing their jobs through some technological improvement, through the merging and consolidation of industries and business, through changes in market conditions and through the inevitable oncoming of old age. Not even the possession of capital is a guarantee of security. Denial of credit or shrinkage in purchase power may ruin a once flourishing business.

The emphasis on selfish motivation which is inherent in present-day civilization further deprives men of happiness by making a bitter class-struggle, with its attendant envy, hate and fear inevitable. The machine workers who constitute the majority of producers in modern industry work fewer hours perhaps than did the artisans in former times, but they have no other interest in their work than as a means of wages. They derive from it no human values. It yields them no satisfaction in terms of personality. The owners of the machines, on their part, have no other interest in their employees than that of obtaining through them as much profit as possible. This means paying the worker as little as possible, and dismissing him as soon as he can be replaced by one who can bring greater profit. The only way the worker can protect his job is by combining with his fellow-workers, and carrying on perpetual war against those who would exploit him. Under such circumstances, he can hardly have peace of mind, to say nothing of happiness.

Realizing that honest toil and industrious pursuit of a calling or business will not guarantee any stable level of life, men are caught up in various speculative fevers, in the hope of getting wealth that will make security possible. But few escape ultimate loss of all upon which they had staked their happiness. The same desire to get rich quickly and easily leads to the organization of illegitimate "rackets" that prey upon business and exact toll, without rendering any service whatever, thus adding another element of danger and instability.

One of the worst effects of economic insecurity, as a menace to happiness, is its tendency to undermine family life. Young people do not feel justified in assuming the responsibilities of married life and the care of children, when their own economic status is so uncertain. They therefore tend to form casual sex relations or to develop sex habits which, while they may afford pleasure, are so unrelated to the whole complex of human instincts that are biologically intended to insure the propagation of the species, and the care, nurture and training of the young, as to preclude happiness. Youth, which was once regarded as the age of romantic idealism, tends to become an age of smart sophistication and blasé cynicism. The situation of modern youth is indeed deplorable. At a time when nature demands that they seek to mate and provide for the needs of a generation waiting to be born, they are hardly in a position to provide even for their own needs. The resulting frustration and disintegration of personality undermine happiness.

Another menace to the achievement of personality, and hence of human happiness, is to be found in the extreme division of labor which must prevail in a machine age. Under more primitive conditions the toil in which a man engaged for his livelihood could employ all his bodily and mental powers. It was therefore accompanied with that sense of physical well-being which proceeds from the harmonious activity of body and mind, when occupied with the sort of work for which they are organically fit. But the introduction of machinery and of efficient organization necessarily involves the limitation of the majority of workers to some specific routine which deadens interest in the work done and frustrates all creative energy. If, however, the worker felt that he had a voice in the conditions of production and distribution of the product, he would manage to find a degree of self-fulfillment even in monotonous and difficult labor. Evidence of the truth of this statement is to be found in the zeal for the hardest kind of manual work, such as draining swamps and building roads, which one finds among Palestinian *haluzim*. Where the tendency among factory workers and exploited laborers generally is to engage in as much sabotage as they can, the Palestinian *haluz* is motivated by a sense of *kedushat ha-abodah,* of the sanctity of labor as a creative force fashioning the Jewish civilization of the future. But the consciousness of being a mere tool for some one else's profit renders the work one does mere drudgery, which uses up the greater part of the energy one needs to get any happiness out of life. Walter Rathenau [**] maintained that industrial democracy would not remove the evil of drudgery. He therefore advocated the interchange of labor in order to distribute such drudgery more equitably. His plan, however, could never be carried out without industrial democracy.

Modern business methods make for the destruction of personality, since those who appropriate the profits of industry are not free to give play to any ethical considerations in the conduct of their business. They are not free under competitive conditions to retain in their employ men whose services are no longer needed, regardless of what the loss of the job may mean to the employee. They cannot be squeamish about ruining a competitor, for fear they may themselves be ruined. Honest candor in salesmanship is a luxury that few indeed can afford. It is a sad commentary on the way the consumer is treated in modern business, when we know that the Bureau of Standards of the United States Government is legally forbidden to inform the public of the quality of the goods sold them, because it is the "right" of a business man to conceal the true quality of the goods he is selling. The need of viewing every competitor with distrust and fear, every employee as a tool and every customer as a "sucker," does not make for the sort of social relationship which can afford true satisfaction. These same people, in their leisure pursuits, demand and comply with rules of good-sportsmanship. They recognize the validity of "fair play," as necessary to the fulfillment of their personal ideal. But fair play

[**] *Cf.* Rathenau, Walter: *The New Society,* N. Y., 1921.

is confined mainly to play; there is scarcely any fairness in business.

Moreover, the preoccupation with economic anxieties and battles leaves but little energy for the cultivation of cultural and spiritual interests, either on the part of employers or employees. Thus the majority of people are prevented from ever knowing the higher joys of the spirit. The breakdown of the observance of Sabbaths and Festivals among the Jews, even when they have the opportunity to observe them, is symbolic and symptomatic of the way that preoccupation with economic interests has crowded out even the most joy-giving spiritual activities. Thanks to the profit motive, industry, which after all provides merely the material means of existence, has come to occupy a position of almost complete dominance over all other human interests. "Things are in the saddle."

Another way in which competitive profit-seeking assails the integrity of human personality and destroys human happiness is through its stimulation of artificial wants. The satisfaction of these wants is calculated to gratify individual pleasure impulses, regardless of their effect on the character as a whole. The most costly social evils of our time—war, drink, gambling, prostitution, and the entire gamut of obscene books, plays, magazines, movies and the yellow press —owe their prevalence to their being the source of immense private profit. Leisure hours that should be given to play activities which afford opportunities for self-expression and social communion are devoted instead to stereotyped forms of commercialized amusements, and to the vicarious enjoyment of sport spectacles, rather than to participation in sport itself. For there is no resisting the hypnotic suggestion of commercial advertisement which is effective in molding the habits of people not in their own interest but in that of the advertisers. The trades that minister to these artificially created wants are kept alive by the fact that as civilization advances the penalty for indulging in them is not as apparent as in more primitive life. *From the standpoint of consumption, happiness is contingent on an economy in which the maximum of utility in health and well-being is the main consideration of industry. That is impossible so long as industry is at the mercy of the competitive system, with its stimulation of individual greed and combativeness.*

Although the leisure interests of men might afford some relaxation from the strain of competition, there is a definite tendency, particularly among the well-to-do, to carry over the competitive impulse from the field of business to the arts of consumption. Veblen, in *The Theory of the Leisure Class,* has demonstrated that, with the growth of civilization, the owners of property try to outdo one another in futile extravagance, or, as he calls it, "conspicuous waste." The aristocracy in olden and medieval days was noted for its ostentatious expenditures on gorgeous palaces and luxurious grounds, on adornments of fabrics, jewels and articles of laborious skill." Among the upper classes in modern civilized nations, the tradition of conspicuous waste and competitive expenditures which have not the least element of utility has been reenforced by the numerous inventions of the modern arts of pleasure. Idle travel, racing, hunting, motoring, golfing, yachting, betting and gambling fill the days of the leisure class in the never-ending effort to outdo one another in diverting their surplus wealth and unearned increment into unproductive expenditures. The paradox of it all is that those who lead such lives miss the very happiness they seek, and become involved in an idle round of meaningless performances, in the mere effort to escape boredom.

Among their imitators, the less well-to-do, these idle pursuits in the art of consumption find their counterpart in the wide range of futile activities to shine in the reflected light of those who enjoy the prestige of great possessions. Such

" *Cf.* Amos. 3:15; 5:11; Is. 3:18-23; 9:8, 9; Jer. 22:13, 14, etc.

activities give rise to all the contortions of the human soul into the poses called for by social climbing and flunkeyism. They dissipate recklessly the moral independence which their wealth could secure, for the sake of a condescending smile from the one above them on the social ladder. While they are thus employed, their envy of those more socially privileged and resentment at the snubs, which their own social climbing invites, spoil their enjoyment of their own wealth and, before long, their luxuries begin to pall on them, and they, too, are eaten up with boredom.

To overcome the obstacles that stand in the way of happiness, it is necessary so to reconstruct our philosophy of life and our social institutions as to recognize in the competitive impulse the menace that it is. To reconstruct that philosophy involves repudiating the prevailing view that life is a contest for possessions, power or recognition, and that only the winner is entitled to honor and happiness. The so-called ideal of "the strenuous life" is inherently a straining to outdo, outstrip and outshine one's neighbor. A far wholesomer philosophy is that of "the simple life," in which success is measured by the extent to which one fulfills one's latent possibilities for good. "Who is truly rich? He who is happy in his portion," [44] who sees the good not in what he can appropriate, but in what he can share. He whose main interest in life lies in the expression of family affection, friendship and social sympathy, in the pursuit of beauty and truth, and the worship of the holy, has rendered himself immune to most of the ills that poison human personality and destroy human happiness. The simple life, by its emancipation from the dominance of the competitive motivation, refuses to pay the excessive toll in human happiness that the complex life demands for the petty triumphs of gratified vanity. It cultivates those values that are absolute rather

[44] *Abot.* IV, 1.

than relative, in the sense that they do not require our measuring ourselves against others. In this way we appropriate whatever good the world has to offer, through appreciation rather than through possession, and acquire "treasures that cannot be stolen." [**]

The elimination of the competitive emphasis must be striven for not only in our economic life, but also in those intellectual and spiritual vocations in which the accumulation of property plays an insignificant part. It has been said that "The competition of scholars increases wisdom." [**] But it more frequently wastes in fruitless and wordy polemics energies which could be put to much better use, if the scholars collaborated in a spirit of mutual tolerance and appreciation. The same may be said of the competitive spirit in art and science. As science grows, it becomes more and more the creation of carefully organized collaboration among scientific workers, so that it becomes almost impossible to credit any single individual for such inventions as the radio or the aeroplane. The competitive spirit always throws a monkey-wrench into the machinery of collaboration, and prevents it from contributing what it might to human welfare and happiness. Art also has always reached its heights when it was the expression of a social life. The decadence of modern art is largely due to the fact that it is no longer the expression of the community spirit, as it was, for example, in the Middle Ages, but has been made an accessory to the "conspicuous consumption" of the wealthy. Wherever genuine art exists, today or at any time, one may be sure that it is the work of an artist whose loyalty to his vision of beauty transcended his desire for the plaudits of the public. If the philosophy of competition were eliminated from the cultural vocations, they could be immeasurably helpful in developing

[**] *Baba Batra* 11a.
[**] *Idem.*, 21a. The spirit of competition is said to have exterminated all but seven of the twenty-four thousand disciples of R. Akiba (Gen. *R.* LXI, 3).

a sounder philosophy of life in our social order generally, and would contribute proportionately to the enhancement of human happiness.

The reconstruction of our social institutions with a view to eliminating from them the competitive element involves recognizing that the time has come to put an end to the haphazard and planless character of our economic and political activities. The so-called ideal of "rugged individualism" in the world of business, and the policy of *laissez faire* in government, are merely attempts at institutionalizing combative selfishness. All this must now be replaced by intelligent planning on a scale of cooperation, which must ultimately embrace the whole of mankind. Such planned cooperation must be sensitive to the personal rights of men, but must be firmly iconoclastic toward alleged property rights which are not rights at all. Moreover, it must interpret personal rights as the right to a personal share in the life of society, but not as the right to further personal interests at the expense of society or other persons.

All these truths are by no means alien to the Jewish tradition, though only our modern knowledge of human life could have made possible the unfolding and application of all that is latent in that tradition. That all these truths are a revaluation and not a transvaluation of Jewish tradition is evidenced by two passages, one from Scripture, which has a bearing on the significance of the *Sukkah,* and the other from the rabbinic writings, which has a bearing on the significance of the "four species of plants."

The passage from Scripture reads thus:

"Therefore turn thou to thy tents [87]
Keep mercy and justice;
And wait for thy God continually.
As for the trafficker, the balances of deceit are in his hand;
He loveth to oppress.

[87] This translation is based on an emended reading.

And Ephraim said: 'Surely I am become rich, I have found me
    wealth,
In all my labors they shall find in me, No iniquity that were sin.'
But I am the Lord thy God from the land of Egypt.
I will yet make thee to dwell in tents,
As in the day of the appointed season." [58]

The rabbinic passage is based on the verse, "He builded
His vault upon the earth." [59] The original for "vault,"
agudato, which the Rabbis take to mean "his band," enables
them to regard that verse as emphasizing the significance of
human cooperation and as implying that such cooperation
manifests the reality and presence of God. [60] Hence, they
teach that the "four species of plants," when held together in
the act of worship, symbolize the truth that when men
achieve unity, they bring God's *Shekinah* down to earth. [61]

[58] Hosea 12:7-10.
[60] Sifrē on Deut. 33:5.
[59] Amos 9:6.
[61] *Menahot* 27a.

VII

GOD FELT AS A PRESENCE

SHEMINI AZERET commemorates no particular event, and is observed by no distinctive rites. Although coming immediately after the festival of Sukkot, it is declared to be a holiday in its own right.[1] These facts constituted an enigma sufficient to elicit from the ancient Rabbis explanations in keeping with their general outlook.

According to one of these explanations, God is represented as a bountiful master moved by the lavishly generous homage of His faithful servants. As they are about to depart after many days of festivity, He asks them to stay one more day, thereby indicating how He regrets their leaving. This eighth day added for communion with God is, accordingly, the way God expressed His reluctance at Israel's parting from His precincts.[2]

Although the childlike naïveté of this explanation cannot satisfy the modern Jew as an answer to the question why he should observe Shemini Azeret, the sentiment which it expresses is more significant than would appear at first glance, and affords a clue as to what Shemini Azeret can mean to us today as a contribution to our knowledge of God. For the author's expression of God's reluctance to part with Israel was born of his own reluctance to part, as it were, with God, with that sense of being in God's presence which he experienced in *azeret,* the assembly of the congregation for religious worship.

[1] *Jer. Sukkah* V, 7; *Jer. Hagigah* I, 6.
[2] *Rashi* on Lev. 23:36; *Cf. Pesik. R. K.* XXX; *Pesik. R.* LXXXIV.

243

I

Public worship as a means to awareness of God's presence

Shemini Azeret is significant to us in that it calls our attention to the part played by public worship in enabling us to experience communion with God. For *God must not merely be held as an idea; He must be felt as a presence, if we want not only to know about God but to know God.* "Taste and see that the Lord is good," [*] says the Psalmist. Religious souls have never been satisfied with an awareness of God merely as an intellectual concept. They always craved a religious experience in which the reality of God would be brought home to them with an immediacy akin to our awareness of objects through the senses, and with an overpowering emotion that stirred every fibre of their being. In our various interpretations of God as the Power that makes for certain desirable goals, there is one point that is not taken into account, and that is that we may accept these goals, without identifying the Power, that makes for them, as God, as the Spirit that so possesses us as to compel our adoration and worship. It is, therefore, necessary to devote one festival to communion with God, for its own sake, in order to satisfy the need of identifying that Power as God. Shemini Azeret serves this purpose. In so doing, it converts the teachings of the other Festivals from theology into religion.

The purpose in the various attempts to reinterpret the God idea is not to dissolve the God idea into ethics. It is to identify those experiences which should represent for us the actual working of what we understand by the conception of God. Without the actual awareness of His presence, experienced as beatitude and inner illumination, we are likely to be content with the humanistic interpretation of life. But this interpretation is inadequate, because it fails to express and to foster the feeling that man's ethical aspirations are part of

[*] Ps. 34:9.

a cosmic urge, by obeying which man makes himself at home in the universe. Without the emotional intuition of an inner harmony between human nature and universal nature, without the conviction, born of the heart rather than of the mind, that the world contains all that is necessary for human salvation, the assumptions necessary for ethical living remain cold hypotheses lacking all dynamic power. They are like an engine with all the parts intact and assembled, but lacking the fuel which alone can set it in operation. *The dynamic of ethical action is the spirit of worship, the feeling that we are in God and God in us,* the yielding of our persons in voluntary surrender to those larger aims that express for us as much as has been revealed to us of the destiny of the human race. It is only this emotional reaction to life that can make humanity itself mean more to us than a "disease of the agglutinated dust."

In rabbinic literature, the awareness of God, not merely as a concept of the mind but as a Presence in and around us, manifest to us by its emotional effect on our whole being, is expressed by the term *Shekinah*. References to the *Shekinah* are, therefore, suggestive of the nature of this experience and the conditions under which it can take place. The *Shekinah* is significantly associated with public worship. The verse, "They shall make me a sanctuary that I may dwell in their midst." [4] is paraphrased in the authorized Aramaic version of the Rabbis, "They shall make a sanctuary before Me, that I may cause My *Shekinah* to dwell among them." [5] The reason that ten men are required as a quorum for public worship is stated to be that "wherever ten men gather for prayer the *Shekinah* is with them." [6] True, biblical passages are adduced to show that, under certain circumstances, the *Shekinah* may rest upon a smaller gathering and even upon a man in his solitude, but it is generally conceded that the multitude of those gathered together adds to the probability

[4] Exod. 25:8.   [5] *Targ. Onk. ad locum.*   [6] *Berakot* 6a; 21b.

of their experiencing a manifestation of the *Shekinah*.[7] The Rabbis [8] associated this thought with the verse in Proverbs.[9] "In the multitude of the people is the King's glory." Just as the subject of a human monarch, when he participates with a throng in saluting and acclaiming his king, is made aware of the reality and majesty of the sovereignty that the king exercises or symbolizes, so the worshiper is made aware of the reality of God and His sway over the human heart, when he joins with the throng in public worship.[10] Indeed, in countries where the king reigns, but does not rule, almost his whole function is to lend his person to such public ceremonies that make the sovereignty of the nation a real influence, experienced in the life of the individual as a wholehearted identification of himself with the nation.

To appreciate fully the meaning of the awareness of God as a Presence, one must actually experience the influence of public worship. Inasmuch as such experience takes possession of the whole personality, it partakes in each individual instance of the uniqueness of that personality, and hence is never wholly communicable. To analyze it can never do it full justice. Nevertheless, some of the communicable elements of this experience may be described, as an intimation of what one who has not experienced such communion with God may expect of it.

Participation in public worship makes one feel at home in the world. In our efforts to maintain and preserve our individuality, we are too often aware of our natural and social environment by the resistance it offers to these efforts. This makes us feel lonely and forsaken, as though we were marooned on an island inhabited by a strange and savage people, with only our individual resources of body and mind on which to depend. The odds then seem so tremendously against us that it hardly appears worthwhile to struggle with

---

[7] *Cf. Mishnah, Berakot* VII, 3.
[8] Prov. 14:28.
[9] *Ibid.*, 53a.
[10] *Cf. Sifrē* on Deut. 33:5.

our fate. The responsibilities of life are too burdensome, unless we are aware of a supporting and sustaining power outside our individual selves on which we can count. This awareness is present when we find ourselves in the fellowship of others who have similar interests, acknowledge similar responsibilities, and respond appreciatively to similar values. Realizing that others share our needs, our hopes, our fears, and our ideals we no longer feel dependent entirely on our own efforts for our salvation. A trickle of water cannot move a mill-wheel, but when these trickles flow together and become a gushing torrent they can. The presence of others participating with us in articulating our common ideals assures us that we are not separate drops of water, but parts of the mighty current of human life.

Even this is inadequate to explain the effect of public worship on the spirit of the individual worshiper. Two shipwrecked men in a row-boat on an angry sea have more than twice the chance of saving themselves than each would have in a boat for himself. Not only can each count on the strength of the other, but, not being alone, he is less likely to be stupefied by fear. He himself, therefore, by reason of the companionship, becomes more resourceful, steadier and more efficient in his rowing. The presence of a comrade thus enables him to discover and take advantage of circumstances favorable to his saving himself, which would otherwise in his panic have escaped his notice. The presence of a friend in the boat, makes even nature seem more friendly, more capable of responding to his needs. He is more aware that, not only in man but in man's natural environment he has invisible allies on whose help he can count: his oars, his boat itself, the remainder of his food and water supply, a favorable wind or current, and somewhere within reach, if his efforts can hold out long enough, the hospitable shore or a rescuing ship. Thus public worship not only enhances our strength by its suggestion of human cooperation, but by banishing morbid fear it gives us renewed confidence in nature itself, enabling us to see in it as well as in humanity the immanence of God. Thus public worship makes us feel not only that we have brothers on earth, but that we also have— to use the traditional metaphor—a Father in heaven, a Power in nature that responds to human need, if properly approached.

Again, public worship aids us by liberating our personality from the confining walls of the individual ego. Imprisoned in self, we easily fall a prey to morbid brooding. Interference with our career, personal disappointments and disillusionments, hurts to our vanity, the fear of death—all these tend so to dominate our attention that our minds move in a fixed and narrow system of ideas, which we detest but from which we see no escape. With a whole wide world of boundless opportunities about us, we permit our minds, as it were, to pace up and down within the narrow cell of their ego-prison. But participation in public worship breaks through the prison of the ego and lets in the light and air of the world. Instead of living but one small and petty life, we now share the multitudinous life of our people. Against the wider horizons that now open to our ken, our personal cares do not loom so large. Life becomes infinitely more meaningful and worthwhile, when we become aware, through our participation in public worship, of sharing in a common life that transcends that of our personal organism.

A sense of common consecration to ideals inherited from a distant past and projected into a remote future means that we have in a sense made ourselves immortal. For death cannot rob our life of significance and value to us so long as we are interested in passing on to our posterity a heritage of culture and ideals. The past before we were born and the future after our death are a part of us, and every moment is eternal that embraces them. Through our worship as part of a religious community that outlives all its members, this sense of our life's triumph over death and all manner of frustration is brought home to us. We thus experience an expansion of our personality, an enlargement of the scope of its interests and its capacities. It is as though by surrendering our souls to God, we admit God into our souls and partake of His infinity and eternity.

Thus the presence of the multitude in public worship creates an atmosphere that profoundly influences the individual participant. It stirs in him emotions of gratitude and confidence that he could not experience in isolation. He knows his life to be part of a larger life, a wave of an ocean of being. This is first-hand experience of that larger life which is God. Such first-hand experience of God is real, even though the individual who has the experience is devoid of the understanding and knowledge necessary to give it a correct interpretation and proper application. The child burning his hand in the fire experiences the reality of the fire, although he may know nothing of the scientific laws governing combustion. A scientist may know all these laws without ever necessarily having burnt himself. But in that case he knows less of the reality of fire than does the burnt child. That is the difference between knowing God philosophically in His manifestations and experiencing Him religiously in worship.

Both approaches to a knowledge of God are equally necessary. Some people imagine that the religious experience of God is invalidated by the fact that it is demonstrably a psychological effect of the presence of the multitude. This is like saying that our emotional response to the music produced by a violin is not a real experience of music, because it is after all but the effect of the scraping of horse-hair on catgut. The implication of such disparagement is that our awareness of God in worship is really only an awareness of the worshiping crowd. But this is a falsehood analogous to our identifying our awareness of the music with our awareness of the instrument, whereas we know that it is possible for us to enjoy music while quite unmindful of the instrument that produces it.

2

Why individual religion is not enough

That man can experience God in a worshiping throng proceeds from an inherent characteristic of human nature. The human being is so constituted that his life must alternate between the sense of separate individuality and that of having his individuality dissolved in the group. His tendency to gregariousness is instinctive, and all that we identify as constituting the higher life of man would be inconceivable without the operation of this instinct. This does not mean that the manifestation of gregariousness itself constitutes the higher or spiritual life, any more than that all operations of the sex instinct are worthy to be called love. But, like the sex instinct, so too the gregarious instinct is of the very matrix of the spiritual life. Out of it all human cooperation is born. That is why God, as the Power that makes for cooperation, is directly experienced in group worship.

Participation in public worship means that, for the time being, one's personality is dissolved in the crowd. The very elemental character of this experience reveals the operation of that power which, *when moralized and ethicized,* makes for cooperation. There is no virtue to religious worship in and of itself. The fact that we feel the presence of God is no guarantee that we are in rapport with the character of God as the Power that makes for righteousness. The feeling of togetherness is the raw material of religion, just as the undifferentiated sensations of the new-born infant are the raw material out of which he later fashions his world of sensory objects and their relations in thought. This feeling is early recognized as God-feeling. As social experience clarifies the objectives of human behavior, and the conception of God is accordingly ethicized, this God-feeling becomes an ethical force. But on the higher level of spiritual thought and conduct, as on the lower level, the feeling of togetherness is indispensable to the realization of God, for without it we cannot experience God at all.

There are people who in the strength of their ego-consciousness are loth to submit to the experience of being depersonalized or deindividualized. They resist it as men have been known to resist being anesthetized, even when in need of anesthetics. They will accept as valid only a religious experience that is personal to themselves, a conscious product of their individual meditation upon their life experiences. Nevertheless, it remains true that the sort of surrender of individual isolation experienced in public worship is as basic and essential to the higher life of man as is his very body. Its dynamic consists of the fact that the human being craves for it. That is why all religions, some partly, others entirely, aim to achieve this effect in their adherents.

Individual religion that seeks to be self-sufficient and avoids recourse to public worship, lest it lose its self-sufficiency, is apt to destroy itself and to work harm to the one who depends on it. Individual religion is subject to this danger, strangely enough, because it is the product of self-consciousness. It is only man who can reach the high level of self-consciousness. That is his distinction, when compared with other animal species. Yet it is impossible for him to remain alone at that high altitude for any length of time without suffering violent reaction. To climb to the top of the Jungfrau or Mount Everest is, no doubt, a thrilling experience, yet the air is altogether too rare for one to remain there long. The danger which attends individual religion that aims to be self-sufficient and to dispense with public worship and all similar expressions of group religion is due to the sinister consequences known to result from any attempt which involves too long a period of self-consciousness. Such self-consciousness leads to the assumption by the individual of full reponsibility for all his personal acts. The assertion of his spiritual autonomy, which is the ultimate objective of personal religion, demands that every act of his justify itself by its consequences both to himself and to others. But nothing short of omniscience could foresee these consequences. It, therefore, follows that no matter how conscientious a man is in endeavoring to envisage them, he must sooner or later beat his head, as it were, against the walls of his own personal limitations. Hence personal religion that maintains its aloofness from all forms of communal worship usually is apt to end in pessimism and world-weariness, sometimes even reaching a point where one's sanity is threatened. The very concern about reaching a correct decision in life's crucial issues may lead only to indecision. "Thus conscience doth make cowards of us all."

Hence we need something that will relieve the strain of self-consciousness, something that will enable us to achieve and conserve the spiritual values derived from individual religion, without having to undergo the tension of too long a state of self-consciousness. Personal religion may give us a theistic interpretation of life, one that supplies our minds with reasons or grounds for being strong, courageous, loyal and cheerful. But to experience the reality of God, we must actually feel strong, courageous, loyal and cheerful. When we associate ourselves with our fellow-men in public worship, we actually do, in consequence of our gregarious nature, have these feelings. This does not mean that personal religion is of no avail. Personal religion and communal religion represent two phases of a necessary vital rhythm that oscillates between isolation of the self and merging of the self with others. We must recognize that experiencing the reality of God, as we do through congregational worship, does not necessarily mean that we experience Him then in His fullness. We may still lack the wisdom to single out those forces in the life of society or in our own persons through which what we experience as strengthening, encouraging and vitalizing may be channeled. Religion does not end with experiencing the reality of God. That is where religion begins. In utilizing this experience to personal and social advantage, every man's personal religion counts. But no one can dispense with the experience of God that comes with public worship, without weakening the dynamic power of whatever religious convictions he may hold.

What happened to the various philosophical religions or religious philosophies proves the inadequacy of purely personal religion that dispenses with the social experience of community worship. The greatest among the thinkers have tried repeatedly to achieve a religion which would help the individual orient himself to the cosmos and build up an ethical system that would train his judgment and fortify his reason to know and do what is right. The hopes cherished by the founders of such systems, that they have at last charted for each one his path in life, have all too often turned out to be an illusion. Their successors gradually ended up as pessimists, who doubted the very worth of life itself. This was the case with the first Greek philosophers, whose successors were the Sophists. Their failure is registered in the sinister connotations of the word "sophistry." Later, Socrates and Plato undertook on their own account to lay the foundation of individual religion. Yet their successors, after many generations, had to resort to various mystery religions and finally joined either Christianity or Islam. In the course of the last one hundred and fifty years, a similar fate befell three different attempts that were made to establish individual religion. Kant's system ended up in Schopenhauer's pessimism, Hegel's deeply religious philosophy in materialism and mechanism, and the high hopes which the evolutionists entertained in progress ended up in the despair so magnificently articulated by Bertrand Russell in his *Free Man's Worship*.

Perhaps it is more than a coincidence that the Book of Kohelet is read on the Sabbath preceding Shemini Azeret, or on Shemini Azeret itself. It seems to indicate what must be the outcome of reliance upon individualistic search for the true way of life. In the cry, "Vanity of vanities!" the human soul testifies to its inability to endure its aloofness. But associated with our fellows in giving common expression to our spiritual aspirations in worship, we are most likely to gear our energies to the high expectation implied in our ideals, thus calling forth the best that is latent in us. Contrast with the despairing cry of Kohelet, the testimony of an ancient Psalmist who experienced God through sharing in the devotions of a worshiping throng:

"As the hart panteth after the water brooks,
  So panteth my soul after Thee, O God.
  My soul thirsteth for God, for the living God:
  'When shall I come and appear before God?'
  My tears have been my food day and night,
  While they say unto me all the day: 'Where is thy God?'
  These things I remember, and pour out my soul within me,
  How I passed on with the throng, and led them to the house
      of God.
  With the voice of joy and praise, a multitude keeping holiday.
  Why art thou cast down, O my soul?
  And why moanest thou within me?
  Hope thou in God; for I shall yet praise Him
  For the salvation of His countenance." [11]

How are we to explain the reason why all efforts to establish religion on a basis of individual self-sufficiency have resulted in failure? And why, on the other hand, have religious systems that made provision for communal expression of religious sentiment in worship tended to survive?

We are aided in finding an answer to this question in the

[11] Ps. 42:2-6.

light of what modern psychology has taught of the nature of self-consciousness. We now know that self-consciousness is the outcome of inner conflict. Individual religion, which is self-conscious religion, can be arrived at only by those in whose minds there is continually going on a struggle, whose souls are the battlefield of contending inner forces. The greater one's mental development, the more subject one is to contradictory tendencies, and the more susceptible to mutually exclusive influences. The more intelligent a man is, the more likely is he to be engaged continually in making peace between reason and impulse. The inhibitions, that curb the impulses of mediocre personalities whose behavior is determined by conventional standards of respectability and traditional tabus, fail the greater personalities who seek to govern their conduct by self-determined standards of value. The Rabbis were remarkable psychologists in observing that the greater the man, the more powerful his impulses.[18] If he is able to manage his impulses, it is because he can see his life as a whole, and is therefore aware that to surrender to any one of his impulses at the expense of the others is to fulfill himself only in part, and to frustrate his true and complete self. But all that implies a continuous state of inner warfare, with seldom a truce.

It is such natures that are also subject to the conflict of loyalties. In normal times they will often find themselves at a loss whether to yield to the claims of the family circle or of the State. In times of civil disturbance, when the State is conquered by an enemy nation, there arises the problem whether to obey the new government or to conspire with those who seek to overthrow it. With the specialization of groups, or the sharpening of economic issues, the question arises which group has a greater claim upon one's loyalty, the vocational group or the political group.

Furthermore, those who are endowed with superior mental

[18] *Sukkah* 52a.

development are amenable in equal degree to the knowledge
and influence of tradition and to the evidence and force of
new experience. It is in minds like theirs that the battle
between the past and the present, between the new and the
old, is fought out in all matters pertaining to religious beliefs
and social customs and standards. Men of that type usually
possess social imagination and they cannot help contrasting
what might and ought to be with what actually is. They are
unhappy because of the inertia of their surroundings and
men's persistence in mental and moral perversity.

There are some who possess such high intelligence as to
be able to resolve these conflicts. They are the constructive
thinkers and philosophers. But even they do not attain that
inner equilibrium, unless they exercise a tremendous amount
of spiritual energy. Their individual religion or ethics is
thus basically an act of will, a *tour de force,* a choice deliberately made of the more desirable good in face of overwhelming and heart-breaking odds. Only those of exceptional
energy can long abide in their choice. In those, however, who
possess character of only average force, the enthusiasm of
the original decision or choice dies down and they soon react
to life with a sense of tedium and weariness which issues in
a feeling of futility, meaninglessness and emptiness.

It should not be difficult for us to understand, in the light
of what has already been said, how public worship acts as an
antidote to the strain of self-consciousness, how it recharges,
as it were, the spent energies of the world-weary and depressed. It resolves the conflict between reason and impulse
by enabling us so to identify ourselves with those with whom
we worship in common that we absorb their experiences,
their needs and their interests. This tends to restore our
mental balance, because it necessarily weakens the onset of
our selfish urges. *To be united with a community in a spirit
of religious devotion is to be united with it in a spirit of love.*
In the same way as one who is deeply in love acquires a

profound sense of sympathy with all living things, even with inanimate nature, so when one is united with his group in a spirit of worship, one loses for the time being all hatred, selfishness and meanness, and is imbued with an understanding and sympathy for all those things that elicit man's devotion.

3
The arguments against public worship

Our appreciation of the value of public worship need not lead us to deny a danger that inheres in it. In all forms of human association there is the danger of crushing individuality. This applies to religious no less than to secular associations. The traditional liturgies used in public worship sometimes express social attitudes which may conflict with the highest ethical ideals held by the individual worshiper. Or they may voice an intellectual outlook antagonistic to the acceptance of newly discovered truths which to the individual worshiper are incontestable. A worshiping throng that uses such a liturgy may thus be influenced by it to the detriment of the worshipers and of society. It may tend to identify God with that which is ungodly, and turn the energies generated by common worship to the glorification of an idol.

But *aloofness from public worship is not the way to deal with the danger of idolatry, any more than withdrawing to a hermitage is the way to remedy social evils.* Whatever danger to individuality may inhere in all forms of human association, religious no less than secular, it still remains true that no individuality is possible except through the medium of association. The articulation of the ideals of the group in a traditional liturgy may reveal to the individual inadequacies in the group's traditional ideals, but this does not mean that he rejects these ideals in their totality. Meantime, his participation in public worship enhances his appreciation of the highest implications of those ideals of the group which he does accept as valid. This will serve to intensify his determination to correct the inadequacies he has found rather than merely permit himself to be discouraged by them.

The correct way to deal with the dangers inherent in public worship is, therefore, to seek to influence the members of our group in the direction of our own ethical convictions and to make them aware of the importance of revising the liturgy to conform to our deepest spiritual insights. In the meantime, it is possible to worship even with a community the majority of whom oppose our ideas, provided we are so intimate with our people that we not only know both their good and evil traits but also sense their potentialities for good. *The religious community is based not so much on common ideas as on common interests, common experiences, common hopes, fears and yearnings; it is a community of the heart rather than of the mind.* Hence its members can worship God in common, experience together the sense of His presence, even though they may have the most diverse conceptions of Him and of the nature of their communion with Him.

The presence of the multitude in worship creates for all a sense of mystery, an awareness of the insufficiency of the self and its dependence on a transcendent Power that we call God. But how that mystery is understood depends on the worshiper's individual cultural development. To the less cultured, the mystery of God's presence is that of a superhuman energy operating behind the phenomenon. To the more cultured, the mystery is the poetic apprehension of the phenomenon as representative and symbolical of the power behind all life and experience. But, regardless of their cultural outlook, as long as they worship together, each helps the other to experience God.

Recourse to public worship is sometimes deprecated by pointing out other ways in which men may experience a similar awareness of God, a similar exaltation and enhance-

ment of the self through the surrender of the self. Thus
there are drugs such as opium and hashish which are known
to produce this state of mind. Likewise delirium and epilepsy
often give rise to a sense of God's presence. The comparison,
however, ignores the obvious difference between these phenomena and the experience of communion with God through
worship, in that disease and recourse to drugs are abnormal.
They are not experienced in the course of the healthy functioning of man's psycho-physical organism. Hence their
after-effects are often disastrous to him. But public worship
is a manifestation of the healthy gregarious instinct of the
human animal and contributes to his well-being as does the
normal functioning of any human instinct.

Moreover, this comparison completely overlooks the fact
that community worship always associates the spiritual
energy engendered by the presence of the multitude with
group memories, hopes and yearnings of deep cultural and
ethical significance. This discriminates the experience of
public worship not merely from the state of mind produced
by drugs and certain diseased conditions, but also from the
sense of exaltation accompanying participation in the actions
of a mob. For a mob is under the sway of the passion of a
moment, and thus enhances a selfish impulse that a group
may hold in common, and breaks down the inhibitions that
might deter the individual from yielding to this impulse. It
therefore is destructive of the integrity of personality. But
the religious community has a longer life and wider interests
than any of the individuals constituting it. Hence the common interests that it articulates constitute an integrating
influence upon the individual and society.

Emerson, in his essay on the "Oversoul," expressed very
well the integrating influence of communion with God. "We
live in succession, in division, in parts, in particles. Meantime within man is the soul of the whole; the wise silence;
the universal beauty, to which every part and particle is

equally related; the eternal One." But Emerson was apparently unaware of the extent to which communion with God is dependent on the social experience of community worship.

Some spiritually minded people, particularly such as have strongly developed esthetic emotions, find communion with God in nature, and regard this as a substitute for community worship. They remind us with Bryant that "the groves were God's first temples." That such communion is possible need not be denied. The Rabbis tell us that the reason God addressed Moses from a thorn-bush was to teach us that no place was void of the *Shekinah*.[18] This statement, however, overlooks the fact that the sense of at-homeness in the universe which is fostered by community worship, as has already been shown, is essential to our full enjoyment even of natural beauty. There is clear evidence for this in the fact that in the oldest epics and sagas there is little love of nature. Primitive men were aware of nature mainly as helping or hindering the satisfaction of their practical needs. A deeper appreciation of nature develops with the growing conviction of a benign spirit immanent in nature as in man, and it is the experience of community worship that has convinced man of the reality of this Spirit. To the Psalmist, the heavens declared the glory of God, but then the Psalmist was also acquainted with the glory of God through the experience of public worship. To those to whom nature means most, natural objects are symbols of reference to human experiences, and most of all to those experiences that have social significance. Even granting that a hermit in his solitude experiences through his contact with nature an awareness of God's presence no less poignant than that of a worshiper with the congregation, that experience would not be nearly so significant, for it would not intensify his desire to serve God by the personal integration of his character and his social cooperation with his fellows.

[18] *Pesik. R. K.* I (2b).

4

The prerequisites to public worship as a means of experiencing the divine presence

But at this point the question may well be raised: How is it that, notwithstanding all that has been said of the effect of public worship on the individual, of how it enables him to experience God as beatitude and inner illumination, this experience is far from universal? How many Jews there are whom the services of the synagogue leave cold and indifferent! Surely this is a phenomenon that demands explanation.

The answer is that, in order to be amenable to the influences of public worship, certain prerequisite conditions must be met. The Psalmist who assures us, "The Lord is nigh to all that call upon Him" immediately qualifies his statement by adding, "to all that call upon Him in truth." [14] The qualification is significant. The experience of communion with God is attainable only by those who are sincere in their desire to bring their lives into harmony with the divine. But such desire, if it exists, does not confine itself to verbal expression at particular times and seasons. It manifests itself in daily conduct. The Jewish religion insists on "clean hands and a pure heart" [15] as qualifications for communion with God.

> "Lord, who shall sojourn in Thy tabernacle?
> Who shall dwell upon Thy holy mountain?
> He that walketh uprightly, and worketh righteousness,
> And speaketh the truth in his heart;
> That hath no slander upon his tongue,
> Nor doeth evil to his fellow,
> Nor taketh up a reproach against his neighbor;
> In whose eyes a vile person is despised,
> But he honoreth them that fear the Lord;
> He that sweareth to his own hurt, and changeth not;
> He that putteth not out his money on usury,
> Nor taketh a bribe against the innocent.
> He that doeth these things shall never be moved." [16]

[14] Ps. 145:18.   [15] *Ibid.*, 24:4.   [16] Ps. 15:1-5.

No notion has been so prevalent and so misleading as the one that the mere act of worship has a spiritualizing effect on the human being. Before worship can have any genuine spiritual influence upon us, before it can reveal God to us, we must qualify ourselves by an arduous discipline in deeds of self-control, honesty, courage and kindness. When we come to the synagogue, after having tried our utmost to deal fairly with our neighbor, to suppress our evil impulses, and have made an effort to meet our responsibilities as human beings, then worship can yield its measure of spiritual strength and give us a sense of inward peace. *Communion with God is a reward of holy and righteous living.*

Does this imply that the synagogue has no place for sinners, or that those who have gone astray morally have no right to participate in religious worship? There must be no shrinking from the logical consequences of the principle here laid down. The only condition on which that principle would allow a sinner to enter the synagogue, in the hope of benefiting by its services, would be that he repent in his heart before he takes the name of God upon his lips. "For transgressions that are between man and his fellow the Day of Atonement effects atonement only if he has appeased his fellow." [17]

But there are many Jews who are not unrighteous and nevertheless complain that Jewish religion as they know it does not satisfy their longing to experience the presence of God in the world. They are keenly disappointed because the prayers of the liturgy leave them cold. They point to Catholicism and Christian Science as helping their adherents to acquire a sense of divine presence, and they ask: Why cannot Jewish religion do the same for its adherents? The fact that the Jewish religion does the same for very many of its adherents should rule out the question in the form in which they put it. But their complaint cannot be dismissed insofar as their own experience is concerned.

[17] *Mishnah Yoma* VIII, 9.

The explanation of their failure to experience God in the worship of the synagogue is probably to be found in their relation to the Jewish community. *In order that our participation in communal worship shall enable us to experience the presence of God by bringing into operation our gregarious nature, it is necessary that we feel strongly our identification with the worshiping community and the totality of its interests.* Nowhere is a man more lonely than in a crowd of foreigners whose ways and interests are not his own and with whom he cannot communicate for lack of verbal and other symbols in common. The unfortunate circumstances of Jewish life in modern times has led to the alienation of many Jews from all vital contact with the Jewish people and Jewish civilization. Even though they may have pleasant personal relations as neighbors with the individual Jews who constitute the congregation, they are so cut off from the Jewish past and so unconcerned with the Jewish future as hardly to feel their life to be a part of the corporate life of Israel, which gives status and *raison d'être* to the congregation. They are therefore not in a position to understand or sympathize with the aspirations of the Jewish people as expressed in its liturgy.

The function of the traditional liturgy is to have the Jewish people experience the awareness of that God Whom Israel began to know only after centuries of groping and stumbling, and Whom it is still in the process of learning to identify. The liturgy therefore speaks in terms of Israel's historic experience; its language, its figures of speech, its symbols and its rites are derived from the cultural heritage of the Jewish people. To individuals who are out of touch with the main current of Jewish life, in past and present, that merging of the individual ego with the spirit of the worshiping congregation is therefore impossible, and their craving for communion with God remains unsatisfied. It is significant that in past ages, when Jews led an autonomous communal life, this particular complaint that the individual could not experience God in the worship of the synagogue was unheard of.

Shemini Azeret, by emphasizing the life-enhancing value of communion with God through public worship, recommends to us the wisdom of seeking that experience for ourselves and our fellow-Jews. It should interest us in the effort to make our religious liturgy for all occasions express the holiest ideals that we have derived from the cultural heritage of our people and from our own experience of life. It should impel us to qualify for true communion with God as one of the congregation of Israel, by the consistent pursuit of ethical aims and by a loyal identification of our interests with those of the Jewish people throughout the world. If it fulfills these functions, it will enable us to share the emotions of the Psalmist who said:

"How lovely are Thy tabernacles, O Lord of Hosts!
My soul yearneth, yea, even pineth for the courts of the Lord;
My heart and my flesh sing for joy unto the living God.

.   .   .   .   .

For a day in Thy courts is better than a thousand;
I had rather stand at the threshold of the house of my God,
Than dwell in the tents of worldly men." [18]

[18] Ps. 84:1, 2, 11.

VIII

GOD AS THE POWER THAT MAKES FOR FREEDOM

It is fairly well established that Passover was originally a nature festival. Though it became an occasion for making pilgrimage to some central sanctuary much later than did Sukkot, it antedates the latter as an Israelitish festival. It was observed by the Israelite tribes when they were still nomads, when sheep and goats constituted the main source of their food supply, and when, accordingly, they looked to the yeaning season in the spring with great concern. When they entered Canaan, they found the natives celebrating in the spring an agricultural festival known as the Feast of Unleavened Bread (*Hag ha-Mazot*). Before long these two feasts, the nomadic and the agricultural, were merged. Subsequently, with the rise of the national consciousness, the two main rites of the combined feast, the paschal offering and the unleavened bread, were reinterpreted to fit into the pattern of the story of Israel's exodus from Egypt.

If the foregoing account of the evolution of Pesaḥ is correct, the spirit of Israel has shown almost unparalleled creative power. Not only has it transformed the Pesaḥ from a nature festival into a historic one, but it has so interpreted the event of the Exodus, upon which it bases the festival, as to give that event not merely a national but a universal significance. It is not often that an individual wants to be reminded of his humble beginnings; but that a nation in ancient times should glory in having been held in bondage by another nation is certainly an unrepeated phenomenon.

Yet in the consciousness of the Jewish people the bondage in which their ancestors were held in Egypt has been an ever-present memory, held vividly and related vitally to the entire context of their life. There is only one explanation for this strange phenomenon. The remembrance of the bondage of Egypt and of the redemption from it has served as a means of signalizing the unique character of the God whom Israel worshiped. With Israel's serfdom in Egypt as background, Israel's God stands forth more sharply and luminously as the Redeemer of the oppressed, as the Liberator of the enslaved, as the Defender of the weak against the strong.

During the last two thousand years Jews have never wearied of referring to the Exodus. In the morning and evening prayers, in the thanksgiving benediction after each meal, and in the *Kiddush* inaugurating Sabbath and Festivals, Jews have thanked God for having delivered their ancestors from Egypt. And every year with the return of the Festival they have recounted to their children the story of that redemption. The main motive which has kept alive the memory of the Exodus during the last two thousand years has undoubtedly been the hope that, as God had wrought miracles for Israel in the past, had been gracious to them and had delivered them from bondage, so will He, when the time comes, once again manifest His power on behalf of His people, free them from oppression and restore them to their land.

Changes, however, have taken place in human life which render that simple version of the Exodus and its meaning no longer adequate. Jews are still the victims of oppression. But they have entered into such intimate relationship with the life of the world about them that they can no longer envisage their own deliverance except as a phase of general human deliverance. If miracles are to be enacted as part of the future redemption, they cannot be conceived as similar to those which tradition associates with the Exodus. *The new redemption to which Jews look forward involves the redemption of society in general from present ills. It implies the transformation of human nature and social institutions through the divine power of intelligence and good-will.*

In order that the memory of the Exodus shall enable us to look forward to such a future for Israel and the rest of mankind, it is necessary to delve more deeply into the meaning which the story of the Exodus originally had for Israel. The redemption from Egypt, whenever referred to in the Bible, carried with it implications which caused the character of the God of Israel to stand out in sharp contrast to that of the deities of other nations. The opening sentence of the Ten Commandments sets forth, to be sure, the claim upon Israel's loyalty to God mainly by reason of what He did for His people. But if we take into account the entire historical context out of which the prophetic conception of God emerged, the opening words of the Ten Commandments imply that in redeeming Israel from Egypt, their God manifested the most characteristic phase of His nature. This is apparent from the use made of the allusion to the Exodus throughout the Torah. Thus the laws in Leviticus known as the Holiness Code [1] which relies on the sanction of *imitatio dei*, "Be ye holy, for I the Lord thy God am holy," [2] refer again and again to God as the redeemer from Egypt, and concludes significantly, "I am the Lord who hallow you, that brought you out of the land of Egypt to be your God: I am the Lord." [3] There can be no question that *in the Torah the story of the Exodus has the connotation that to help the oppressed is an essential attribute of godhood.* This is verified by the numerous allusions to the Exodus as exemplifying God's intervention in behalf of those who are the victims of tyranny. [4]

[1] Lev. 19:1; 22:33.   [2] *Ibid.*, 19:2.   [3] *Ibid.*, 22:32, 33.
[4] Exod. 23:9; Lev. 25:17, 38, 55; 19:33-37; Deut. 24:19-22.

From this standpoint alone can we understand aright the entire Exodus epic. We miss the point of that epic, if the stories of the miracles are merely so many wonder tales that tax our credulity. That is because we read it in the light of our own outlook. Pharaoh, whose destruction God encompasses, is to us merely a wilful despot, who knows no pity, but essentially an ordinary human being. We cannot understand why God should be represented as deliberately making him stubborn, so as to wreak all the greater punishment upon him. But no such ethical problem could have arisen in the minds of those who fashioned this epic, for, to them, Pharaoh was not just an ordinary human being. To them he was a pretender to godhood; he played the god; he ventured to measure himself against the God of Israel, Whose purpose with His people he sought to frustrate.* That this was the conception of Pharaoh is evidenced from the later prophetic conception of the Pharaohs in general. Thus Ezekiel, addressing himself to the Pharaoh of his day, says: "Behold, I am against thee, Pharaoh, King of Egypt, the great dragon that lives in the mud of the river, that hath said, 'My river is mine now and I have made it myself.' " * This fact makes the contest between Pharaoh and YHWH a contest between the embodiment of arrogant tyranny, on the one hand, and the Power that makes for redemption, on the other.

I

The meaning of freedom

The conception of God as the redeemer of the oppressed has revolutionized the meaning and function of religion, and has placed it at the service of the ethical impulses. To appreciate the far-reaching significance of this conception, we

---

* The interpretation in Romans 9:17-24 is bad exegesis and worse theology.
* Ezek. 29:3.

have to bear in mind that in other religions God was reckoned with mainly as the power that makes for fecundity,
whether of the soil, of animals, or of human beings. The
Jewish religion does not minimize the importance of identifying as divine the forces in the physical environment that
make for physical survival and well-being. It has not altogether obliterated the nature aspect of Pesaḥ, which survives
in the practice of having it fall in the spring, and in the
counting of the *Omer,* which begins on the second night of
the Festival, to mark the barley harvest.[7] Nevertheless, the
Jewish religion has very definitely subordinated nature's
revival, as a manifestation of God's power, to the revival of
the human spirit through freedom. Pesaḥ is preeminently
"the season of our freedom." This is in marked contrast
with the trend of the other religions which insisted upon
focussing man's attention on the miracle of the dying and
rebirth of vegetation. The great vogue, during the first
three centuries of the common era, of mystery religions
which centered about Isis, Tammuz, Adonis or Dionysos,
tells the story of what God meant for the most civilized races
of the ancient world. All these mystery religions held out
the hope of personal survival and salvation, by drawing
upon the analogy from the self-renewing processes of nature. Christianity owes its early popularity largely to Paul's
success in converting the simple faith of the early Jewish
Christians into a mystery cult. By placing Christ's death
and resurrection at the center of Christian interest and mystic communion, Christianity has reenforced the tendency of
religion to confine religion to man's individual yearning for
immortality instead of placing it at the service of his ethical
strivings. In the face of this retrograde tendency, it remains
Israel's task to accentuate the primacy of that aspect of
God's nature which has a bearing upon the relationship of
men and groups to one another, and upon the art of their

[7] *Menahot* 65b on Lev. 23:15.

living together in peace and cooperation. The festival of Pesah is henceforth needed to stress the truth that God manifests Himself in human life as the Power that makes for freedom.

The need for stressing this truth exists not only because we are liable to be mistaken in our conception of God, but also because we are liable to misconceive the meaning and function of freedom. To most people there is something inherently incompatible between religion and freedom. They take for granted that religion's main business is to bridle freedom. Thus Solomon Reinach defines religion as "a sum of scruples which impede the free exercise of our faculties." * Even thought must be restrained, if it is to move in the channels of religion. Freedom of thought is usually associated with irreligion, and a freethinker is a synonym for an atheist. Even those who do not go so far as to look upon freedom as the antithesis of religion, tend to limit the province of freedom to politics.

What men think of political freedom these days is enough to make the visionaries of the eighteenth and nineteenth centuries, who gave their lives for it, turn in their graves. It is highly fashionable to bait and mock it, and to hold it up to ridicule as a childish illusion which has done the race more harm than good. The institutions of democracy and representative government based upon the ideal of political freedom, so the argument runs, have exhibited men's gullibility and impotence to a degree never suspected. The policy of *laissez faire* which that ideal sanctioned has most often meant: Don't interfere with the strong, while they are busy exploiting the weak.

In the face of the misconception of freedom, due to its being regarded either as license or as a political illusion, Pesah with its affirmation that God is the Power that makes for freedom emphasizes the thought that *freedom is at the*

* *Orpheus,* trans. by F. Simmonds, N. Y., 1909, 3.

very root of man's spiritual life, and is the prime condition of his self-fulfillment, or salvation. The ancients recognized that fact and formulated it as best they could.in the doctrine of free-will, which is based on the realization that there can be no responsibility without freedom. Freedom is not only a prerequisite of the spiritual life, but is also its reward, as when the Sages say: "No man is free but he who occupies himself with the Torah." [9] But the conception of free-will, too, has fallen upon evil days. It does not speak in the mood of today, which seeks evidence of causality in human behavior as well as in other phenomena of nature. Likewise what is meant by freedom as an achievement or reward requires elucidation in terms of current thought.

The ideal of freedom assumes that, potentially, human beings and human groups have something unique to contribute to the totality of life. That ideal further assumes that God is the Redeemer, is the Power that makes for the discovery and realization of that potential uniqueness in individuals and groups. This conception of freedom is ethical and religious. It is ethical, because it directs attention to the ethical potentialities in persons and communities, which are in need of being recognized and stimulated. It is religious, because it helps us get a deeper understanding of God as He manifests Himself in human experience. It is this conception of freedom that gives worth and sanctity to human life. The teaching of R. Johannan b. Zakkai [10] to the effect that God can be served only by free moral agents, and not by slaves, points to the truth that *the meaning of religion can be grasped only when social life is based on freedom.*

The problem of freedom, conceived in these spiritual terms, is a problem (1) in the significance of individuality or selfhood, and (2) in the liberation of personality.

[9] *Abot* VI, 2.   [10] *Kiddushin* 22b.

2

The significance of individuality

The poet and philosopher R. Judah ha-Levi points out that, when God came down on Mount Sinai to give the Torah to Israel, He did not say, "I am the Lord your God who created the world and all that is in it." Instead, He said, "I am the Lord your God who brought you out of the land of Egypt, out of the house of bondage." [11] God's purpose in revealing Himself to the Israelites was to give them the laws by which they were to live. From that standpoint it was more important for them to know that God had redeemed their ancestors than that He had created the world. The knowledge that God had redeemed them from bondage did more than merely place them under obligation to keep His commandments. It gave them to understand that what God expected of them was not arbitrary, but was in correspondence with His own essential nature. The spirit and purpose that underlay the laws emanated from the very nature of God which He displayed in redeeming the Israelites from slavery. "And thou shalt remember that thou wast a bondman in the land of Egypt, and that the Lord thy God redeemed thee; therefore I command thee this thing this day." [12]

Translated into our own way of thinking, the foregoing implies that it is more important to experience the reality of God as the Power that makes for freedom than merely to know that there is a God. To experience the reality of God means to realize that life is worthwhile, in spite of all that mars it. Its worthwhileness is due not so much to the actual, realized good, as to the infinite potentialities that are still latent and that will in time come to fruition. To be aware of that, to find zest in living by reason of this realization, is to know God. To experience the reality of God as the Power that makes for freedom implies that it is only

[11] *Alkhazari* I, 25.   [12] Deut. 15:15.

when we enjoy freedom that we are in a position to find life worthwhile. Freedom is therefore an indispensable requisite to that experience of God's reality which is revelation.

The freedom which occupies so central a place in man's higher life is not the freedom of one or more dominant impulses, desires or passions, but of our whole being. Only when we call into play each and every power and tendency within us under the urge of some symphonic will or purpose are we free. It is only then that our personality functions, only then are we something more than the resultant of forces of which we happen to be the meeting point. When the whole of us acts through every part of us, we are initiators of action, creators and not merely passive and helpless automatons. When we are given a chance to live thus, we evolve individuality, that inalienable, untransferable element of singularity which renders each human being an unrepeated and unrepeatable entity in the entire universe.

Mankind has turned a complete somersault in its way of thinking. Before the dawn of science, man was an animist. He ascribed *personality,* or individuality like his own, to everything he saw around him. Trees, stones, springs, hills —to say nothing of the heavenly bodies—were not merely things but persons, centers of self-originated action. Man now goes to the other extreme of denying self-origination even to living things. He considers his own personality an illusion. Obsessed with the so-called method of science, he looks upon everything as the effect of everything else, and as having no voice whatever in and about itself.

The method of science has, indeed, helped man decipher many an enigma of the physical world. But with all that, this method may prove to be a distraction, a source of partial truth, and a means of falsifying fact, if regarded as the only method of interpreting experience. It is certainly important for man to know that his life is determined by the forces of heredity and environment. The part that the physical constitution, or the glands, play in character and career should not be underestimated. But no more fatal error can be committed than that of overlooking the element of personality. There is in every human being something irreducible which renders him a monad, a world in himself, a microcosm which, as the mystics were wont to say, reflects the macrocosm.

The principle of individuality is by no means limited to human beings. The minutest atom in creation has something that distinguishes it from every other atom. The mere fact that it occupies a different position in space and time gives it a certain uniqueness. There is not a thing in the entire range of being of which this is not true. But there is something unique to human individuality as such. Human individuality is not fixed in its measure and quality. It has the power of unlimited growth. Every experience contributes something to its development and prepares the way for further growth through experience. To differentiate human individuality from the individuality of other beings, we shall call it selfhood. That is the selfhood referred to in the dictum of Hillel: "If I am not for myself, who is for me?" [13]

"If a man strikes many coins from one mould," say the Rabbis, "they all resemble one another, but the Supreme King of Kings, the Holy One, blessed be He, fashioned every man in the stamp of the first man, and yet not one of them resembles his fellow. Therefore every single person is obliged to say: 'The world was created for my sake.'" [14] This was their way of emphasizing the truth that the individual is a center of reference, an end in himself and fully responsible for what he does with his life. Hence the important ethical implication that he must not be made the tool of another. Felix Adler expresses this thought in his definition of personality: "It is a unique excellence. It is one of the infinitely possible modes of being, worthwhile as such, unduplicated anywhere in the world, never recurrent,

[13] *Abot* I, 14.   [14] *Mishnah Sanhed.* IV, 5.

utterly individual and yet of which it is the supreme property to react in such a way upon all other spiritual natures
as to make possible in turn the distinctive excellence in each.
The personality is that which has its own life and which produces, evokes the essential life in all other personalities, lives
in them, and experiences the pulse beats of their life in itself.
. . . This then is the supreme commandment of the moral
life: To act so as to personalize others, to put them in possession of the self that is their very own, and in so doing
fall heir to that which is your very own, become a person,
a spiritual nature yourself." [15]

The most serious indictment of modern civilization, as of
all the civilizations that have preceded it, is the fact that the
vast majority of human beings are held in subjection and
that the growth of their personalities is stunted and warped
through being made to serve the selfish interests of the few.
The failure of civilization to make men free is not to be
ascribed entirely to the greed, rapacity and aggressive selfishness of the dominant classes. A large share of the blame
must fall upon our political, economic and cultural institutions which are accepted on their face value without regard
to their consequences in terms of human welfare. If that
evil will ever be remedied, and human welfare will become
not merely the avowed, but the intelligently and sincerely
sought-after, purpose of all social laws and institutions, the
criterion of human welfare itself will have to be the extent
to which it releases the personality in human beings. Men
are not born free; they have to be made free. *The right into
which one is born is only potential freedom; but actual freedom is an achievement with the aid of civilization which is
based on the religious evaluation of personality.*

The history of slavery helps us realize both the essence
and the problem of freedom. The historians point out that
slavery arose as a change in the method of disposing of

prisoners of war. Originally prisoners of war were offered
up to the gods of the victors or slain outright, until it occurred to the far-sighted among the captors that it would be
more advantageous to allow the captives to live and work
for them. Looked at from the standpoint of antiquity,
slavery was thus an advance rather than a retrogression. In
the first place, it kept alive a great part of the race that would
otherwise have been exterminated. And secondly, it enabled
the privileged classes to bestow resources and leisure upon
those who were qualified to create the higher cultural and
spiritual values of human life.

Slavery thus came at the point in human development at
which man had already acquired the power to make use of
tools. The distinctive trait of human intelligence is that it
enables man to make use of tools. At first he knew only to
make use of inanimate tools, like the flint-axe and the war
club. Later he learned to utilize animals in the capacity of
tools, the dog for hunting, the ass and camel for burdens,
etc. A new process of development set in when man discovered that he could use his own fellow-beings as tools for
the carrying out of his purposes. To be a slave means essentially to be used as a tool. *When a man is made to subserve
a purpose of which he is unaware or in which he is not interested, he is a slave.*

Unfortunately for the struggle for freedom, the institution of slavery contributed in ancient times to human progress. When man had but few mechanical labor-saving devices, he depended largely upon sheer man-power to produce
the surplus necessary to make of his life more than a hand-
to-mouth existence. If there had been no slaves then to do
the drudgery, the higher values of life would never have
entered the consciousness of man. The great achievements
in ancient art, poetry, literature and philosophy were made
possible by the leisure enjoyed by the few talented individuals at the expense of the multitudes who lived and worked

like beasts of burden. Despite, however, the important part played by slavery in ancient times as a force for progress, no one would frankly venture to justify its continuance, even in mitigated form. But a habit once formed persists in the realm of the subconscious, even if in the realm of the conscious we condemn it. Men have not really extirpated their belief in the need of slavery, at least in a sublimated form. They still subscribe to the need of having the masses of men serve as the tools of the chosen and gifted few. They still act on, even if they disavow, the principle of aristocracy as essential to human evolution.

It is for that reason necessary to nurture the sense of justice which rebels against all forms of human bondage, to foster with the aid of the Jewish religious tradition that something in us which tells us that every human being is meant to be the master of his own destiny. The first and the most solemn protest against human bondage is the declaration that the God of Israel is essentially the Redeemer of the oppressed. As believers in the God of Israel, we must hold to the conviction that slavery must be abolished not only in name, but also in fact. A human being must have a purpose to live for, a purpose which his whole being consents to and shares in. All normal human beings, even the drawers of water and hewers of wood, have in them the potentiality of living for a purpose in the spirit of freedom. This does not mean that every human being can become intellectually and spiritually qualified to set up a purpose of his own. It is not given to everyone to exert initiative, or to possess originality. With the variegated character of human ability, some will have to lead and others to follow. But following does not mean slaving, so long as one knows and freely accepts the wherefore and the whereto of his actions, and of all that they imply in terms of the highest and most universal ethical purposes. Hence, *when we look to God as the Power that makes for freedom, we expect that He will give mankind no rest until it puts an end to the order of social living which makes it possible for a human being to be drudging and slaving for aims in which he has no part or parcel.*

The element of selfhood or individuality with which we must reckon inheres not only in each individual person but in each group of persons, whether it be a purposive group, a church, or a nation, that has something unique to give to human civilization. This is why true democracy cannot merely mean the rule of the majority; it must provide equally for the rights of the minority. Democratic constitutions have generally recognized certain rights of the individual which are inalienable and which not even the State, as expressing the will of the majority, is allowed to override. But modern nations, even when they purport to be democratic, have not given sufficient recognition to the rights of minority groups to express themselves; they continue to thwart minority self-expression and self-determination; they frustrate the element of personality in the members of minority groups.

The freedom which means the release of selfhood consists in the right to be different and the right to be creative. These inherent rights of personality will be resisted so long as we labor under the dangerous fallacy that unity and cooperation are impossible without uniformity. The industrial economy has given rise to mass production, and mass production has led to the ideal of standardizing human beings. The efficiency engineer tries to reduce the number of operations performed by the hands and feet of the worker to the minimum required by the routine of production, in exactly the same way as he tries to effect the strictest economy in the expenditure of fuel for the machine and the elimination of waste through friction and heat. The trained psychologist is used by industry to regiment the minds of workers and consumers to serve the economic interests of the producer. In politics, propaganda is similarly employed to make men like-minded, in the interest of facile control by those in power. Even education, which should aim at furthering the growth of personality and at socializing the selfhood of the individual, is too often but an ill-concealed effort by those who are in power to robotize the minds of the masses.

Although the striving after uniformity has received new impetus since the machine age, it is by no means the product of our day. Long before the age of industry, Jewish, Christian and Mohammedan religions regarded it as axiomatic that there can be only one true religion for all mankind. It is impossible to recount the misery which the attempt to cast all human souls into one mould has brought upon the race. Religious toleration, which has become the accepted principle of the modern State, is the merest beginning in the direction of that freedom which means the right to be different. As a matter of fact, it does not signify the avowed recognition of that principle, but rather a concession to a condition which cannot be dealt with otherwise. Historically viewed, it was only after the internecine religious warfare that followed the Protestant Reformation resulted in a stalemate and issued in sheer exhaustion, that the modern states deemed it prudent to recognize freedom of conscience. But even today that freedom is usually interpreted to mean merely freedom of worship and ritual practice, and is not extended to include free criticism of social institutions, particularly in times of crisis, when untrammeled social thinking is of the utmost importance.

So long as religions themselves will not acknowledge the right to be different as an integral part of their very teaching, so long as they will fail to behold in that right the opportunity for the functioning of the selfhood which makes life worthwhile, dogmatism and bigotry will flourish not only in religion, but in all walks of life. The blindness of religions to this fact is mainly responsible for the discredit into which they have fallen among those elements of the population which find themselves thwarted by the persecution of all social free-thought, as well as among many sensitive intellects who find themselves curbed in their passionate quest for knowledge and truth by the dogmatism of religious creeds.

In addition to the right to be different, the freedom which means the release of selfhood includes also the right to be creative. To be creative socially means to exercise responsibility, to be self-determining. Selfhood in the human being cannot possibly come into play, when it is held in check by those who are afraid to trust it to itself and who, even though it be in a spirit of well-meaning paternalism, regard it their duty to prevent those whom they love from getting out of hand. By instilling in men implicit reliance on an authoritarian tradition or an ecclesiastical hierarchy for guidance in all vital matters, and by discouraging them from facing the facts of life with self-reliance in a bravely realistic spirit, religion renders them a disservice. By relieving men of the responsibility that rests upon them as moral agents, it saps the creative energy of their selfhood. A similar effect is produced whenever loyalty to constituted authority is invoked, in the mistaken belief that blind obedience is to be not only a measure of last resort, but a virtue of the first order, productive of more good to him who exercises it than to the one to whom it is yielded. This is the story of despotism from its most benevolent to its most malevolent forms, despotism in government, in family life, in education and in religion.

As a people, we Jews have suffered more than any other from the deprivation of the right to be different and the right to be creative. We should miss more keenly the joy of evolving material and moral values that we could call our own, not in the possessive sense but in the creative sense. We should yearn more intensively for the right to social and spiritual self-determination. We should never have committed the colossal blunder of identifying the political equality, which has been granted to us, as the dawn of the messianic era. Political equality, instead of releasing Jewish selfhood, has inhibited it. This does not mean that we can do without political equality; it means that political equality is not enough. *Political equality has given us merely formal freedom as individuals; but in demanding as the price of that freedom the surrender of our historic civilization, it has robbed us of the right to be different, and destroyed the chief prerequisite to our cultural and spiritual creativity. Not until we win the right to foster our Jewish civilization to the full in our ancestral home, and to some extent in the diaspora, can we consider ourselves truly free, either individually or as a group.*

3
The liberation of personality

The conception of history implied in the Jewish religion is that the trend of human events makes for the emergence and development of personality. History cannot be set down as a senseless phantasmagoria, if it is true that there is more of reason, more of character, more of the sense of justice, more of the power to mould environment, more of the faculty to create arts and sciences and political systems, more of human sympathy than there was on this earth five thousand years ago. All of these human gains find their embodiment in soul and personality.

The sculptor with chisel in hand stands before a block of marble and begins to hew. Presently there emerges the outline of a human form. After a while we behold distinct features of a face, in which we recognize character. If the sculptor happens to be a Michaelangelo, the cold marble soon grows resplendent with the beauty of the conception in his mind. Likewise, it appears, the great world Artist keeps on hewing at the vast quarry of human potentialities, until there gradually emerge human souls, each stamped with an individuality of its own. All the strife and pain and agony in the world may be part of the divine process whereby personalities, men and women with souls, are brought into being, are liberated from *Tohu* and *Bohu,* the void of meaninglessness and purposelessness.

But the very process of liberation, or release, implies the overcoming of resistance. This resistance takes on various forms. Not until we learn to identify those forms can we fully appreciate the meaning of God as the Liberator of the element of personality. One mistake commonly made hitherto has been to assume that man's resistance to the process of divine liberation is due solely to the functioning of the Evil *Yezer,* when actually there are at least three main sources of resistance to the attainment by every human being of the full stature of personality of which he is capable. They are, the will to power, the bodily hungers, and the vast reservoir of mechanical energy opened up by the machine. Another mistake has been to think of the resistants to personality as negating and foiling the divine purpose with man. The truth, however, is that they are resistants in the sense that the marble is to the sculptor; they challenge the divine in man, yet they are the very substance out of which the divine in us fashions personality, as the divine in the world fashions the cosmos out of the universal *Tohu* and *Bohu.*

The first type of resistance to be recognized as obstructing personality was the will to power, as manifest in the tyranny exercised by the few strong over the many weak. This type gives rise to all forms of oppression, of exploitation, of injustice. It comprises all forms of slavery, from the most flagrant and brutal to the disguised but, nonetheless, oppressive kinds that still flourish in the world. The subjugation of one people by another, whether it express itself as ruthless conquest of the kind made familiar again by the recent Italian exploit in Ethiopia, or as economic imperialism which means foreign control of markets and natural resources, generally involves the suppression of human individuality and the stunting of personality. This tyranny becomes even more unbearable and dangerous, when it takes the form of controlling men's minds. All forms of heresy-hunting are detrimental to the development of personality. A legislature prohibiting the teaching of evolution, or a university suppressing radical thought, is but a continuation of that same spirit which in the Middle Ages burned heretics at the stake. That one man should have power over another to his hurt was one of the reasons that led the ancient Sage to despair of the meaning and values of life.

"But I returned and considered all the oppressions that are done under the sun; and behold the tears of such as were oppressed, and they had no comforter; and on the side of their oppressors there was power, but they had no comforter. Wherefore I praised the dead that are already dead more than the living that are yet alive; but better than they both is he that hath not yet been, who hath not seen the evil work that is done under the sun." [10]

It is undoubtedly true, as the Marxists contend, that the tyranny of man over man has been all-pervasive in human history. It is equally true that, in the social struggle, the stronger have resorted not only to physical force, but mainly to the instrumentalities of the mind. Those in power have always managed to have the cultural, social and religious institutions embody their will, and keep the multitude in subjection. But the Marxists overlook the significant fact that the rule of tyranny was not always permitted to go unchallenged. At least, as far as Israel is concerned, YHWH as the God of justice and mercy was acclaimed as combating cruelty and oppression. Around the idea of a God of justice

[10] Ecc. 4:1-3.

and mercy there sprang up institutions incorporating the hope of freedom and equality. The priests of Baal to whom Jezebel paid homage confirmed Jezebel in her possession of the vineyard of Naboth, but Elijah who spoke in the name of YHWH denounced her villainy. Whether through ignorance or prejudice, Karl Marx made no distinction between the God of Israel and the Tyrian Baal, but regarded them both alike as the protagonists of the ruling class. He might have known that the principal theme of the Jewish religion is the distinction between false gods and the true God. The God who brought Israel out of bondage executed judgments upon the gods of their oppressors, the Egyptians. They who spoke in the name of the God of Israel long ago tore the veil of hypocrisies from official religion. The God whom Isaiah heralds enters into judgment with the elders of his people and the princes thereof, telling them, "It is ye that have eaten up the vineyard; the spoil of the poor is in your houses." [17] Such a God cannot well be the patron of the elders and the princes. If, instead of condemning religion indiscriminately, Karl Marx had learned to distinguish religion as represented by the God who is the Liberator of mankind from religion as represented by the false gods whom tyranny has created in its own image, he might have aligned himself with the Prophets in helping to bring about the much needed redemption of man the enslaved from man the oppressor.

If Marx could have combined his economic intuitions with a philosophy which views history as a continuous divine process for the release of personality, he would not have fallen into the error of relying wholly on the material wants of the dispossessed to motivate their self-emancipation. Great movements of liberation are not initiated and carried through mainly by those who, by long suffering and oppression, are conditioned against faith in redemption, or even the desire

[17] Is. 4:14.

for it. For the most part, those who are inured to "cruel bondage" refuse to listen to the promise of deliverance. Social revolutions are fomented and led by those whose breadth of social vision and sympathy impel them to indentify themselves, regardless of their own station, with the cause of the oppressed. It was Moses, the Egyptian prince, who emancipated the Hebrew slaves from the tyranny of the Pharaohs; it is Karl Marx, the bourgeois scholar, whose philosophy dominates the proletarian revolt of our day. The reconstruction of our social and economic order along lines more in conformity with economic justice stands much greater chance of success, if we rely not on the envy and resentment of the downtrodden, but on the enlightened passion for justice and righteousness and the exercise of social intelligence.

The oppression of the weak by the strong, however, is not the only hindrance to the full development of personality. We must not lose sight of man's physical hungers. These inherited wants are far more powerful than man's tyranny over his fellow in resisting the emergence of human personality. Without them man's tyranny over man could not be possible. To conceive of God as releasing human personality from the grip of the primal hungers, which function in man with the momentum of a heredity that goes back to the earliest forms of life upon earth, is to understand God more profoundly than when we regard Him merely as the shatterer of men's yokes. As man grew introspective and self-searching, he came upon that deeper understanding of God. Upon looking into his own heart, he became aware of the contending forces using him as a battleground.[18] On the one hand, the imperious passions and appetites that knew no restraint; on the other hand, the will to do what is right and good. Later on, he named the forces within him that

[18] *Cf. Berakot* 61a, especially the statement of R. Simeon b. Pazzi.

would enslave him, the Evil *Yezer,* and his own will struggling to emancipate itself from their power, the Good *Yezer.*

Already in the Torah we note that the conception of God
as Liberator is applied to man's inner struggle against the
tyranny of his instincts. Thus, the reason given for the
observance of *zizit* is "that ye turn not aside after your own
heart and your own eyes after which ye use to go astray.
. . . I am the Lord your God who brought you out of the
land of Egypt to be your God." [19] But it was with the rise
of spiritual individualism during the early centuries of the
common era, that men's minds were generally directed
toward this inner bondage. God, in His function of Liberator, appeared then chiefly as the Redeemer of man from
this power of evil. [20] This view of redemption for a time
removed it from the field of political economic interests and
transferred it to the region of man's soul. [21] Redemption thus
became a problem of individual salvation and other-worldliness. To be redeemed by God meant thenceforth to be released from the power of the physical and earthly, which was
regarded as the source of the inner forces that held man in
bondage. Most of the religious institutions were, accordingly, interpreted as means to other-worldliness, where man
was to be free from the slavery of the body.

With modern psychology obliterating the dichotomy between matter and spirit, body and soul, men's interests today
are no longer gripped as in the past by the dramatic conflict
between the Evil *Yezer* and the Good *Yezer.* The ascetic
practices, which the Middle Ages sanctified as the main
method by which God redeemed the soul from the Evil Inclination, have been discredited as worse than ineffectual.
We cannot regard the flesh as the source of all evil, and its
mortification as bringing release from the dominance of the
baser passions. We recognize the functional character of the

---

[19] Num. 15:39-41.   [20] *Kiddushin* 30b.
[21] *Abodah Zarah* 5a; *Shabbat* 105b.

human instincts that govern our bodily activities, and their positive contribution to the preservation and enrichment of human life. But the bondage of man to primitive and irrational impulses, which is symbolized by the Evil *Yezer*, is, nevertheless, a very real one. Unless our instincts can be coordinated and socialized, they will issue in forms of behavior that, while appropriate enough to the life of the jungle, do not make for the free play of creative personality in the complicated society which human history has evolved. Only the functioning of ethical ideals can emancipate humanity from the dominance of those atavistic impulses that work havoc with human life. The functioning of ethical ideals is the activity of God as the soul's Redeemer from sin.

Man had hardly learned to comprehend the tyranny of his instincts when he began to forge a new tyranny, the tyranny of the machine. The machine has augmented his physical power beyond the wildest dream of his imagination. It has multiplied the possibilities of transportation, communication and mass production a thousandfold. But it has also increased to a corresponding degree the range of opportunities for oppression, conflict and destruction. There are plenty of technicians to master the complicated details of each machine, but few if any know how to bring the machine process as a whole under control, how to gear, so to speak, the machines into each other and to human needs so that they might collectively contribute to human welfare and happiness. So far the machine process has proved to be man's Frankenstein. It feeds on the personality in the human being. Man the toiler becomes a robot; man the executive becomes a calculating machine. All considerations of justice, kindness, humanity must be sacrificed to keep prices down and dividends up. If the industrial struggle were waged not merely against those who have seized the mastery of human affairs and who exercise it irresponsibly and selfishly, but against the inherent ruthlessness of the machine process, and in the interest of human values, victory would not only come sooner, but it would also result in the *complete* emancipation of the human spirit. Vaughan Moody did not exaggerate when he described the machine in the following lines:

"Thru his might men work their wills.
 They have boweled out the hills
 For food to keep him toiling in the cages they have wrought.
 And they fling him hour by hour
 Limbs of men to give him power,
 Brains of men to give him cunning; and for dainties to devour,
 Children's souls, the little worth, hearts of women cheaply
       bought;
 He takes them and he breaks them, but he gives them scanty
       thought."

The problem of human values has to be dealt with in its entirety. Man has to be emancipated from the more cruel and insidious tyranny of his passions and instincts; he has to learn to control the machine which at present holds him in bondage; he has to learn to exercise the right to be himself, insofar as by being himself he can serve society best.

The emancipation of human personality is to be achieved not by destroying but by subduing the forces that have thus far held it in bondage. If God is Liberator, He also manifests Himself in the wisdom of the race. Wisdom consists in utilizing the forces that exist in the world. The strong man's love of power need not be destroyed or suppressed; it could be transformed into the desire to guide and uphold the weak through a political order that spells commonwealth and cooperation instead of dictatorship and despotism. Not by asceticism can we hope to become free from the dominance of the instincts, but by wisely controlling them and subordinating them to the rule of reason. Likewise, it is futile to denounce machinery, as did some nineteenth-century visionaries. Properly controlled and utilized, the machine could evoke undreamed of powers of human personality.

Every people has its men and women who hope and strive for the complete manifestation in human life of God as Liberator. But it was Israel's privilege to have been the first to herald that aspect of God's self-manifestation, and it is Israel's responsibility to demonstrate through its own life the validity of its message. *Jews should, therefore, celebrate the festival of Pesah as a stimulus not merely to effect Jewish self-emancipation, but also to further universal self-emancipation from all forms of bondage whereby man suppresses the personality and individuality of his fellow.*

4

The relation of freedom to life

It appears that the Torah has but little sympathy with the attitude of those Israelites who would rather have remained in bondage than face the dangers of the Wilderness. Most people prefer to be let alone. Men resist freedom, when the price they have to pay for it is hardship and suffering. This is true not alone of freedom from bondage at the hands of others, but also of freedom from bondage to one's own ignorance and superstition. When knowledge introduces us to new problems and difficulties, we are as averse to it as we are to taking risks of life in the wilderness. Most people prefer the safety of slavery to the adventure of freedom, and the bliss of ignorance to the thrill of knowledge. If this desire to be let alone were the primary trait of the human being, if it were so deeply rooted in his nature as to be ineradicable, we should have to despair of human self-fulfillment. But the fact is that this tendency which prevents man from achieving self-fulfillment is not of man but in man, not an integral part of his soul, but a negative inertia that invades his soul. Though the behavior of the average man may, at least under ordinary circumstances, be dominated by the motto, "safety first," the creative genius of the race that in every age gives human history its impetus and direction has always found its most perfect expression in personalities who followed the rule formulated by Nietzsche in the slogan, "To live dangerously." "The freedom of the sky," said Rabindranath Tagore, "is better than the shelter of the cocoon." The well-known paradox about gaining life by losing it is expressed in the Talmudic statement, "He who wishes to live should court death." [22] "Only heroism," said André Malraux, "can inspire us and give our life meaning." And he illustrates that thesis in his novel *Man's Fate*.

The struggle for freedom is only another name for the will to live. Every living thing wants to be moved by the necessity of its own being, by its own hungers and desires. The fear of freedom, though it may have its source in the instinct for individual self-preservation, belongs to the dread of death, which is something far different from the lust of life. It is born of the sense of man's impotence, whereas the desire for freedom, in the sense of the release of selfhood, is born of man's realization of life's potentialities and his own creative potency. Only they yearn for freedom in whom the life urge functions vigorously. Such life urge is the divine in man.

From the way human beings act most of the time, we are tempted to conclude that the life force in them is weighted down by the desire to be let alone. The new-born infant cries as soon as it finds itself released from its mother's body, as though to say; "Why was I not let alone; why was I not allowed to rest in comfort and spared the annoyance and pain of the wilderness of the world?" When, wearied with toil, we lie down to sleep and cannot bear the light in the room or the noise of children, or when we are wakened before we

[22] *Tamid* 32a.

have had our full measure of sleep, how earnestly we beg to be let alone! But the truth is that it is not the life in us, but the lack of energy, that acts thus. As our Sages put it, "Sleep is a sixtieth part of death." ** Suppose we are weak in body and the physician prescribes for us a regimen of food and exercise. The time comes to go through that regimen. How readily we find excuses for omitting to do that which we know to be good and necessary for our health! It cannot be the vitality in us that begs to be let alone. When a man happens to be lost among snowdrifts and, overcome with cold, he suddenly begins to feel a sense of drowsiness, what in him is it that would yield to this fatal wish to be let alone? Surely not the will to live. If avoiding risks were due to the will to live, it ought to make for life. Yet the world is a more habitable place for the human being today not as a result of the universal desire to be let alone, but because a few daring spirits ventured into the unknown, ploughed a path in the fathomless seas, penetrated into the fever-laden forests of the tropics, and knew no fear amid the eternal ice of the Arctics.

Apparently nothing should be so desirable as the truth, yet in reality we dread the truth. Were it not for the inner compulsion which drives us to come to grips with reality, we should never know the truth. Börne satirizes the human tendency to be disconcerted by the truth. He tells the story of Pythagoras who, when he discovered a mathematical truth, was so overjoyed that he offered a hundred oxen to the gods. "Ever since then," he adds, "every time truth is discovered the oxen tremble." Even in the most truth-loving and truth-seeking among us, there is always the inertia of habit which makes the learning of new truth difficult. The very act of mental concentration is attended with resistance; the mind ordinarily avoids organizing its ideas. Not one in a thousand is interested in thinking through any problem to

** *Berakot* 57b.

its ultimate conclusions. We prefer to be inconsistent, so as to save ourselves the trouble of thought.

The sum of human knowledge which we at the present time possess has been won at a cost of tremendous struggle. Centuries had to pass before man was willing to recognize the truth concerning the world in which he lived. Imprisonment, torture, excommunication, death were meted out to those who dared apprise us of the true nature of the physical world. An equally bitter struggle was waged when the truth concerning man's origin began to be known. The most recent revelations of truth are those which have to do with the knowledge of human society. We are afraid to learn the truth about the working of our minds, about the history of religion, about the origins and motives of our social institutions, for fear that the conclusions might necessitate our readjusting ourselves mentally.

The ancient distinction between spirit and matter will help us understand the behavior of the desire to be let alone, the desire to avoid the adventure of new truth and the risks of new freedom. Whatever may be true of matter, from the standpoint of physics or metaphysics, its pragmatic significance in the thinking of the past was that of a symbol for the negation of life, activity, growth. Accordingly, the desire to be let alone is not to be regarded as the functioning of life, but as interference with life, call it matter, or whatever you will. If the Israelites preferred to be slaves in Egypt rather than to perish in the Wilderness, it was because their will to live was so weak and sluggish that it rendered bondage bearable and preferable to death. Had they been of that heroic mould, however, which would have prompted them to prefer death to a life of slavery, it would have meant that their will to live would have shown itself vigorous and aggressive. It was not the will to live that threw panic among the Israelites when the Egyptians were approaching them at the Red Sea. They lacked the redemptive force of courage and faith, which is man's true life. That was the cause of their outcry against Moses for having led them out of Egypt.

5
The divine dialectic of freedom

The Jewish spirit has discerned the aspect of divinity not only in man's ultimate self-realization through freedom, but in the very process by which man wins his freedom. Instead of beholding in human life, as it is actually lived, nothing but a welter of chaos, and looking to some remote and ideal future as the only time when it would take on meaning, ancient Israel achieved a formula which cast the very conflicts of individuals and groups into a pattern that gives them meaning. That formula is that *in spite of man's desire to be let alone, there is a Power within man and above man that gives him no rest*. That Power deprives him of the security for the sake of which he is all too ready to surrender his soul, and thrusts him out into the wilderness where he is compelled to achieve his freedom and reclaim his soul.

How does this come about? By means of that inner contradiction which develops within human bondage. Those in the master class over-reach themselves in their desire to exploit their slaves for purposes in which the latter have neither share nor lot. Before long they fail to afford them even that minimum security for which their slaves forego their freedom. It is then that those in the slave class are compelled to rise in revolt and strike out for freedom. In ancient Israel they had a term for that inner contradiction which gives rise to the dialectic of freedom. They spoke of it as "God hardening Pharaoh's heart." This dialectic accounts for the decline and disappearance of chattel slavery and the breakup of feudal slavery, and it points to the inevitable outcome of our present industrial slavery.

Such is the inertia produced by security on the human

spirit, and such its wish to be let alone, that if the master
class would supply the minimum needs of food, shelter and
clothing to those whom they hold in thrall, human society
would become crystallized into the type of organization that
exists among bees and ants. Mankind would remain per-
manently divided into higher and lower classes of human
beings; the caste system would remain iron-bound and unalterable. Such a caste system would exclude forever the
vast multitudes of the human race from the possibility of
salvation or self-fulfillment. But apparently there is something of the divine in every human being which does not
permit mankind to reconcile itself to so dire a fate. That
divine urge utilizes the Pharaonic tendency of the oppressors
and exploiters to over-reach themselves, as a means of frustrating their most carefully devised schemes. It is true that
their power may hold out for a long time, and that they
wreak much havoc in the meantime; it is equally true that
when their overthrow finally does take place, it is attended
with ruin and disaster. But so long as we can count upon
redemption for the human spirit as the final outcome, we are
heartened by the awareness that life has direction and purpose.

It is erroneous to conceive God merely as a transcendent
being who exists beyond and above human life, as the sun
exists beyond and above the earth, and to believe that to
affirm a divine attribute is to affirm the functioning of God
independently of human striving and endeavor. In our idea
of God as Helper, we identify those forces in human life and
its environment which make for health, happiness and progress as the manifestation of God. Our identification of God
with the Power "that brings forth bread out the earth," does
not lead us to expect our daily bread without toiling for it.
We know that if we want to avail ourselves of this Power
our attitude must not be one of passivity, but one of active

self-identification with it. So also with regard to the attribute of God as Redeemer. It is a mistake to conceive God and man as separate and distinct, with man, on the one hand, enslaved by his physical self, by his fellow-man, or by his own tools, and on the other, God completely transcendent, in Himself absolutely free, dispensing the gift of freedom. God as immanent in human life is manifest in the urge to realize to the utmost the highest potentialities of the human being. To the extent that man is unfree, the God in man is unredeemed. This is the teaching of the Rabbis. To them Israel constituted the part of humanity that was of immediate interest to them. They therefore identified the redemption of Israel with the redemption of God.[44] Hence, so long as men yearn for freedom and strive to attain it, human life is identified with God, with that aspect of the cosmos which spells life and creativity.

It is only this conception of God that gives to the duty of serving Him a meaning far beyond that of merely proclaiming in worship the ideals we associate with His name. One of the main reasons why human struggles for freedom have so often led to disillusionment is that men imagine that the mere formulation of an ideal is itself adequate to its achievement. The verbal tribute to the ideal of "liberty, equality and fraternity," by evoking an emotional response in the French people *as if* this ideal were an accomplished fact, helped to blind them to the tyranny of the Terror and to the subsequent abrogation of their liberties by Napoleon. Similarly, the verbal identification of the cause of the American Republic with the inalienable right of men to "life, liberty and the pursuit of happiness" served to prevent the founders of the American Republic from seeing the inconsistency of their course in adopting a Constitution that tolerated slavery. In our own day the fervor evoked in Russia by communist slogans likewise tends to obscure for the Russian people the

[44] *Mekilta* on Exod. 12:41.

actual discrepancies between the "dictatorship of the prole
tariat" and the classless society which it is designed to usher
in. But when religion as the service of God is identified with
the responsibility of men to strive continuously for the release of selfhood in themselves and others, and for the removal of all obstacles to self-realization, whether they assume
the form of atavistic impulses, human oppression or the
tyranny of the machine, such mere lip-service to the ideal
becomes impossible. We then know that the freedom for
which we are striving is not a final goal but an everlasting
quest, that every victory in the cause of freedom demands
further victories, that there is always occasion to say, "This
year we are slaves; next year may we be freemen," and that
the hope of divine redemption can be achieved only when we
give ourselves whole-heartedly to the task of releasing the divine in our own souls. So conceived, religion ceases to be an
opiate making us resigned to the evils of the status quo, and
becomes a stimulant to every kind of activity that gives
meaning and value to life. This is how religion should function in the process of redeeming human life from all that
would thwart and obstruct it.

IX

"GOD AS THE POWER THAT MAKES FOR
RIGHTEOUSNESS—NOT OURSELVES" [1]

THE festivals of Pesaḥ and Sukkot achieved already in biblical times the synthesis implied in recognizing the power of God both in nature and in history. It was otherwise with Shabuot. No historical event was originally associated with it in the biblical ordinances which commanded its observance. It figures in them as a purely agricultural festival.[2] It was designated as the Harvest Feast [3] and as the Day of the First Fruits.[4] In post-biblical times, however, Shabuot took on the additional function of commemorating the self-revelation of God on Sinai, when He gave the Torah to Israel. Though the exact date of that event is not recorded in Scriptures, tradition has made it coincident with the Day of the First Fruits.[5]

When the Jews ceased to be an agricultural people, the nature aspect of the Shabuot festival receded and served merely as a memory of what once had been, and as a symbol of yearning for the return to the Land where Jews might once again march in procession to the Sanctuary in the ceremony of presenting the first fruits. The historic aspect became the predominant one. The theophany at Sinai became the central theme of the rich arabesque of aggadot and piyutim. The day whereon God had come down to give the Torah to Israel became the day of Israel's nuptials to God.[6]

---

[1] This is Matthew Arnold's well-known formulation of the conception of God in the Bible. (Cf. Literature and Dogma, Ch. I, and God and the Bible.)

[2] Deut. 16:10; Exod. 34:22.　　　　[3] Exod. 23:16.

[4] Nu. 28:26.　　　　[5] Shabbat 86b and Cant. R. on 2:3.

[6] Cant. R. on 3:11.

It was accounted as the day whereon Heaven and Earth had met, and all nature had stood in awed suspense, by reason of the great miracle which was being enacted. All manner of fanciful legends helped to augment ·the Jew's appreciation for the great gift that had come to him from God. The Jew was told how God had offered the Torah to the other nations, only to have them reject it as incompatible with their way of life, and how Israel likewise was disposed to decline it until compelled to accept it on pain of death.[7] Such are some of the ideas that form the aura of the epithet which Shabuot acquired in the liturgy as "the season of the giving of our Torah."

It is easy to understand how Shabuot could be occasion for rejoicing when it marked the harvesting of the wheat, or the ripening of the first fruits. The commandment, "And thou shalt rejoice before the Lord thy God, thou and thy son and thy daughter and thy manservant,"[8] was easy of fulfillment because it coincided with a human tendency and with what had been common practice. Nor is it difficult to understand how the spirit of rejoicing could be transferred to the historic aspect of Shabuot, for to our ancestors the Torah was the greatest gift that God could confer on man, the indispensable means to bliss in this world and to salvation in the hereafter. The consciousness of being the possessors of that gift made them oblivious to the suffering and degradation at the hands of a hostile world, and put them into a far more exalted mood than sufficiency of worldly goods by itself ever could.

But the question is: Can Shabuot thrill the modern Jew as it did his forebears, now that the tradition with which its celebration has become associated is no longer viewed by him as a historic event? The Jewish masses may be unfamiliar with the scientific study of the Bible and with the evolution-

---

[7] *Cf.* Ginzberg, Louis, *The Legends of the Jews,* Vol. III, 77-114 and Notes 175-248 in Vol VI (29-48).
[8] Deut. 16:11.

ary conception of the origin of the Jewish religion. But enough of the negative implications of the new approach to tradition has reached them to take the heart out of their observance of it. The thinking, and not the thoughtless, Jew must after all be the measure of all our planning for the future of Jewish religion, and it is for the thinking Jew that Shabuot has come to be a festival in search of a meaning. The meaning which Shabuot will acquire, if it is to retain anything of its traditional character, can be none other than the one we arrive at by the process of *revaluation*. This involves emphasizing whatever implications the concept of Torah as divinely revealed may prove to have validity and relevance for our day.

I

The association of religion with the moral law

The belief in the divine origin of the laws governing all phases of human conduct, the moral as well as the ritual, was common among all ancient peoples. From the history of religion, we now know that no primitive or ancient people existed without some kind of moral law, and that all moral laws were regarded as having been prescribed by some deity. Even the crudest religions concern themselves with human relationships.[*] A savage tribe in Australia, for example, was discovered worshiping a deity named Daramulun. When the time comes for the boys of that tribe to be initiated, they are made to lie prostrate on the ground before a rudely shaped image of Daramulun, and over their heads are recited solemnly a number of ordinances which bid them honor their elders, respect the marriage covenant and observe the practices of the tribe.

According to W. Robertson-Smith, there was a time in

[*] *Cf.* Westermarck, Edward, *The Origin and Development of the Moral Ideas*, London, 1908, II, 669-737 ("Gods as Guardians of Morality").

the life of the Semitic peoples when the very conception of private property did not exist. As soon, however, as the development of property laws became essential to the maintenance of the group, there arose a whole series of religious sanctions and tabus to prevent encroachment by outsiders.[10] In the hymns addressed to the Babylonian deity Shamash, he is invoked as "Merciful God who lifts up the lowly and protects the weak,"

> "Thou guidest the lot of mankind
> Eternally just in heaven art thou
> The just ruler of the lands art thou
> Thou knowest what is right,
> Thou knowest what is wrong." [11]

The ethical element figures no less prominently in ancient Egyptian religion. The ferryman who transported the departed to the field of the blessed was said to receive into his boat only those who had not wronged their fellows. The Egyptians had a definite conception of a judgment in the hereafter. They assumed that all who departed to the realm of Osiris were judged. A well-known judgment scene in the *Book of the Dead,* pictures the heart of the deceased as being weighed against a feather, the symbol of truth and righteousness, while the deceased himself has to prove his innocence of forty-two different crimes.[12] Homer in the *Iliad* speaks of Zeus as punishing man for pronouncing vicious judgments and distorting the right. Hesiod in *Works and Days* describes at length the part played by the gods in demanding of men that they deal justly with one another. Zeus does not content himself with his own all-seeing watchfulness, but he sends forth thirty thousand watchers to roam

[10] Robertson-Smith, W., *Semitic Origins*, London, 1914, 144-146.
[11] Jastrow, Morris: *Hebrew and Babylonian Traditions*, N. Y., 1914, 259.
[12] *Cf.* Breasted, J. H.: *The Dawn of Conscience*, N. Y. and London, 1933, 255 *et seq.*

over the earth and report what they see of men's deeds. The wrongs or crimes that remain unpunished by man Zeus revenges. These instances could be multiplied indefinitely, proving that the regulation of human relationships is associated with religion even in its early stages.

The fact, however, that the moral law constituted an integral part in ancient religion would hardly warrant the conclusion that the association of the moral law with religion is inherent and indissoluble. For all we know, such association might be natural and even indispensable in the early stage of human development, but might be dispensable as soon as man achieves considerable cultural and social progress. There are, however, sufficient historical evidences to indicate that the dependence of the moral law upon religion is a permanent rather than a passing phase of the human spirit.

The outstanding historical phenomenon which points to this dependence is the rise of the two world religions, Christianity and Mohammedanism. There were undoubtedly many social and political forces that contributed to the spread of those religions, but the most important factor was the need, on the part of the peoples that adopted them,—and the reference, of course, is to those who adopted them voluntarily—of a religious sanction for the elementary principles of right and wrong. As a result of wars and migrations, numerous peoples had become disorganized and demoralized. The gods in whom they had trusted were no longer deemed sufficiently holy or worthy to be the upholders of the moral law. The moral law had to be sanctioned by some god whose nature measured up to the new vistas and the new problems that had opened up to mankind. Having learned that such a god was the God of Israel, the nations transferred their allegiance to Him, and identified themselves as the true Israel, going so far as to exchange their own histories for the history of the Jewish people.

The rise of Christianity and Mohammedanism is instructive for two reasons. In the first place, it indicates that the human mind is so constituted that it has to find the fulcrum for the leverage of the moral law not within but outside human life itself: that is to say, *the moral law must be regarded not as some prudential arrangement or social convention, but as inherent in the very nature of reality.* The human mind loses all sense of security, and suffers from failure of nerve the moment it begins to suspect that the moral law is man-made. This is evidenced by what happened in the ancient world during the first centuries of the common era. As far as the theory and the organization of society on the basis of man-made laws were concerned, the European nations certainly had enough knowledge and experience amassed in the Greco-Roman culture. But all that guidance was without avail because it lacked the only kind of sanction that could give it weight and authority, the sanction of the faith that it was not merely some arbitrary human decree. In the second place, the rise of Christianity and Mohammedanism points to something unique in the Jewish religion which qualified it to take the place of the spiritual vacuum created by the failure of the native cults. That unique element could not have been merely the association of the moral law with religion for, as we have seen, such association was universal. *The unique element in the Jewish religion consisted in the conscious recognition that the chief function of the belief in God was to affirm and fortify the moral law.* It is one thing to obey an inherent principle of the human mind, but it is another to be conscious of that principle and to apply it to a critical situation. The outstanding characteristic of the Jewish religion is its *conscious emphasis* upon the teaching that the moral law is the principal manifestation of God in the world. This teaching is summed up in what is perhaps the most significant statement in the entire literature of religion: *"The Lord of Hosts is exalted through justice, and God the Holy One is sanctified through righteousness."* [19]

As a result of historic vicissitudes, that prophetic teaching found concrete embodiment in the adoption of the Torah as the guiding instrument of national and individual life. The identification of God as the author of righteousness or the moral law was thus translated into the identification of God as the author of the Torah. *We should therefore recognize in the doctrine of* Torah min hashamayim, *of the Torah as divinely revealed, the original prophetic discovery of the moral law as the principal self-revelation of God.*

2

The Jewish contribution to the moralization of the God idea

It is not easy to describe briefly the part played by the Jews in the evolution of religion. The nearest we can come to an accurate description is to say that the Jews have manifested in their civilization certain characteristic attitudes toward reality which have made for a more adequate conception of *godhood* than that evolved in any other civilization. A conception of *godhood* is as different from a static conception of *God* as the idea of manhood is different from the idea of a particular man. In evolving a conception of *godhood*, the Jews have produced standards by which we can determine whether the object of our worship deserves to be called *God*. This has meant more for the development of religion than fixed dogmas or creeds about the nature of God.

The Jewish God idea was not derived by metaphysical inference from observations of the physical world. Out of the clash of metaphysical systems there have emerged attempts to formulate the nature of God in terms of abstract concepts like matter, mind, and causation. Out of the conflict of

[19] Is. 5:16.

ancient Hebrew religion with other religions of those days there emerged the attempt to formulate what God meant in terms of human experience and ideals. The canonical Prophets, who were driven by the prospect of foreign invasions to conclude that YHWH was the only God of the world and that the social conditions in their own land were a violation of His law, were not metaphysicians but pragmatists. Their concern was not with the *being* of God, but with what God *meant* to those who called upon Him in prayer and worship. This pragmatic tendency is likewise evident in the biblical version of creation. It does not attempt to set forth how the universe came into being, but how it was ordered from the standpoint of man's place in it. In other words, the interest in the universe is an interest chiefly in what it means for human life.

By their emphasis on the meaning of godhood, the Hebrew Prophets may be said to have introduced into religion an entirely new way of thinking about God, an entirely new approach to the very method of experiencing His reality. That approach was different from that of the average religionist who could not help thinking in terms of the specific deity or deities his fathers worshiped; and it was different from that of the religious philosophers who, though they achieved an abstract idea of godhood, did not relate that idea to man's everyday conduct, but made it an object only of intellectual contemplation. To the Prophets the thing that mattered was not so much the conception of God, as what experiences in life were regarded as manifestations of His activity, and what forms of behavior seemed consistent with the recognition of His godhood. For they realized intuitively that the conception of God, or the God idea, was necessarily based upon those interests and purposes to which men attached supreme importance. When they tried to habituate their contemporaries to associate with YHWH higher and more socialized interests and purposes than the current ones, they were stressing the importance of holding the kind of God idea which made for a better world.

An interesting example of Hebrew reasoning about the God idea has come down to us in a Psalm, the meaning of which commentators and translators have succeeded in distorting almost beyond recognition. In the eighty-second Psalm, YHWH, who, to the poet, is the God *par excellence*, or Elohim, is represented as rising in the council of the gods, among whom He rules supreme and saying to them, "How long will you judge unjustly, and respect the persons of the wicked? Uphold the weak, the fatherless; let the forlorn and poor have justice; rescue the weak and wretched from the power of evil men. . . . I thought you were gods, all higher beings, yet like mere men, you shall die, you shall perish like some demon."

This Psalm is evidently a dramatization of the poet's conviction that YHWH alone is a true God, because He comes up to the idea of what a God should be, namely, the champion of the weak and the helpless against their oppressors. Since the other claimants to godhood fail to come up to this standard, they are no better than human beings. They are merely ordinary demons, spirits that terrorize human beings with their constant demand of offerings of all kinds and, as such, they will perish. This kind of reasoning is not directed at the metaphysical essence of God. It is merely a clarification of the idea of God in terms of His relation to human life, or in terms of those ideals which in the opinion of the Psalmist, who was evidently a disciple of the Prophets, should govern human life.

The Jewish religion, in which the prophetic impulse still throbs, is fundamentally not a system of metaphysical beliefs about God, His existence, His infinitude, omniscience, and the whole string of algebraic adjectives which fill the theological works of the Middle Ages. *The Jewish religion is an attempt to set forth the God idea by selecting those purposes*

*and possibilities in the life of the Jewish people in which
there is most promise of good, and making God, as it were,
sponsor for them.* Only by understanding Jewish religion in
this way will we ever get to know the true relationship between it and the rest of Jewish life. It is merely a particular
quality or emphasis given to those elements in the entire
cultural content and historic career which give unity and
meaning to the life of the Jewish people, both as individuals
and as a group.

This should not be interpreted as implying that the belief
in God is purely subjective, a figment of the imagination
rather than an interpretation of reality. One might as well
say that, since the awareness of color is a subjective experience, it is entirely a creation of the eye, and that no objective
reality is responsible for the eye experiencing color, as to say
that, since our idea of God is determined wholly by our own
limited experience of life's values, there is no objective reality which is responsible for the values which we experience.
*The word "God" has thus come to be symbolically expressive
of the highest ideals for which men strive and, at the same
time, points to the objective fact that the world is so constituted as to make for the realization of those ideals.*

3

*How to recapture the consciousness of the divine sanction
for the moral law*

In our own day we are witnessing a recurrence of spiritual
disintegration, due to the destruction of ancient landmarks,
the shifting of populations, the breaking up of old loyalties,
the intensification of class conflict, and the hearsay knowledge of inferences superficially derived from modern science.
Once again people have begun to demand the why and the
wherefore of standards of action which hitherto, if not
always lived up to, were at least never questioned. If civili-

zation is to survive, we must find a way of reinstating men's faith in the moral law. Cold logical reason will not do it. There is no way of proving by any kind of logical process that we should forego anything our heart desires for the sake of a duty or ideal. The thoroughgoing cynic who scoffs at all virtue may strike most of us as a repulsive creature who is a trifle mad, but his arguments show no flaw in logic.

All attempts to base a code of ethics upon scientific inference reduce themselves to two lines of reasoning. One is that without morality society is impossible; the other is that it is for our best interest to abide by the established rules of human behavior. Neither of these arguments carries one very far in one's devotion or enthusiasm in behalf of the right against the wrong. In theory, the welfare of society has the first claim on us. But in actual practice that claim seems to be in constant conflict with what the individual considers his own good. The exercise of prudence in that case not only destroys a whole universe of values and thereby impoverishes the life of the individual; it is itself a broken reed. The belief, for example, that honesty is the best policy is at the breaking point when one can play safe and the chances of discovery are very remote. Virtue when pursued from interested motives ceases to be virtue. It deteriorates into mere respectability, and is often corrupted into rank hypocrisy.

What is ordinarily called "experience" is unreliable as a means of validating the moral law. This becomes evident when we recall that in many instances men make use of "experience" to tear down the little that still survives of faith in the supremacy of ethical standards. On the one hand, there are those who, upon a superficial knowledge of the laws of biological evolution, conclude that morality is unnatural because it tries to change the course of evolution. It has been described as the invention of slaves and weaklings to keep down the strong and master class of humanity. Thus every man who finds himself in a privileged or advantageous position is encouraged to exploit his advantages ruthlessly, regardless of the harm he does others, because his very possession of these advantages is testimony to his superior "fitness," and his might validates his right.

Again morality has been recently attacked in pseudo-scientific terms by those who dabble in psycho-analysis. Taking their cue from Freud, who demonstrated that many of our nervous ills were due to self-repression, they have elaborated the theory that most people's troubles are due to their having a conscience, or, as they call it, "a moral censor." Hence they would do away with restraints. Their advice with regard to the conscience is that, if you cannot dismiss it altogether you give it at least a holiday. Such are the quagmires into which we are led, if we allow ourselves to be guided solely by experience. To be sure, we need the knowledge of experience to guide us in our conduct, but of itself that knowledge lacks the imperative that could impel us to choose any course of action which involves personal sacrifice, however fraught with consequences for the general good. We need only recall the case of the ancient Sophists to realize to what lengths reasoning on the basis of what is ordinarily called experience might go in destroying the very sense of moral values and condemning all moral distinctions as relative or artificial.

Fortunately, something other than mere reasoning based on "experience" governs human life. Men may disagree as to what is right and wrong, but they cannot help viewing life under the categories of right and wrong. Even those who say they deny the validity of the distinction between right and wrong must assume it in their conduct. They resent a "wrong" done to them and clamor for their "rights"; they experience a sense of mortification if caught in a lie, regardless of whether they suffer any practical penalties in consequence or not. No one in his senses can ignore the difference between selfishness, greed and impurity, on the one hand, and justice, purity and good-will, on the other.

But whence comes this ineradicable need for recognizing the validity of the distinction between moral good and moral evil? There can be no doubt that this need arises not from any specific urge or desire, but from the whole man, from the totality of our being, from that which we designate as personality, as soul. The imperative character of the moral law could never have arisen from what we have in common with the rest of animal life. Its origin is undoubtedly the human differentia called the soul, which the human being has succeeded in achieving over and above the animal complex in him. But if that is true, do we not come back full circle to the original premise sensed in all religions and articulated in the Jewish religion, that the only sanction for the moral law is the reality of the divine? For *human personality, with its reference to goals of human behavior beyond our capacity, yet demanding our fullest devotion, points to a power that makes for righteousness—not ourselves.* The authority which the moral law derives from the inherent worth of personality is truly divine. Without such authority the moral law is without foundation.

The recognition that personality is the indispensable sanction of the moral law links the meaning of Shabuot with that of Pesah. In the mind of the Jewish people there was always an awareness of the close relationship between the two festivals. The Torah enjoins counting the days between the offering of the *Omer* of barley which on Pesah marked the beginning of the barley harvest, and the offering of the loaves of the first wheat of Shabuot.[14] In accordance with the change in emphasis from the agricultural to the historical significance of the holidays, this counting of the days between the second day of Pesah and Shabuot was interpreted as expressive of the historic connection between the two

14 Lev. 23:15-17.

events which they respectively celebrated—the Exodus and the Revelation.

Thus Maimonides explains the reason for counting the *Omer* as follows: "Shabuot is the day of the giving of the Law, and by reason of the exalted and important character of the day men count the days from the beginning of the Pesaḥ until its arrival as one who looks forward to the coming of his beloved, the desired of his soul, counts the days until her arrival. This is the reason for counting the *Omer* from the day of the exodus from Egypt to the day of the giving of the Torah, which expresses the intent and purpose of this exodus, as it is said, 'And I brought you unto me.' " [15] Translating this thought into more modern idiom, we might say that the work of emancipation from Egyptian bondage did not find its fulfillment until the people consecrated themselves to the service of the moral law at Sinai. For only the freeman can serve God; only he who has achieved free creative personality, only he who is fully emancipated from bondage to primitive drives inherited from a subhuman existence, can recognize the divine authority of the moral law. "The law engraven on the tablets spells freedom, for only he is free who occupies himself with the Law." [16] The social conduct of man is determined by two polar forces, both of them divine. The one is the force making for individuality, and the other the force making for sociality; the one expresses itself in the quest for freedom, the other in the quest for law. Neither can be dispensed with. Each is necessary to the other. Man, to fulfill his manhood, must recognize the divinity of both. As the *Azeret* of Sukkot stresses the godhood of the Power that makes for cooperation, so the *Azeret* (the term by which Shabuot is designated by the Rabbis) of Pesaḥ stresses the godhood of the Power that makes for freedom.

[15] *Moreh Nebukim* III, 3.   [16] *Abot* VI:3.

4

The moral law, as applied to the life of nations, in need
of divine sanction

The need of a divine sanction for the moral law is felt
not alone in the application of that law to our dealings as
individuals; that need is felt perhaps even more strongly in
the application of the moral law to the collective life of peoples. No nation can achieve the full stature of its nationhood,
true fulfillment of its national individuality, except in a
world in which nations as well as individuals subject themselves to moral law. This is evident in the nemesis which
pursues vigorous nations when they embark on a career of
imperialism. There comes a time when the energy of the
nation which formerly went into creative activity to enrich
the life of its citizens is entirely concentrated on extending
and holding its possessions. The machinery developed to
keep conquered provinces in subjection is turned by military
leaders upon the citizens themselves and deprives them of
freedom, initiative and responsibility. In this demoralization
one finds that source of inner corruption and decay which
eventuates in the collapse of the empire. The story of the
rise and fall of one empire after the other fits into this
pattern.

It is of tremendous importance for the nation, as for the
individual, to be aware of the divine source of those moral
laws by which alone it can fulfill its nationhood in a world
of nations. If the individual needs faith in the divine character of the moral law in order to inspire him to subordinate
merely selfish interests to social ones, how much more is this
true of the collective personality of the historic group! The
mere fact that the interests of the group demand sacrifice on
the part of the individual invests group interests with an aura
of sanctity even when they may conflict with the interests of
society as a whole. To kill for one's country seems meritori-

ous where killing for personal reasons does not, precisely because it may involve dying for one's country. No nation in the world today, not even the Jewish nation, is guiltless of having rationalized, justified and glorified aggressive warfare. But when Jewish religion abandoned henotheism for monotheism, it took the first step in recognizing the universality of the moral law as designed to apply to all humanity.

If, then, the Torah is to serve the function of defining for the Jewish people its status in the world as a nation, the Jew must utilize it as did his fathers for helping him to discover and implement the moral law which he acknowledges as divinely authoritative both over his individual and his collective life. He need not assume that the Law, as tradition has bequeathed it to him, is the final revelation of God's ultimate purpose; but he must use that tradition to the utmost, in learning from it whatever an honest critical study of it can suggest as to what the moral law demands of him, as a man and as a Jew. When we reflect that the Torah tradition is the embodiment of Israel's quest through the ages for the moral law that expresses the will of God, it appears absurd to entertain even for a moment the thought that tradition may be valueless to us in our continuation of this quest which our nature as human beings imposes on us. The Torah is not infallible; but even its errors, when submitted to study and analysis, may prove instructive and enlightening. We learn the moral law as we learn natural law, by trial and error. If we study the Torah in this candid yet reverential spirit, it will continue to be a means of revelation to us, disclosing to us those spiritual values which, since they constitute the value of life, are the only possible evidence of God.

When Saadia said, "Our nation is only a nation by reason of its Torah," [17] he thought of nation in terms of a theoc-

[17] *Emunot Ve-Deot* III:17.

racy, and of Torah in terms of a supernaturally revealed document. But his statement is no less true, if we conceive of nation in the terms of democratic nationalism, and of Torah in terms of a Jewish civilization. The fact still remains that whatever national status the Jew maintains he owes to the Torah.

One of the reasons why many Jews, particularly among our young idealists, rebel against the status of nationhood for the Jewish people is the unsavory connotation that the term "nation" has acquired in our day by reason of the common abuse of nationalism. National patriotism has been so often appealed to by imperialistic states in order to make the masses of the people sacrifice themselves in military adventures for the benefit of the governing classes, that many have become wary of all appeals to national loyalty. They know only too well that, in the name of nationalism, peoples have been whipped into maniacal fury against other peoples whenever their real or fancied interests were opposed, resulting in warfare that frequently left both sides exhausted and solved none of the problems that lay at the heart of the conflict. Why should Jews seek the status of a nation? There are too many nations in the world as it is.

Such an argument, however, can be based only on a conception of nationalism that is derived from nationalistic philosophies which are diametrically opposed to nationalism as developed by the Torah tradition. In the story of Samuel, when the people asked for a king, saying, "Let there be a king over us, that we may also be like all the nations," Samuel was reluctant to accede; and the biblical author considers the request of the people a sin against God. He represents God as saying: "They have not rejected thee, but they have rejected Me, that I should not be king over them." [18] Why was Samuel opposed to Israel's being "like all the other nations"? Why was the prophetic attitude, reflected in the book

[18] I Sam. 8:7.

of Samuel, so antagonistic to the monarchy? It was because all other nations regarded themselves essentially as fighting units. Their nationhood asserted itself only *vis-à-vis* other nations in attack and defense. Group survival was the sole objective of their national organization, and to this end the individual was expected to sacrifice himself at any time. Monarchy was the most efficient form of government for military purposes. It could impose an iron discipline that more democratic institutions could not exact. When the Israelites were hard-pressed by the Philistines in the days of Samuel, the need for military efficiency asserted itself, and the more democratic forms of social control by tribal "judges," who exercised powers in emergency subject to the consent of tribal leaders and elders, had to yield to the institution of the monarchy.

But the monarchy, with the national objectives that it implied, did not come to enjoy in Israel that privileged sacrosanct position that it occupied among the surrounding nations. The Prophets were "tribunes of the people" who, by identifying God with the championship of the wronged and oppressed, developed a totally different ideal of nationhood from that which dominated the political life of the world in their day and which has worked so much havoc in our own. For them, God, Whose will is expressed in the moral law, was the true King of the nation. The regulation of life in conformity to His will is the national objective, and kings, princes and priests can claim authority only insofar as they conform to the divine law of righteousness. It is awareness of these objectives of the national life that makes Israel "a kingdom of priests and a holy nation." [19]

Thus Jewish nationhood functions, like the moral law itself, as an instrument for social cooperation and personal self-realization. Its aim is not mere survival through attack and defense, but civilization, the humanizing and socializing

[19] Exod. 19:6.

of its people for their own good and that of mankind generally. In the effecting of this end, the Torah was the main instrument. Through it the people were able, even after the destruction of their political State, to develop a community life that enabled the common past of the Jewish people to function as inspiration for a common future, in which the ideals that were rooted in the Jewish civilization would be realized. Thus Jewish civilization survived the destruction of the Jewish State; thus it happened that, as Israel Zangwill put it, the Jewish people was twice resurrected to say *kaddish* over its own grave.

5
Righteousness to be translated into law

The term "Torah" is so frequently translated "Law" that we are apt to lose sight of the fact that the Torah is much more than a code of laws. Indeed, all the basic elements of human culture are represented even in the written Torah, to say nothing of the oral. The written Torah contains folklore and a world perspective; it outlines a national policy; it prescribes ethical and religious conduct; it lays the foundation of a system of jurisprudence; it does not even disdain to deal in matters of etiquette. The Torah, especially as developed in life and interpretation, can therefore without exaggeration be regarded as the full equivalent of what we understand by a national civilization. But the fact that Torah is so commonly translated as "Law" is significant. The Torah does emphasize the importance of law, and discussion of the legal aspects of Jewish civilization, known as the *halakah,* looms large in the literature of Torah. *The Torah seeks to translate righteousness into law. All modern efforts at social reconstruction prove Paul* [20] *to have been wrong in maintaining the primacy of faith-righteousness, and are a vindication of*

[20] Romans 10:1-10.

*the Jewish religion which insists on the primacy of law-
righteousness.*

The progress of mankind is a movement from the notion
that the world is governed by arbitrary whim to the realization that this is a law-governed world. Law-mindedness is
that attitude of mind which seeks out the inherent nature of
the realities it copes with in order to discover their potentialities for the achievement of truth, beauty or goodness.
The attitude of law-mindedness toward physical realities has
given us science. The change from the notion that the elements of nature are controlled by an arbitrary will to the
discovery that those elements act in accordance with pre-
dictable and uniform laws has increased a thousandfold the
possibilities of health and life, has made the world infinitely
more habitable and has immeasurably increased our capacity
for growth and development. Law-mindedness in matters of
human creativity has given us the arts. It was due to the discovery of the great uniformities in the physical form of man,
and the unsparing self-discipline which the Greeks cultivated
in the arts, that they became the world's exemplars in human
creativity. The long years of apprenticeship and training to
which the musician, painter and sculptor must submit in
order to achieve success proves that those laws which its
devotees conform to have not been arbitrarily devised by a
few master artists, but are inherent in the very nature of the
beauty which man seeks to create.

Jews may be said to have contributed to human values the
intuition that social life is not the plaything of arbitrary
human wills, but is subject to intrinsic laws which cannot be
violated with impunity. This law-mindedness, applied to human relations, gives rise to law-righteousness. Law-righteousness has little, if anything, in common with that efficiency in social organization which multiplies laws on the
statute-books. It is rather the recognition that social give
and take must conform to certain fundamental laws that are

as intrinsic to human nature as the law of gravitation is to matter, and that by reckoning with those laws the human being can achieve a fullness of life from which he is otherwise precluded. The Jews were not expert either in the discovery of the laws of physical nature, or of those governing the fine arts, but they possessed a deep insight into the inherence of law in the art of living together.

A survey of the contents of the Torah reveals that it provides the art of life with a technique, based upon those forces of human nature which come into play in the various relationships that go to make up our social and spiritual existence. The laws into which righteousness is translated in the Torah may be divided into the following three groups:

Love: There are various precepts in the Torah, which can best be described as an attempt to articulate the laws which inhere in the element of good-will that exists in human nature, so that this element shall be permitted to function to the utmost extent in all human relationships, and in the relationship which each one occupies to life as a whole. The development of the traits of kindness, sympathy, and above all, gratitude, is the purpose underlying such precepts as those of loving and honoring parents, refraining from envy, loving our neighbor, treating the stranger with consideration, having pity upon all forms of living creatures. To this category belongs the entire system of ritual observances, the purpose of which may be said to be the evocation of an attitude of thankfulness toward life as a whole, an attitude which is bound to radiate good-will in all our specific relationships.

Justice: The genius of Israel represents the first conscious endeavor to arrive at and articulate the laws pertaining to the production and distribution of wealth from the point of view of the social welfare of all the people. There are numerous provisions made for honesty, fair dealing and just reward. The Torah may be said to have given the initial impulse to the discovery of the laws which inhere in the relation of man to the possession of goods and the rendering of services. We are, as yet, very far from having acquired the technique of the art of life in the matter of justice, as periodic economic crises testify. Economic law is not made by legislatures; it has its roots in human nature and human needs. To live justly is to discover that law and to live up to it.

Purity: A third class of regulations in the Torah represents the endeavor of Israel's genius to arrive at and articulate the laws that inhere in the relationship between man and woman. These laws never degenerated into mere negative restraints that might have evolved into the classic Christian exaltation of celibacy. That relationship never assumed in the Torah tradition the character of a necessary evil. On the contrary, it was regarded as not only essential for the perpetuation of the human race but as indispensable to human happiness and self-fulfillment, and as constituting an occasion for the manifestation of God's Presence.[11] Only such a realization of the inherent character of the human sex relationship could liberate personality from bondage to primitive passions that tend to assert themselves in forms of behavior inconsistent with human welfare.

In the art of living, even as in the scientific quest for truth or in the artistic search for beauty, there can be no finality. The *specific* laws of the Torah, having originated in response to particular social situations have, for the most part, become inoperative and must give way to laws to be formulated in keeping with the highest ethical standards of our day.[12] In

[11] *Sotah* 17a.
[12] Rabbi Dr. Isaac Herzog, in his recent work "The Main Institutions of Jewish Law," (xx-xxii) defends the Orthodox view that the Torah laws are unalterable. In answer to the statement that many of those laws are incompatible with modern civilization, he argues that such incompatibility is imputed to them, on the assumption that they are meant to be put into effect. But no such thing is intended. The reason they cannot be put into effect is that they presuppose prophetic direction, supernatural divine manifestations, the reinstatement of animal sacrifices, and duly ordained judges. "Had Jewish law," he adds, "continued along normal

the distress caused by modern economic crises, a literal application of the Mosaic laws expressing benevolent concern for
the poor would be of little service. The laws designed to protect the slave, the hired laborer, the debtor, and the stranger
from forms of exploitation current in the biblical era, would
certainly be inadequate to express the demands for social
justice in our age, when technical and mechanical progress
has made possible the abundant production of all the necessities and many of the luxuries of life, provided we can justly
distribute the work and the product of work among men.
Likewise the laws of purity, to be made applicable to the
modern situation, would have to reckon with the social equality of the sexes, with the requirements of an optimum population and with modern discoveries in the realm of the
physiology and psychology of sex. But law-mindedness would
find in the correlation of the study of the laws of human
nature with the highest interests of mankind much valuable
guidance in developing and applying the legal machanism of
social control for our modern communities.

Whoever is at all familiar with the history of post-biblical
teaching knows that Jewish law was developed by interpretative modification and other techniques. In the past, however,
such development was slow and scarcely conscious of itself.
In theory it was assumed that the law had always meant what
the Rabbis and Sages, influenced by the needs of their day,
interpreted it to mean. Society changed slowly, and no concept of history as a process of human evolution existed in
anybody's mind. The law cannot develop today by such un-

---

lines of development, capital punishment would probably have entirely
dropped out of practice, though the law of the Torah would not have been
altered in theory." (xxi) Apart from the mystifying evasion of the
main issue, the foregoing argument is not likely to be of much help to
Jewish life or Jewish religion. In the first place, one is amazed at its
frank acceptance of a permanent contradiction between the theory of law
and its practice. And secondly, one might question our claim to being a
modern civilized people, if we were seriously to maintain that the Torah
law, for example, which renders a Jew who lights a cigarette on the
Sabbath subject to capital punishment is theoretically valid for all times.

conscious processes. Life moves with too rapid a tempo to admit of this. Moreover, since we have become aware of the way legal institutions come into being and develop, it is a psychological impossibility for us to become unaware of it. We cannot, therefore, pretend that the law always meant what we feel it should mean today. Law-mindedness must, therefore, in our day express itself in the continuous effort to reconstruct our legal institutions so that they continue, in the changing circumstances of life, to express the fundamental laws of human association, continue to make for a maximum of good-will, justice and purity. But, if Judaism is to be true to itself, it must continue to concern itself preeminently with the *halakah,* with the regulation of human behavior to conform to the moral law to the extent that we have discovered it.

6

Why humanism is not enough

The modern outlook on life tends to be humanistic rather than theological. The modern spirit tries to solve all human problems by reliance on the power of intelligence. It looks for guidance to the human understanding rather than to any traditional body of doctrine or law, which is assumed to be supernaturally revealed. This is a complete reversal of the attitude which prevailed in the past, when God and His revelation were taken for granted, fundamentally on the basis of tradition; all ethical and philosophical thinking was then an attempt to elaborate the logical and practical implications of supernaturally revealed precepts. It is therefore inevitable that many in our day should question whether the God idea and the religion associated with it are needed altogether, whether worship may not be a mere relic of the past, without meaning or function in modern life. They argue that, since the main function of religion in the past was to validate what, according to tradition, was the ideal life and the ideal world, and since we today find that tradition can no longer guide us, religion is bound to hinder rather than help human adjustment. Nothing is to be gained by evoking the God idea.

The fundamental error of humanism consists in assuming that there can be only one conception of God, which must remain fixed and static, and that we either accept the traditional view of Him as the author of the specific laws and customs which have come down from the past, or leave God entirely out of our reckoning. The truth, however, is that by the same process by which the human mind comes to think more clearly about man and the world, it learns to think more clearly about God. A brief review of the different meanings that God has had for men at different levels of civilization will make evident that *what God means to us depends mainly upon our ideal of human life, or life as it ought to be, and that the way we conceive that ideal depends upon which of the following levels of civilization we have attained:*

(a) If we are so minded as to expect that every fleeting impulse of the individual ought to be fulfilled, we are living on the impulse level of civilization. That is the level on which primitive man probably lived in prehistoric times. Whenever he had a wish that he could not fulfill by some simple and direct action of his own, he would invoke the aid of some deity to fulfill it for him. Children and naïve people today often have similar expectations. God represents to them the assurance that these wishes are attainable. But whoever realizes the folly of such expectations, whoever understands that the fulfillment of our desires is limited by natural law and human society, must look upon such a childlike conception of God as superstition.

(b) On a higher level, men recognize that what ought to be frequently involves sacrificing individual desire and conforming to the accepted norms and standards of the society in which they live. The appetites, whims and passions of the individual must be subordinated to the regulations, laws and institutions that are held sacred by the ethnic or religious groups to which one belongs. This represents the authoritarian and moral level of evaluation. At this level, the first glimmerings of universal law and order give rise to the conception of God as the author of duties and customs which must be obeyed implicitly. In the belief that God metes out reward for obedience and punishment for disobedience, man expresses his first intimations of life as an orderly instead of a whim-governed process. That belief marks the beginning of man's realization that society as a whole, rather than his own ego, can determine what ought to be. But that belief is contradicted by experience. The orderly process which he thought he sensed in human life is often flagrantly lacking in the apparent fortunes of both the righteous and the wicked. The problem is solved for a time by transfering the scene of ultimate reward and punishment to a posthumous life in another world.

(c) But the level of authoritarian morality is by no means the highest level on which conduct may be evaluated. For there comes a time when the laws, customs and mores of the society to which one belongs interfere with the fulfillment of yearnings and hopes which emanate from what is best and holiest in one's self. Such interference leads to revolt against accepted standards. The revolt is further inflamed by the discovery that the sanctions for those hampering institutions are without foundation in reality. It is then also that men begin to question the godhood or the existence of the deity whose will had been accepted as the chief sanction of the standards of human conduct. Society cannot long remain in this state of maladjustment. As soon as the process of recovery begins to set in, two things take place simultaneously: the social institutions are revalued and reconstructed to meet the new conditions that exist in society, and correspondingly a new conception of the God, who is regarded as sanctioning the laws and standards man must live by, is evolved. When this takes place, both religion and morality advance from the authoritarian to the ethical level. That happened in Greek civilization when Socrates and his disciples flourished. That also happened in Israel when the Prophets whose writings are embodied in the Bible came on the scene. Ethically and religiously, the contribution of Socrates and his disciples proved to be far less significant to the world than that of the Prophets. Henceforth also it is the contribution of the Prophets that will have to serve as a precedent for every revolution in moral and religious standards, which is to culminate in spiritual progress.

The Prophets achieved their purpose by refusing to regard God as the author of social practices and standards merely because they were accepted as authoritative. They insisted that only those laws should be obeyed as God's which commanded men to deal righteously with one another and to cease exploiting one another. From their ethical level of evaluation, the religion of their contemporaries was nothing but morally corrupting and vicious idolatry. A being who could be invoked in support of unjust laws and institutions could not be God. But instead of repudiating YHWH, they repudiated the unjust social institutions and pagan religious practices that were regarded as having His sanction. As for YHWH, Him they loved and adored all the more passionately as the Power that made for the kind of personal life and the type of social order which their ethical genius led them to envisage as both desirable and possible.

In all the mutations which the conception of God undergoes as we advance from lower to higher levels of purposive behavior, that conception functions chiefly as an expression of the belief: first, that what ought to be is in keeping with the very nature of things, and, secondly, that what ought to be will ultimately be realized. *God may therefore be defined*

as the Power that endorses what we believe ought to be, and
that guarantees that it will be.

Viewed thus, the belief in God is just as indispensable on
the ethical level of human thinking as on the authoritative
and moral. In relying on reason and experience to inform us
what is, we imply, not that reason and experience create what
is, but that they discover its true character. What is exists in
the objective world of reality. Likewise, we rely upon reason
to inform us of what ought to be, because it discovers certain
desirable potentialities of human nature. Reason must assume the fulfillment of those potentialities, if it is to regard
them as imposing specific obligations upon us. What can
never be realized cannot possibly constitute an aim which we
should feel obliged to strive for.

So long as the state of our knowledge could suggest no
way by which men at a distance could communicate directly
and immediately with one another, it would have been meaningless for anybody to say that people ought some day be
able to talk to one another across a continent or an ocean.
For, even assuming that such an idea had presented itself to
the fantasy of men, it could have had no motive power, since
it could have suggested nothing that men might do for its
realization. But when men began to learn something of the
nature of electricity, new possibilities began to present themselves. The potentialities of the telegraph and telephone
loomed on the horizon, and their invention became a reasonable ideal for scientists, the moment such an ideal could suggest experiments looking to the eventual utilization of electricity as a means of communication. Today international
peace is an unattained ideal. If we are convinced that the
ideal is not only unattained but unattainable, it ceases altogether to be an ideal for us, since we cannot possibly have
any responsibility to contribute to its realization. But if we
see, in the measure of human cooperation already achieved,
the potentialities of further achievements that could eventu-

ally result in international peace, we may be moved by them
to explore these possibilities. But we can conduct such ex-
plorations only on the assumption that there are conditions
which, if we can discover and conform to them, will result in
international peace.

This is the process by which men have achieved whatever
desired ends they have set up for themselves. All ideals rest
on the assumption that there exists in reality that which, if
we can discover it, assures their realization. In some instances, our assumption may prove incorrect. If so, our ideal
must be abandoned as illusory and invalid. But we can never
abandon all ideals, since it is part of our nature to have purposes in life. The formulation of ideals is an indispensable
part of the process by which our long-range purposes are
realized. Therefore, on the ethical level of idealistic evaluation, no less than on the impulsive and the authoritative level,
we feel the need of reckoning with what has always been the
implication of the God idea, that whatever ought to be can
be, and ultimately will be, realized. This does not point to a
static goal, to a single and final consummation of human purpose in "one far-off divine event toward which the whole creation moves." The events of life create new problems, new
wants, new ideals in an eternal process. The goal of the
ideal is ever a flying goal, but the process of expectation and
achievement goes on, and God is the name we give to the
reality that underlies this process. Our God is the Eternal;
belief in Him is a necessary concomitant of all idealistic
endeavor.

But not only these abstract considerations point to the un-
reasonableness of a godless humanism. In the actual effort
to live in conformity with what we regard as the right kind
of life, we experience so many difficulties due to temptation,
failure and discouragement that, without the assumption or
faith that our effort is in keeping with the inherent nature of

reality, and is in the direction of what will finally come about, we could not possibly have the courage to go on trying. Wrongdoing often leads to success, honesty to bankruptcy, sacrifices are wasted, and loyalty is undemanded. There is so much of defeat and frustration, lingering disease, death of friends in the prime of life, so much unnecessary suffering and heartless wrongdoing, that if we are not fortified by faith in a Power that endorses what in our most illumined moments we believe to be right, and that makes for its realization, we cannot regard the ought as more than idle fancy, and the hope of a better world as anything more than a mirage.

Particularly in an age when rapidly changing conditions of life accelerate the obsolescence of laws, institutions and mores, men are oppressed by a feeling of inner conflict. They feel that much which passes as law and morality is mere pretense, yet they are afraid to break with law or custom for fear of scandalizing their neighbors. This is the age of neuroses. "The neurotic is, so to say, the first human type who lacks a support of an ideology of God of whatever kind, and is thrown entirely on his human qualities on which he tries to live and cannot." [11] *The resolution of inner conflict demands a faith that identifies the very spirit of revolt against existing conditions with the divinely creative forces at work in the universe.* This would make it possible for the social revolutionary, notwithstanding his maladjustment to contemporary society, to feel that he has a place in society as an evolving organism. Belief in God, as here conceived, would save men from the illusory rationalization of the neurotic and from the cynicism of the frustrated and world-weary. It would arm the ethically malcontent with iconoclastic zeal, for only the believer in God can destroy the idols to which society renders undeserved homage. Though the society in which such a man lives may collapse about him, he

[11] Rank, Otto: *Modern Education*, N. Y. 1932, 141.

does not feel involved in its fall, since he is confident that the ideals that give meaning and purpose to his life will survive and help to reconstruct a new and better order out of the debris of the old.

This gives us a clue to the psychological basis of the traditional belief in the world to come (*ha-olam ha-ba*). We must bear in mind that the world to come was nothing more than the crystallization of the ancient man's conception of what ought to be. To the extent that what ought to be is infinitely more important than what is, the ancient man was far from mistaken when he placed the center of gravity of his existence not in the here and now but in the world to come. When we recognize this psychological implication in the traditional emphasis upon the world to come, most of what the ancients had to say about the world to come loses its bizarre character. The fact that the beatitude of God's Presence is reserved for the world to come is in accord with what experience teaches concerning the true relationship of the belief in God to our ethical strivings. Even the statement [14] about the things which bear dividends in this world, and the stock of which is laid up in the world to come, can easily be equated with the ethical approach. It can be interpreted to mean that to live in accordance with what ought to be is to invest in the world to be. *As an investment, the good life implies the existence of a Power that endorses the risks and sacrifices man makes for the sake of the future.*

Whence do we derive this faith in a Power that endorses what ought to be? Not from that aspect of the mind which has to do only with mathematically and logically demonstrated knowledge. Such faith stems from that aspect of the mind which finds expression in the enthusiasm for living, in the passion to surmount limitations, a passion which is uniquely human. Those who possess this enthusiasm, and who consequently strive for a better world, are believers in

[14] *Mishnah Peah* I.

God. The fact that many lack this enthusiasm does not invalidate the truth, any more than the fact that it took the genius of an Einstein to discover the principle of relativity should lead us to cast a doubt upon its truth. This enthusiasm is man's will to live the maximum life. *Just as the will to live testifies (in an intuitive, not in a logical sense) to the reality of life, the will to live the maximum life testifies to the realizable character of such life.* A world in which the maximum of human life is attainable cannot be a meaningless world. The upshot of all that men have tried to express when they affirmed the existence of God, is that the world has meaning, for *God is what the world means to the man who believes in the possibility of maximum life and strives for it.*

It is a mistake to lump together into the one category of disbelievers and atheists all who say they do not believe in God, and to classify as believers all who profess theistic belief. A significant classification would divide men into two distinct groups holding two directly opposed attitudes toward life. Those who consider life as a meaningless vanity, as "a tale told by an idiot, full of sound and fury, signifying nothing" are the real atheists, though they may prate of God. But those who, at great danger and cost to themselves, are identified with some cause of social reform or humanitarian benefit, enjoy and communicate the experience of life's worthwhileness, despite all its tragic waste and ugliness, must be classified with religious believers. They act as witnesses of God, regardless of what they say. In their desire to break with the limited traditional conception of God, they may proclaim themselves atheists, yet they are the first to accord genuinely divine honors and adoration to persons, texts and events through which the world promises to come one whit nearer to their hearts' desire. It has been said of Buddha that he was an atheist who became a god. The truth is that in trying earnestly to prove that life had no meaning, Buddha succeeded in giving meaning to his own life, thereby contradicting what he had set out to prove.

When men break through their narrow and prejudiced conception of religion and begin to realize that it is inevitable for the conception of God to reflect one's mental and ethical development, they will learn to identify as divine that Power in the world which impels them to make it what it should be. The name of God will then stand for a truth about reality, not in terms of a division between natural and supernatural, but in terms of normal human experience. That truth is that life has meaning and as such deserves that we give to it, whether despite or because of the evil that mars it, the best that is in us. Men's hearts will then be filled with that exuberance and gratitude which the Psalmist felt when he called upon his soul to greet and praise the Lord: "Praise the Lord, O my soul; and all that is within me, praise His holy name!" [55] They will determine, with the Psalmist, to make their lives a hymn to God: "I will praise the Lord while I live; I will sing praises unto my God while I have my being." [56] Theirs will be the faith which even death cannot extinguish, for despite death they will triumphantly proclaim: "Magnified and sanctified be His great name in the world which He hath created according to His will." [57]

[55] Ps. 103:1.   [56] Ps. 146:2.   [57] *The Kaddish.*

X

JEWISH RELIGION AS A MEANS TO JEWISH NATIONAL SURVIVAL

THE striking feature of the celebration of Hanukkah is the fact that, although the occasion which it commemorates was incidental to a successful war of independence fought against an oppressive foreign ruler, that occasion itself was neither a victory on the field of battle nor a political transaction that gave official recognition to the hard-won independence of Judea. Hanukkah commemorates the rededication of the Temple at Jerusalem to the service of the God of Israel after it had been deliberately defiled by the Grecian rulers. "Not unto us, O Lord, not unto us, but to Thy name give glory for Thy lovingkindness and Thy truth!" [1] These words voice the attitude of the Jews who won the war of liberation. This was their interpretation of those events in which their lives and, in many instances, their deaths were involved. Their military feats were to them nothing to glory in, and even their political independence was significant mainly as it afforded an opportunity for the untrammeled expression of their religious idealism. The glory of the victory, therefore, belongs not to any man or men, but to that spirit which invested Jewish life with such meaning and sanctity that it became worth living and dying for. It was God's victory, and those who experienced it were convinced that it was the spiritual influences at work in Jewish life that proved decisive in the conflict between the Jews and the Greeks.

To be sure, in accordance with the conceptions of their age

[1] Ps. 115:1.

they thought of those influences in supernatural terms.
"Thou didst deliver the powerful into the hands of the
weak," we read in the special Hanukkah prayer, "the many
into the hands of the few, the unclean into the hands of the
pure, the wicked into the hands of the righteous, and the pre-
sumptuous into the hands of those that engaged in Thy
Torah." We today cannot believe in any supernatural intervention determining the issue of a battle. But in the conflict
between opposing civilizations, the issue is not, in the long
run, determined by military operations. Judaism survived
the crushing defeat of Bar Kokba, as it did the heroic victory
of Judah the Maccabee, and in both instances because of the
religious element in Jewish civilization. It was not, as the
Maccabees themselves probably thought, that their God gave
them the victory; but it was their devotion to the service of
their God that gave significance to their victory and made the
memory of it worth preserving.

The fruits of the military victories won by the Hasmoneans were short-lived. They obtained it only with the help of
Roman diplomatic intervention that ultimately made them
dependent on Rome. But the fruits of their spiritual victory
we still enjoy. How little would Hanukkah mean to us today,
if it commemorated only the battle at Emmaus or Beth
Horon, and how much it has come to mean by reason of its
commemorating the rededication of the Temple at Jerusalem!
This has made Hanukkah, indeed, a Festival of Dedication,
when *the Jewish people each year rededicates itself to that
religion which is at one and the same time the objective of
its national life and the instrument of its national survival.*
No battle flag could have symbolized the triumphant achievement of the Hasmoneans nearly so well as the *menorah* with
is light ever-increasing, as the eight days of Hanukkah succeed one upon the other. In their darkest moments, when the
memory of past triumphs would otherwise have been but "a
sorrow's crown of sorrow," the Hanukkah light could con-

vincingly convey the thought expressed by the poet Bialik
when he said:

> "What though the foe prevail! vain is his victory.
> For I have saved my God and my God hath saved me."

I

The survival power of a religion that invests its sancta *
with universal significance

But if the Jewish people today is to benefit from the
observance of Hanukkah, it is not enough that we accept
without reflection the thought which its observance conveys
to us that religion is both goal and means of Jewish survival.
In their contact with western civilization, modern Jews are
confronted with problems very similar to those which confronted our people during the Hellenistic period. If Jews
are to save Judaism from being submerged by this western
civilization, as their ancestors in the days of the Maccabees
saved it from being submerged by Hellenism, they must
understand just what is meant by conceiving of Jewish religion as the goal of Jewish civilization, and just how they are
to proceed in utilizing it as a means of survival.

There can be no question that the ability of the Jewish
people to resist the inundation by Hellenistic culture, a flood
that no other civilization which came under Greek rule could
withstand, was due to their being able to fall back upon their
religion for support. If they had not felt that they were
fighting God's battles and that, therefore, the issues at stake
were of transcendent importance, they would not have been
able to summon that tremendous energy and courage without
which the victory could not have been achieved. But this
does not mean that religion was the whole content of their
civilization; that they could dispense with such other elements
as land, culture and communal organization. What it means

* For the meaning of *sancta* see Preface, p. vii, and Introduction, p. 18.

is that all these other elements were invested with that sort of religious significance which had survival value. Their land became the Holy Land, their literary classics Holy Scriptures, their communal organization the Congregation of God.

Nor is the fact that they assigned a religious significance to the various elements of their civilization in itself sufficient to account for the survival of the Jewish people. All people tend to hallow, and thus associate with religion, whatever they prize most in their civilization. This must have been no less the case with the various oriental states that succumbed to the wave of Hellenism which swept the Near East in the wake of Alexander's army. Whatever elicits from a people a sense of reverence and loyalty may be said to be invested with religious significance. But not everything that calls forth reverence and loyalty has equal survival value. The temples of the Greek gods were also approached with reverence and loyalty, but their cult has not survived. To account for Judaism's surviving not only the Hellenistic crisis, but the many other crises both before and since the Maccabean war, when Judaism was confronted with the challenge of other civilizations, we must understand what sort of religion it is that possesses survival value.

The history of the Jewish religion points to the truth that *the religion which invests with universal import the* sancta *of the civilization in which it functions has most survival value.* A religion does so when it enables these *sancta* to elicit loyalty not merely to one's people, but also loyalty to what is regarded as the deepest and holiest of *human* interests. If a religion elicits loyalty merely to a particular nation as a political entity, it must share the political fortunes of the nation. Should the nation lose its political independence, the opportunity for expressing loyalty to the nation would be diminished. If the institutions of the conquering civilization can satisfy as many human interests as those which the conquered civilization had satisfied, the individual will transfer not only his political but also his spiritual allegiance to the conquering civilization. In such a case, the conquered civilization is doomed. *The secret of the survival of Judaism in the face of the successive challenge of Canaanite, Babylonian, Greek, Roman and Arabic civilizations is the fact that in all these epochs the Jewish religion invested the* sancta *of the Jewish people with such universal, ethical and spiritual significance that the issue involved was felt to be not only the saving of the Jewish people, but the saving of all that made human life worth living.* A brief review of these historic struggles with other civilizations will show the process by which Jewish religion effected the survival of the Jewish people.

2

How Judaism met the challenge of one civilization after another

When the Israelites settled in Canaan, they found themselves in the midst of a people far advanced in all the material elements of civilization. The early Israelites were a nomadic pastoral people; the Canaanites were an agricultural and commercial people. In the conflict between Baalism, the religion of the Canaanites, and the cult of YHWH, the national god of the Hebrews, the former had the advantage of possessing local altars and temples hallowed by ancient tradition and associated with a ritual that was deemed indispensable to the fertility of the land and the prosperity of its people. YHWH had at first only a tent and a portable ark. As Israel had to adjust itself to its surroundings by also becoming, to a great extent, an agricultural and commercial people, it was inevitable that many, particularly of the ruling classes, should accept the religion of Baalism.

One must bear in mind that in those early days the gods were generally worshiped mainly for the practical benefits which their influence was supposed to assure their worshipers, for material prosperity and for protection against their foes. YHWH, being as it were an imported deity, could not be conceived as equally potent with the local *baalim* to supply the necessary rain and sunshine for the crops. Nevertheless, the religion of YHWH survived and Baalism perished. How was this result achieved? Was it by the thoroughness of the Hebrew conquest and the extirpation of all traces of the earlier religion? Certain passages of the Bible seem to accord with such a view, but biblical criticism has shown conclusively that there was no such thoroughgoing conquest, and that the Hebrew State was the result of a gradual fusion of Canaanite and Hebrew elements. The decisive victory of YHWH must therefore be accounted for otherwise.

The real explanation is that the Hebrew Prophets identified the cause of YHWH with the free and democratic social ideal of a pastoral people, which was challenged by the luxury, greed, licentiousness and cruelty that characterized the more complex and economically differentiated civilization of their day. Since Baalism was associated with that iniquitous civilization, Baal could not be deemed worthy of worship. They thus identified the cause of YHWH against Baal with the triumph of justice, freedom and peace, all of them universal human values. In consequence, the traditional *sancta* of the people were changed or reinterpreted to express these universal values. The God of Israel came to be considered the only god worthy of worship, and thus tended to become eventually the one and only God of our present religious tradition. Prophecy changed the character of YHWH worship from a cult that sought to further by quasi-magic means the probable fortune of private or public undertakings to a mode of life that endeavored to render the moral law supreme in human society. And the Torah was largely rewritten to express the social idealism of the worship of YHWH in terms of concrete legislation that sought to reduce as far as possible the economic and social inequalities that prevailed.

In the Babylonian exile Judaism met the challenge of Babylonian civilization and survived by the same process. It is hard for us today to appreciate what the loss of the Temple and of the Judean State meant to the Jews of those days. Nowhere in the world was there the conception of a god whose influence transcended all territorial limits. Of what avail was it that the God of Israel was more worthy of worship than any other, if He was powerless to save His people in a critical juncture of their history? The defeat of Israel had to be interpreted according to popular belief either as the defeat of Israel's God, or as evidence of His having abandoned His people. In either case, communion with Him was impossible. "How can we sing the Lord's song in a foreign land?" [*] was a sincere expression of the spiritual dilemma in which the Jews exiled in Babylonia found themselves. Those who could not reconcile themselves to the belief in YHWH's impotence were convinced that they were the victims of an inexorable sentence of doom pronounced upon them by reason of the sins of earlier generations of their people. "The fathers have eaten sour grapes," they said, "and the teeth of the children are set on edge." [*] When they saw the pomp and splendor of imperial Babylon, it seemed to them that all hope of Jewish survival was lost. Many of them doubtless threw themselves upon the protection of the powerful Babylonian gods as their fathers had upon that of the local *baalim* of Canaan, for they saw no future for Judaism.

But again the Jewish people and its civilization were saved by the process of giving a universal significance to the traditional *sancta*. Since the pre-exilic Prophets had taught that Judah would be destroyed and its people exiled by reason of

[*] Ps. 137:4.   [*] Ezek. 18:2.

their sins, the Babylonian exile was deemed a vindication of their teaching and an evidence that YHWH had influence not only over the destiny of Israel but over that of all peoples. His kingship would one day be asserted not merely over Israel but over all nations. The teaching of the Prophets that God desires "love and not sacrifice" [*] assumed a new meaning, now that the sacrificial cult had, of necessity, to be suspended. Worship lost something of its sacramental character and became a more intimate communion through prayer and praise. The origin of the synagogue was probably a response to this need, and represents a universalization of the cult, by making it independent of any specific holy place or mediating priesthood.

To combat the notion that the exile was a punishment of the sins of the fathers, a doctrine of individual retribution and of the opportunity and obligation of repentance began to assume an important place in Jewish religion. The Torah which had been formulated as an authoritative guide for the conduct of public affairs came to be taught and studied as a method of personal communion. Palestine did not cease to hold a place in the affection of the people and to be regarded as the Holy Land. Indeed, they looked forward with confidence to the eventual restoration of the nation to its soil. But its holiness assumed a deeper meaning. It meant that the privilege of living upon it and enjoying the more complete communion with God which they associated with life in the Holy Land, demanded a community life organized in all its details to give effect to God's Torah. Since the monarchy had proved a bar to such a development, the post-exilic State was envisaged as being without a king. [*] God, the God of all the world, was the true King of Israel who had asserted His kingship not by giving Israel victory and special privileges over other people, but by giving them His Torah for a guide,

[*] Hos. 6:6; Amos 5:21-24; Is. 1:11-17.
[*] *Cf.* Ezek. 45:16, 17 *et seq.*

and the special responsibility of bearing witness to His rule.

The dawning consciousness of a universal mission for the Jewish people is an expression of the effort of the Jewish people to meet the challenge of Babylonian civilization by making Jewish civilization yield values that were of universal import. With Judaism assuming such transcendent importance to the world, Babylon and her gods could no longer impose on the imagination of the Jewish people. They mocked her image worship and met the challenge of her worship of the heavenly bodies by asserting that God, the God of Israel, was the Creator of heaven and earth and all they contained.[*]

When the conquests of Alexander the Great brought the Jewish people under Greek domination, they came for the first time into contact with a civilization which, like their own, had created human values of universal significance. The universal significance of Grecian philosophy, literature and art need hardly to be dwelt on here; volumes have been written to expound the influence of Hellas in stimulating the intellectual and esthetic activity of all nations that have come into contact even with the posthumous remains of Grecian civilization. In the period during which the issues that came to a dramatic climax in the Maccabean revolt were gradually defining themselves, Judaism was faced with the challenge of Hellenism on two fronts, as it were, the one in Egypt, the other in Palestine. The reaction of the Jews to the impact of Hellenism on these two fronts differed, but their experience on both fronts is of great significance to us.

The city of Alexandria in Egypt was the most populous and the most spiritually active center of Hellenism in the world at that time, and the Jews were a considerable part of Alexandria's population. It was a psychological impossibility

[*] Jer. 10:1-16; Is. 46 and 47.

for them to have segregated themselves from Hellenic influence. It would have been about as difficult to isolate them from Hellenic civilization as it would be to isolate the modern Jew from the influences of occidental civilization. A process of assimilation was inevitable. But "assimilation" is an ambiguous term. It may be used in an active sense and in a passive sense; it may mean assimilating, and it may mean being assimilated. *A minority group may appropriate elements of the culture of the majority and so relate them to its own* sancta *that they stimulate the creativity and will to live of the minority.* That is active assimilation. On the other hand, it may be so overawed by the achievements and prestige of the majority civilization as to accept the standards of the latter uncritically, lose its own self-respect and abandon its national *sancta* altogether.[7] In that case, it is doomed to extinction.

For several hundred years the dominant reaction of the Jews of Egypt was that of active rather than passive assimilation. The universal values of any civilization are communicable and can be readily assimilated by any other, without loss of its identity and to the advantage of its cultural creativity. The translation of the Bible into all the languages of the world has not inhibited the growth of national civilizations but, on the contrary, has in many instances proved the first stimulus to literary self-expression in the vernacular. Similarly, whatever was of universal import in Greek philosophy and art could have been appropriated by Jews, to the enrichment of their own culture.

In Egypt this actually happened. The Neo-Platonic philosophy which was then current impressed the Jews profoundly and set them to studying anew their own national writings in search of implications that might have bearing on the philosophical problems which engaged their attention.

[7] *Cf.* Ahad Ha-'Am: *Selected Essays* (translated by L. Simon) Phila. 1912, 107.

By the use of the allegorical method of interpretation they were able to convince themselves that the Torah, in its teachings, had anticipated the wisdom of the Greek philosophers. Their contact with Greek thought did not therefore result in an abject subservience to Greek standards, but led them to seek new meanings in the traditional culture and institutions of Judaism. The writings of Philo combine a deep reverence for Jewish tradition and an appreciation of its religious values with the logic and orderliness of Greek philosophic thought.

In this attitude toward the Jewish tradition, Philo was not alone, but was typical of the Hellenistic Jewry of his day. Their interest in Jewish scriptures was such that it led to the first translation of the Bible into a foreign tongue. The Greek translation known as the Septuagint was made in order that the Jews for whom Greek had become the vernacular might retain their knowledge of the biblical literature. They took pride in the opportunity it afforded of familiarizing the Greek world with the nobility and grandeur of the Jewish religion. They applied to the event the verse in Genesis: "May God extend Japheth and may he dwell in the tents of Shem," [*] which in accordance with their allegorical method of interpretation they construed to mean that, henceforth, the beauty of the Greek should have a place in the Jewish house of learning. When conditions in Jerusalem led to the desecration of the Temple, they did not hesitate to erect a temple in Leontopolis where the traditional sacrificial worship could be performed, showing, at the same time, their attachment to the traditional ritual and their freedom from any localized conception of God which would have made the erection of a temple to His worship elsewhere than in His land unthinkable. [*]

In Judea, the impact of Hellenism upon Judaism had different consequences. Judea was never a seat of Greek culture

[*] Gen. 9:27.   [*] Cf. Is. 19:19-25.

at its highest, such as, outside of Greece proper, Alexandria became. The superficial qualities of a civilization are much more communicable than its deeper and loftier values. American slang and American jazz spread much more readily than the spirit incarnated in such typical Americans as Lincoln, Emerson or Whitman. To the Jews and other people of the conquered territories, the soldiers and camp-followers of the Greek armies represented Greek civilization and set its standards, just as the natives of India probably think of English civilization in terms of Tommy Atkins rather than of the notable names in the roster of England's spiritual achievements.

The Hellenistic movement in Judea was not inaugurated by a group of idealists. It originated with a little clique of Jews who acted as tax farmers. Serving as intermediaries between the main body of the Jews and the foreign rulers, they found it to their advantage to curry favor with the ruling classes. It was part of their tactics to flatter their masters and to play the sedulous ape. This imitation fortified their economic position, and enabled them to maintain authority over the rest of the Jews.

The Jewish Hellenists believed that the possession of wealth and power established the superiority of the Greek civilization over the Judaic one. They were ignorant of their own culture and were not in a position to acquire any of the finer cultural products of Greek life, because their masters themselves were uncultured. The only standards by which they could measure the worth of a civilization were wealth and military prestige. Since the Greek overlords possessed both, Greek manners and Greek customs were regarded by the Jewish Hellenists as superior to the Jewish way of life. These Hellenists cared nothing for Greek thought or art, of which they probably knew very little, if anything at all. They were enamored of the militarist spirit of the Greek civilization and of the voluptuousness which it had assimilated from the oriental kingdoms it had conquered, and not of the "sweetness and light" of Greek culture.

The aping of Greek ways was confined to the upper classes that could hope to be admitted into the society of the ruling powers, in consequence of their obsequious devotion to Hellenism. The peasants and artisans who constituted the bulk of the Jewish population, noting this tendency, only learned from it to associate Hellenism with the oppressive regime and the social arrogance of the politically favored. If that was Grecian civilization, their own tradition stood on a much higher ethical plane. They therefore resented with vehement protest any expression of irreverence on the part of the Hellenists for the Temple, the priesthood, or other *sancta* of Jewish religion. When the protest against Hellenism reached a point that made the Hellenists fall back upon the intervention in their behalf of the Grecian king, Antiochus, a revolutionary situation was created, and the Hasmoneans became the champions of the revolutionary cause.

But between the beginning of the penetration of Hellenism into Judea and the triumph of the Maccabean arms, there were dark days when the spirit of the people was sustained solely by the intensity of their religious convictions. Whoever reads the Psalms that were written in this period notes how, again, as in the time of the struggle against Baalism, YHWH is the champion of the poor and wronged, of the *anavim* and *evyonim* against the *zedim* and *geyonim*, the arrogant and the haughty. The apocryphal and apocalyptic literature of the period shows a tendency to identify the "Day of the Lord," when God's rule over Israel would be asserted, as a cosmic day of judgment for all the peoples of the earth, when all would be compelled to acknowledge His sovereignty. To bear witness to His kingdom, Jews in great numbers suffered martyrdom rather than violate His covenant.

The disparity, however, between the fortunes of the righteous and those of the wicked led to grave questionings. The glib certainty of the prudential wisdom of piety and devotion could no longer be maintained. The prevailing answer to the question, which sustained the religious spirit of the age, was faith in the resurrection of the righteous to life in the world to come (then known as "the end of days") which would be ushered in by the Day of Judgment. Though this supernatural solution of the problem of evil is alien to our way of thinking, we should not be blind to the universal significance which that solution of the problem of evil had when first promulgated, and to the important part it played in the religious crisis during the Judean revolt against Hellenism. That solution made it possible for men even in the darkest ages to refuse to accept the existing status of human life as ultimate and representative of what ought to be, even when they did not know how to improve it.

The Torah thus became for the Jewish people a gospel of salvation, which they were not only to retain for themselves but for mankind as a whole. It is no mere coincidence that, with the success of their resistance to paganism, the Jews initiated the movement for making proselytes to Judaism. Christianity, the influence that reconstructed western society out of the chaos caused by the collapse of the Roman Empire, was a definite outcome of this movement.[19]

The Jewish proselytizing movement which developed after the Hasmonean rebellion was an expression of the tendency to give universal meaning to Jewish nationalism. Since the Torah was revealed to Israel as a way of salvation for the individual by which he could triumph over death itself, ethical considerations demanded that membership in the Jewish people be held open to all who would be willing to abide by the Torah. Thus the very conception of Israel's covenant with God was given a new and more universal import. Abraham, who was conceived as having committed his posterity to

<hr />

[19] Matthew 23:15.

this covenant, is henceforth depicted in Jewish traditional lore as a missionary who, having come to believe in the one and only God of the universe, spreads his doctrine among men. The Jewish proselyte is permitted to address God as "Our God and the God of our fathers" although his ancestors worshiped other gods and he himself was not descended from the "holy seed." If we contrast this attitude with that of Ezra who insisted on the people's divorcing their Samaritan wives, although the Samaritans had accepted the God and Torah of Israel, we can see the progress that had been made in universalizing the concept of Israel.

The recognition of the acceptance of proselytes, as an implication of the universal import of Jewish nationalism, explains the evolution of the meaning of the term *ger* from that of "sojourner" to that of "proselyte." The convert to Judaism is one who, although originally a guest of the Jewish nation, is so attracted to the way of life in which the Jew sees the promise of salvation that he is willing to commit himself to it and integrate himself in the national community. Although the circumstances of history later dampened the missionary ardor of the Jews, access to the privilege of Jewish nationhood has never since that time been denied to any one who seeks it on these terms.

Although emphasis has here been given to the significance of the new function of Torah as the key to salvation conceived in terms of resurrection and a new world-order to be inaugurated by a day of divine judgment on mankind, the tendency to other-worldliness was as yet quite free from ascetic implications. It was used to comfort the victims of persecution and to encourage self-sacrifice even to the point of martyrdom rather than submission to the profanation of all that was holy to the Jewish people. Its function was that of an anodyne, not of an opiate; to deaden the pain and ache in the interest of vigorous and efficient action, not to divert attention from the need for action nor to paralyze the protesting will. To merit salvation after death, one had to defend with one's life all the *sancta* of Judaism, the land, the laws, the language, all the elements of the national life.

The Hasmonean war was in every respect a struggle for liberty. To those who fought it, liberty meant the right to live in accordance with a divinely revealed way of life that spelled salvation. Because the Jews felt that way of life to be supremely important to them as individuals, because it satisfied their deepest human needs as the degenerate Hellenism which was its alternative could not, they were able to conceive and carry out the movement of revolt. History provides clear evidence of this in the fact that, as soon as the first victories of the Hasmoneans had won from their oppressors the concession of religious liberty and the revocation of the persecutory decrees, great numbers abandoned the fight. Although the Hasmonean leaders deemed it necessary to press the fight for complete independence, the war languished, and it was only the intervention of Rome that made possible the attainment of independence.

This, then, accounts to a large extent for the survival of the Jewish civilization, though it was oft menaced by civilizations that commanded much ampler resources of economic, political and military power. By making their civilization indispensable to the individual for his self-fulfillment as a human being, Jewish leaders inspired such faith in the value of Jewish life that the Jewish will to live as a collective entity expressed itself in an unusual capacity for adaptation to the changing conditions of life.

The illustrations that have been given of how Judaism met the challenge of Canaanite, Babylonian and Greek civilization make it unnecessary to discuss at length the spirit in which Judaism survived its subsequent conflicts with the Roman and Arabic civilizations. Although the rebellion against Rome, unlike that against Syria, resulted in crushing defeat and dissolution of the Judean political state, *Judaism survived because the Jews identified their yearning for the Messiah, that was to redeem them from Rome, with their faith in the establishment of the Kingdom of God throughout the earth.* They pitted against the iron discipline of Roman imperial power an even stronger discipline of voluntary conformity to the Torah of Israel, devoting themselves with passionate zeal to its elaboration and application to every detail of their lives. The Academy of Yabneh, the apparently unimportant concession which R. Johannan ben Zakkai was able to obtain from Rome, and the other later centers of Jewish learning were able to set up a spiritual government which united Jews everywhere by a common standard of social behavior and elicited from them a disciplined loyalty to their national traditions and aspirations.

Although their dogged adherence to their own way of life brought upon the Jews the hostility and oppression that is the usual lot of unassimilated minorities, the very measures that were used against them were to them evidence that their life was more in tune with the divine will, and hence destined to eventual triumphant vindication. "Better to be of the persecuted than of the persecutors" [11] expresses the universal ethical significance of passive resistance offered by the Jewish people to the *force majeure* of victorious Roman imperialism and of the imperialisms that followed upon it.

The challenge of Arabic civilization was of a different quality. It resembled more the challenge of Alexandrine Hellenism, in that it offered an alluring culture as an alternative to that of Jewish tradition. In fact, it was in a sense a renewal of the challenge of Hellenism. The Aristotelian philosophy which the Arabs learned from Hellas offered to the best minds among the Jewish people an attractive alternative to their traditional lore, much of which could not stand the critical analysis to which the new philosophic habit of

[11] *Baba Kama* 93a.

thought acquired from Arab teachers subjected it. But the Jewish people met the challenge as Alexandrian Jewry had met the more direct impact of Grecian philosophic thought. They developed a Jewish philosophy of their own that reinterpreted their religious tradition in more universal categories of philosophic thought. Jewish philosophers like Maimonides found in Jewish Scripture support for a philosophic conception of God wholly free of those anthropomorphic attributes which had brought Jewish tradition into disrepute. They stimulated a renewed and fruitful reexamination of the whole field of Jewish learning, with the aid of a newly acquired knowledge of grammar and logic. Similarly, the poets among the Jewish people were moved by the wealth of Arabic poetry to renewed creativity, by applying Arabic verse forms to the writing of Hebrew poetry, and thereby helped to enrich the Jewish liturgy with a wealth of poetry that articulated the spiritual ideals of their age. The efflorescence of Jewish culture in medieval Spain and other centers of Arabic civilization was Judaism's answer to the challenge of Arabianism.

3

How Judaism should meet the challenge of modern occidental civilization

What can the Jews learn from their past experience with challenging civilizations? How can it guide them in making their adjustment to occidental civilization? There is no possibility of their isolating themselves from its influence. What must they avoid and what must they do in order to insure that its influence will contribute to the survival and not to the extinction of Jewish civilization?

In the first place, it is important that Jews avoid the mistake of those Judean Hellenists who indiscriminately aped everything that was characteristic of the dominant alien civilization, without any regard for the *sancta* of their own Jewish civilization. We have the modern equivalent of these Jewish Hellenists in the Jew who is willing to identify himself with the worst features of our western civilization, with its deification of Mammon, its worship of success, its glorification of mere bigness, its apotheosis of power. We must not forget that the careerists and social climbers among the Judean population under Syrian rule almost succeeded in destroying Judaism altogether. Fortunately, they were repudiated and rejected by the mass of Jews who resented their betrayal of the most sacred institutions and ideals of their people.

The tendency to social climbing is so widespread among all peoples that it is commonly regarded as a human weakness which we are ashamed to own up to, but which we readily condone in ourselves and in others. Thus even the Prophet Elisha did not regard it as highly objectionable. He was ready to reward the kind hospitality which the Shunemite woman had shown him by commending her to the court where he had considerable influence. Her reply is significant in its implied rebuke of all social climbing. She answered with simple dignity, "I dwell in the midst of my own people." [11] Such an attitude is as rare as it is refreshing. Few people can resist the temptation to advance their social standing in the eyes of others, even though it involves an obsequious dependence on the favor of others and the severance of long-standing social ties that bind one to one's "own people." But if we judge the tendency to social climbing by its consequences, we find these to be so detrimental that we ought to take this offense out of the category of venial delinquencies and treat it as a form of moral perversity. Social climbing undermines the entire order of spiritual values. It places a premium upon success, regardless of the methods whereby that success is attained.

[11] II Kings 4:13.

The principal danger to Jewish survival derives from the tendency to social climbing. Uppermost in the mind of the social climber is the eagerness to dissociate himself from any group or class that is lacking in social prestige, and to associate himself with any class that possesses it. The Jews as a minority group that is continually made the scapegoat for all existing evils by those in power cannot confer social distinction in a predominantly Gentile society. Hence the habit of social climbing issues in an attitude of mind that seeks flight from Judaism wherever possible, and that would rather welcome than otherwise the dissolution of the Jewish people as a collective entity, since its existence is an impediment to their recognition by the "society" to which they aspire to belong.

The craze of modern Jews for social climbing takes on manifold forms. In its worst form it exists as an obsession to escape Judaism altogether, to cut oneself off entirely from Jewish affiliation, to seek admission into Gentile society, to become a member of some prominent church. In its milder form, which attacks a large number of respectable and professed, and even active, Jews, it takes the form of the fear of being too Jewish. One can diagnose oneself by this very simple criterion. He who is afraid of being too Jewish has a touch of the malady of social climbing, and unless he takes measures to check that malady at once, it is sure to get worse. Unfortunately, it has already gone too far in many of our own people whom we would never have suspected of suffering from that spiritual ailment.

If Jews are to remain true to Judaism, they must develop a conscience in the matter of social climbing. They should realize how grievous a sin it is; that it is as contemptible as the action of those who, in a crowded hall, catch sight of an incipient fire and, instead of taking measures to extinguish it, start a stampede for the door and climb and elbow their way to the street, not caring whom they mangle in their eagerness to escape.

Hanukkah should teach Jews that history avenges itself on the social climber. The careerist who sacrifices the vital interests of his people and their civilization to his personal ambition or vanity, purchases his brief enjoyment of social success at a price of being branded with eternal infamy in the inexpungeable records of history. The Psalmist declare that "the meek shall inherit the land." [11] The issue of the Hasmonean revolt was certainly a vindication of this thought. Ambitious self-seekers may enjoy a brief day of glory as a result of their efforts to raise themselves above their fellows, but it is not their achievements that establish the permanent values of a people's civilization. These are almost always the result of creative forces generated by the experience of the humble and oppressed. This is certainly true of Jewish history. *The Jewish people has shown a pronounced tendency to slough off its ambitious upper classes and exalt those who identified themselves with the humbler elements of the population.* Thus when the descendants of the victorious Hasmoneans tended to deteriorate into a worldly aristocracy, they too were repudiated, and the national heroes of the Jewish people were drawn from the ranks of the popular Pharisaic party. Eugene V. Debs once said: "I do not want to rise above the masses; I want to rise with them." In saying this, he expressed a sentiment that is in harmony with the spiritual attitude of Israel's great Prophets and Psalmists. Certain it is that the Jews who today seek to advance in influence and power by abandoning their Jewish people and repudiating their Jewish cultural heritage are choosing for themselves as inglorious a role in Jewish history as that played by the Hellenists in the events which Hanukkah recalls to us.

But if an indiscriminate acceptance by Jews of all the elements of the dominant western civilization would be fatal

[11] Ps. 37:11.

to the survival of Judaism, an indiscriminate rejection of all
it stands for, even if possible, would only be ruinous. No
nation today, least of all one that has to live as a minority
group in the midst of peoples of other nationalities, can be
economically, socially, politically or culturally self-sufficient.
The only course, therefore, that is open to Jewry, if it is to
meet the challenge of western civilization in a manner that
will permit of Jewish survival, is to react to the modern situation as the Jews of Alexandria met the challenge of
Hellenism. *Jews must discover what there is in western civilization that has universal import, must relate these aspects
of it to the traditional* sancta *of Judaism, and thus integrate them in the very fabric of Jewish civilization.* Such a
course is bound to stimulate the spiritual creativity of the
Jewish people and issue in the production of new cultural
and social values that are distinctively Jewish because they
are born of the collective experience of the Jewish people.
Only by enriching Jewish life with whatever of truth, beauty
and goodness can be found in modern life regardless of their
source, will it be possible to make Judaism of sufficient importance to the individual Jew to justify the efforts he must
expend on its preservation. No fear need be entertained that
this will impair the continuity of Jewish history or the
identity of the Jewish civilization. Just as the personality of
the individual is enhanced rather than impaired by a sincere
intellectual and emotional communion with others on the
highest possible ethical level, so the collective personality of
a people is enhanced and not impaired by its exchange of
cultural experiences.

No policy could be more detrimental to Jewish survival
than one which would reject a true idea, a beautiful form or
a just law on the ground that it did not originate among
Jews. Such a defensive national chauvinism is not infre-
quently indulged in. In the reaction against the first manifestation of the tendency to slavish imitation of the ways of

the Gentile in the interest of careerism, which characterized the period of the Emancipation, there was a tendency to discountenance the reading of all literature except that of the traditional Torah. The esthetic improvement of the Jewish liturgy has been hampered by prohibiting any innovation that may have been suggested by the practices of other faiths, although not inherently antagonistic to Jewish ideals, merely on the ground that they were *hukkat hagoy*, "the practice of the Gentiles." The interest of the Synagogue in the social issues that agitate the modern world has been deprecated on the ground that these are not "Jewish" problems, and the Synagogue should not concern itself with any such extraneous interests. The unwisdom of such a course is clearly demonstrated in the experience of the Jewish people in Russia. Although the Synagogue, unlike the Russian Church, could not be held responsible for the oppression of the laboring masses of Russia, since it lacked all power to oppress, nevertheless, because it held aloof from the larger social issues that affected Jew and Gentile alike, it was implicated by default in the sins of the old order. The Synagogue could not retain the loyalty of the Jewish masses whose economic interests, being identical with those of non-Jews, it regarded as irrelevant to Jewish religion. The above analysis of how the Jewish people in the past met the challenge of contact with other civilizations than their own shows that they did not resort to a turtle-like withdrawal into their own shell. On the contrary, they sought to reinterpret their traditional *sancta* by finding in their tradition those implications which would support the new spiritual insights that they gained from their contact with the outside world. *Paradoxical as it may seem, if a nation wishes to survive, it must not make survival itself its supreme objective, but rather aim at the achievement of the highest intellectual, esthetic and social good that alone makes national survival important to its individual members.*

The advocates of a secular nationalism often err in assuming that by giving emphasis to the content of Jewish civilization, to such component elements as land, language and communal organization, we insure the nation's survival. But this is not enough. Only when these component elements are given religious significance of universal import can they be depended upon for their survival value. The possession of a land can be easily forfeited, unless a people looks upon that possession as affording the opportunity for a social life of supreme value to them, because of the ideals it incorporates. The preservation of a language is not assured, until the literature of that language affords such supreme esthetic and intellectual satisfaction, by reason of the truth and beauty it expresses, that it is cherished as the vehicle of spiritual values. And the bonds of communal organization are easily loosened, unless the collective experiences afforded by communal living are of a sort to enhance the value of life for each individual of the community, by helping him bring to fruition whatever personal and social gifts he is endowed with. *Only by fostering such a religious orientation to life as will issue in the affirmation of the holiness or supreme worth of life, can any nation generate a national will to live adequate to its survival, in the face of challenge or persecution.*

The dependence of the Jewish people on Jewish religion for survival is obviously true of the Jewish diaspora. If Jews were to eliminate all forms of public worship, all ritualistic acts in association with such personal events as marriage, birth and burial, all religious indoctrination through Jewish schools and other cultural agencies, it is almost inconceivable that the secular aspects of Jewish life would retain their interest for the Jewish people even for a generation. But even in Palestine, Jewish survival is dependent upon religious sanctions. The motive that has been the dynamic force behind Jewish achievement in Palestine has been a faith in the destiny of man to achieve a better social order than has yet been achieved anywhere, one in which nationalism would function not as an aggressive military or economic force in the hands of predatory interests, but as a civilizing agency utilizing the cultural traditions of the various peoples for intellectual growth, esthetic enjoyment and social communion. Combined with this motive has been the faith that the Jewish people, if given a chance to develop in contact with nature and under autonomous political conditions in its own land, could and should make a significant contribution to this goal. Such faith is, in the truest and deepest sense of the term, religious. Were this faith to become inoperative, Palestine would soon become but another Jewish ghetto, with no more appeal to the loyalty of the Jew, with no more power to stir his imagination or to elicit from him that self-forgetful devotion which the Palestinian enterprise has so far happily evoked, than any other center of Jewish population.

In view of this truth, it is to be deplored that so little attention has been given in Palestine to the problem of articulating in an appropriate ritual the religious idealism of the new Palestine. Doubtless, a not unjustifiable discontent with the over-emphasis on ritual in the past, and a true perception that the ritualistic forms handed down by tradition no longer express the actual religious ideas and sentiments of the modern Jew, have led to an impatience with ritualism as such. This, however, is a mistaken attitude. The psychological effect of the liturgic expression of religious ideals has a profound influence in keeping them in the foreground of our consciousness, and preventing them from being shoved aside by the clamorous demands of less important but more insistent personal interests. Palestinian Jews, even those who profess indifference to religion, are today moved by religious motives, but, if they were aware that the motives which move them are religious, they would immeasurably augment their force.

4

*The reconstruction which the Jewish religion must undergo
to function as a means of Jewish survival*

But if the Jewish religion, whether in Palestine or in the
diaspora, is to save Jewish life in our day, it must be reconstructed. The Jewish religion must be brought into rapport
with the best achievements of modern civilization and rendered expressive of the most universal human values. It
must be made rational, ethical and esthetically creative.

The Jewish religion must be made to conform to the demands of rationality. One of the most outstanding achievements of western civilization is the discovery of the scientific
approach to reality. That approach represents an achievement of universal import, as its influence even on such old
civilizations as those of the Far East demonstrates. By its
aid, man has achieved unprecedented control of nature and
the promise of greater power in the control of human nature
itself. It is a sin against the integrity of human nature to
utilize for practical purposes the products of scientific
thought, without accepting as valid the insights that underlie
scientific processes. Some of these insights are the assumption of the universality of natural law which no miracle can
set aside, the assumption of the reliability of human reason
in applying to truth the criterion of logical consistency, the
respect for empirical data and the recognition of the need for
validating theoretic ideas by reference to them. This means
that we may no longer refer to the Bible or any authoritative
text as a standard of truth superior to reason and observation. It means that free-thinking must no longer be condemned as irreligious, for to do so would be a reflection on
religion. It means that we must give up all attempts to
formulate dogmas, that is to say, authoritative religious doctrines which are presumably beyond critical inquiry. Faith, to
be sure, has an important function to perform, inasmuch as

the most vital decisions of men have often to be based on assumptions that can neither be proved nor disproved, yet faith must justify itself pragmatically by showing that whatever it asks us to accept as a basis of our conduct answers some experienced need of human nature. *To fail to reconstruct Jewish religion in harmony with the fundamental postulates of modern science is to sin against the light.* "The seal of the Holy One, blessed be He, is truth." [14] A disregard for truth as modern experience has revealed it to us has the inevitable effect of identifying religion with superstition. If Jewish religion should ever be generally identified with superstition, its doom would be sealed. The interest of Jewish survival, therefore, demands that Jewish religion be reconstructed in a spirit of the most rigorous intellectual honesty.

Jewish religion must be made to harmonize with our highest ethical demands. One of the affirmative contributions of modern civilization is its emphasis on the power and responsibility of men to shape the social order with a view to the maximum of self-realization of the individual and the maximum of mutual cooperation among individuals and groups. In the past, the impotence of man to change the social order was taken for granted, and the yearning for a better state of society expressed itself in the hope that God, by an intervention in the natural order of things, would bring life into conformity with the ideal either on this earth or in a heaven to which the soul would be transported after death. The duty of man was limited to conformity with a supposedly revealed divine law not of his own making. If the operation of that law worked unhappiness on earth, there was nothing that man could do about it, except hope for compensation in another world. That is no longer the case. Man looks upon himself as an efficient cause and a responsible moral agent for bringing a better world into being.

[14] *Shabbat* 55a.

The main significance of the democratic movements of modern times must not be sought in the political machinery of representative government, which has too frequently broken down under the impact of economic forces. That significance must be sought in the ethical implication of democracy that every man has a share of responsibility, and hence should be given a corresponding measure of power for determining the character of the social order of which he is a part. This ethical concept remains valid, notwithstanding the strain to which democratic institutions have been subjected in recent years, and the consequent resurgence of arbitrary and tyrannical authority in many countries of the world.

Not only has the trend of modern civilization been in the general direction of emphasizing the ethical responsibility of the individual, but it has also been in the direction of widening the scope of relations within which man's ethical responsibility is expected to function, until it includes the whole of humanity. In the past, the nation was the widest unit to which a man owed ethical allegiance. That nations had ethical relations to one another was hardly conceived. Aggressive warfare was not condemned even in theory. Although the practice of nations in the modern world shows little ethical motivation, the growing interrelatedness of all nations has led to the conception, in theory at least, of nations being responsible for maintaining the peace of the world and protecting civilization against the disastrous effects of internecine warfare.

The religious tradition of Judaism, like that of other religious civilizations, is still couched in terms of conformity to a revealed law, and still tends to put on a supernatural intervention the responsibility for social change. This must not be. Jewish religion must identify God as the spirit that, immanent in human nature, urges men by means of their ethical insights to fulfill the destiny of the human race. It must not use the hope of a hereafter as an excuse for inactivity in the removal of remediable evils. It must not justify any social injustices, even if they conform to the traditional law. It dare not, for example, withhold from woman equal status with man as responsible ethical personalities, merely because the traditional codes which are supposed to be revealed accord her an inferior status on the ground that "women are light-headed." [18] No reliance on God must be made a plea for the evasion of social responsibility, and no appeal to precedent must be used as a justification of injustice.

The disrepute into which religion has fallen with the laboring masses of the Jewish people who see in it "the opiate of the masses" illustrates the danger to Jewish survival of not bringing Jewish religion into harmony with the best ethical and social thought of the modern world. If the Jewish religion is to recover the lost allegiance of those of its sons who have turned from it in disgust, or even retain the loyalty of those who still adhere to it, it must clearly be reconstructed to make it motivate the highest ethical conduct. Only then will it command the devotion that is necessary to make it an instrument of Jewish survival.

Finally, Jewish religion must be reconstructed esthetically. One of the most characteristic aspects of modern civilization is its glorification of art. To be sure ancient religion also availed itself of artistic expression. The embellishment of houses of worship, craftsmanship in the production of objects of ritual significance, the development of liturgic poetry and music, all attest the urge to give esthetic expression to religious motifs. But in the past, the motive for artistic expression was theocentric. It was designed to please the Deity. Today it is designed for the satisfaction it affords as a form of self-expression, a method of communicating to others deep emotional experiences to which the artist attaches value. So long as men held a theocentric view of life, artistic ex-

[18] *Kiddushin* 8ob.

pression tended to be bound by conventions often as rigidly prescribed by religious law as any other phase of the ritual. In modern life, with its humanistic emphasis, art has been freed from subservience to religious convention, and has been made to enhance the significance of every conceivable object of human interest. But even this so-called secular art involves something of a religious mystic experience of which modern religion should be appreciatively aware. For esthetic experience essentially involves a perception of meaning and significance that adds to the value of life. It is a sort of *giluy shekinah,* a revelation of value, of a spiritual quality, or divine aspect in things. To produce art is to be creative, to give new meaning to reality. Since the experience of value in life constitutes our knowledge of God, all sincere art is sacred. In the past, religion emphasized "the beauty of holiness"; modern religion must also emphasize the holiness of beauty.

The lack of appreciation of this significant truth in the past is attested by the total absence from traditional Jewish education of the cultivation of esthetic expression. Even the forms of artistic expression in association with religion had no place in the curriculum of the Jewish school, except for the traditional cantillation of the scriptural readings. That, in spite of the lack of all educational encouragement to artistic expression, there was as much of it as we actually find, testifies to the fundamental importance of art as answering the need of the spirit. If Jewish religion deliberately cultivated the esthetic powers of the Jewish people, it would bind them to it with ties of gratitude and reverence that would go far to insure every necessary effort on their part to perpetuate Jewish life.

These are some of the ways through which the challenge of our modern occidental civilization to Judaism could be converted from a menace to Jewish survival into a positive aid to Jewish survival. Such a way of meeting the challenge would be utilizing the traditional method through which Judaism survived the impact of Hellenism and of the various other civilizations that seemed for a time to endanger the existence of the Jewish people and its civilization. If the observance of Hanukkah can awaken in us the determination to reconstruct Jewish life, by informing it with a religious spirit characterized by absolute intellectual integrity, unqualified acceptance of ethical responsibility and the highest degree of esthetic creativity, it will indeed be a Festival of Dedication. It will mean a cleansing of the temple of our faith to render it again fit as a habitat for communion with God. *So long as the Jewish people is thus linked in communion with the Eternal, it can look forward to an eternal life for itself.*

5

The status of the Jews as a minority group a source of spiritual values

Whatever the historic origin of Purim, the meaning which Purim has for the Jew derives from the story told in the book of Esther. The events recorded in that book have always been regarded as constituting much more than a passing episode in the career of the Jewish people. They are typical of what the Jews have had to endure in the various lands of the dispersion during the last twenty-two centuries, and of the many miraculous escapes in which they beheld divine intervention. "In every generation men arose to annihilate us, but the Holy One, blessed be He, delivered us from their hands." [10] The need for such consolatory reflections can scarcely be questioned. Jews need only recall what is happening to their brethren in many European countries today to realize that the successors of Haman are legion, and that his policy has become the professed purpose of political

[10] *Pesah Haggadah.*

parties. The message of *Megillat Esther* is just as timely as ever.

Nevertheless, Jews have come to a point where the mere iteration of the Purim story is no longer sufficient to hearten them. Formerly Jews took for granted that it was their destiny to be a people apart and that, regardless of the misfortunes that befell them, they were in rapport with the scheme of things by remaining apart. With that as their firm belief, all they needed was the reassurance that God was exercising His providence over them. They found such reassurance in the book of Esther.

Nowadays, however, there are Jews who question whether that destiny is as inexorable as their fathers assumed. Dissociation from Jewish life no longer carries with it the stigma of disgrace among fellow-Jews. There are others, who, despite the present recrudescence of barbarism among some of the most civilized nations, cannot get themselves to believe that anti-Semitism is more than a passing phase of a temporary world disorder. There are still others who, on the contrary, are inclined to treat anti-Semitism as a chronic attack of irrationalism and want something more than thoughts of consolation. They want to know what attitude to take and how to act in the face of the hostility which they encounter on every side because they are Jews. The mere record of a former deliverance from enemies as told in the Purim story, even if we assume its complete historicity, offers little of assurance to the modern Jew in the face of present perils, and still less of guidance.

It is therefore necessary, as it is appropriate, to make of the Feast of Purim, and of the special Sabbath preceding it, an occasion for considering anew the difficulties that inhere in our position as "a people scattered and dispersed among the nations."[17] It is important that Jews know the nature of these difficulties in order that they may the better equip them-

[17] Esther 3:8.

selves to meet them. Those days should make Jews conscious of the spiritual values which their position as a minority group everywhere in the diaspora should lead them to evolve, and of the dangers which they must be prepared to overcome, if they expect to survive as a minority group.

The purposeful development of spiritual values out of the status of a minority group presupposes a correct understanding of what it is that exposes the minority to the ill-will of the majority. A mistake which is commonly made is that of attributing such ill-will to innate prejudice. In the first place, it is questionable whether prejudice, not in the sense of judgment arrived at without sufficient evidence but in the sense of antipathy and hatred, is innate. Secondly, even if antipathy be innate, this does not mean an innate tendency to hate all other groups as such, but only such groups as have conflicting interests with one's own. Group antipathies are cultural products fostered by those who have some interest at stake, either prestige, power or income.

There is a striking passage in the book of Esther, which gives the dramatic setting of group antipathy:

"When Haman saw that Mordecai bowed not down nor prostrated himself, then was Haman full of wrath. But it seemed contemptible in his eyes to lay hands on Mordecai alone; for they had made known to him the people of Mordecai; wherefore Haman sought to destroy all the Jews that were throughout the whole kingdom of Ahasuerus, even the people of Mordecai." [19]

The general law which is illustrated in that situation is that antipathy among groups which live together originates with some one in the majority group finding his interests or ambition thwarted by some one in the minority group. The whole of the minority group is then implicated. The injured party obtains the aid and sympathy of the rest of his people in bearing down upon his opponent, and is acclaimed for ward-

[19] *Ibid.*, 3:5-6.

ing off the menace which his opponent's people harbored against his own.

All forms of racial, religious and national antipathy begin in some such way. They are, in the last analysis, the ill-will which the conquering group entertains toward the conquered group, whenever the latter, as a whole or through some of its members, crosses the ambition, pride or greed of the former. For, with society organized on the basis of power, a majority group regards itself as the potential, if not the actual conqueror of the minority group, and treats it accordingly. When, therefore, the minority refuses to be subservient to the will of the majority and demands that it be treated on a plane of equality, the pride of the majority is hurt, and the cycle of hatred and persecution, on the one side, and resentment and fear, on the other, begins its mad career. In this cycle, mankind is at present deeply implicated.

Out of the reaction of Jews in the past to their status as a minority everywhere in the diaspora there evolved a remarkable philosophy of life or system of spiritual values. It is remarkable not only for its influence in sustaining the courage of the Jew in desperate situations, but for its inherent worth. Being in the minority, Jews were expected to accept the life-pattern of a conquered people. They were expected to adopt the standards imposed on them by the majority, with good grace, if they could, or with sullen resentment, if they must. They did neither. Instead, they formulated a philosophy of life which prevented the conquest from being consummated.

The core of this philosophy was their insistence that their God, and not the God of the majority or conquering people, would ultimately triumph. Other conquered nations commonly interpreted the defeat of the nation to mean the defeat of the nation's God by the god or gods of the conquerors. Not so the Jews. Instead of seeing in their situation ground for denying their God and the authority of His sovereignty,

they developed a new criterion of godhood that revolutionized the generally accepted values of life. In their astounding
affirmation that theirs was the true God and not the deity
worshiped by the majority, and that He would one day assert
His rule in spite of all appearances to the contrary, there was
the clear implication that godhood was not synonymous with
might, but rather with justice to the oppressed and downtrodden.

Even at the very beginning of the dispersion, during the
period of the Babylonian exile, the Prophet Ezekiel com-
forted his people in these words: "I will feed My sheep, and
I will cause them to lie down, saith the Lord God. I will seek
that which was lost, and will bring back that which was
driven away, and will bind up that which was broken, and
will strengthen that which was sick; and the fat and the strong
I will destroy, I will feed them in justice." [19] In similar vein,
the Rabbis interpret the words of Kohelet, "God seeketh that
which is pursued," [20] to mean "God is on the side of the
persecuted." [21] *Because the Jews conceived world unity in
terms of a Kingdom of God, they were the one minority
people which refused to accept the practical logic of their
position and to merge with the majority, and which formulated a new spiritual dialectic that called for the treatment of
minorities as equals.*

The Jews have clashed with world imperialism since the
days of Persia, and therefore brought down upon themselves
the most bitter and malignant forms of group antipathy.
Persia, with its one-hundred-and-twenty-seven provinces,
strove for universal empire. The Macedonian Empire was
projected by Alexander as bringing the light of Greek life
and wisdom to barbaric mankind. Pre-Christian Rome, especially as visioned by its outstanding thinkers, the Stoics,
hoped to see all mankind united under her aegis. And finally
the Church and the Mosque each maintained the right to im-

[19] Ezek. 34:15-16.   [20] Ecc. 3:15.   [21] Ecc. *R. ad locum.*

pose by force the salvation upon which it claimed to have a monopoly. All these great empires and their peoples could not bear that a small people like the Jews, whom they could easily crush, should presume to challenge their ambition by regarding themselves as forerunners of a universal kingdom which would supersede theirs. Haman, Manetho, Apion, Cicero, and their successors voiced the resentment of wounded pride. But the Jews, though worsted physically, came forth spiritually unconquered. The high ideals and wisdom of life which they evolved out of their struggle for existence amidst a hostile world were adequate compensation for all they had gone through.

The world imperialism of the Church has been superseded by modern nationalism. While the transition was being effected, the Jews could breathe more freely. There was a tendency, for the first time in history, to abolish the conqueror-conquered relationship toward them and to treat them on a basis of equality, despite their being in a minority. But before long modern nationalism came to be seized upon by the ruling classes as a means of rendering their privileges secure against attack by those they exploited, and of rallying their fellow-citizens to help them wrest and hold privileges and concessions in their own and in foreign lands. As part of this use of nationalism, it became necessary to find a scapegoat for all the miseries and deprivations of the exploited. The Jews being an outstanding minority and forced by prejudices of long standing to hold in the general economy the position of middlemen, are made the convenient scapegoat for the sins of the exploiting classes. They are pointed out as parasites and held responsible for the poverty, the insecurity and the misery of the masses.

Under these circumstances, the Jews of today should do deliberately what their ancestors did unconsciously. They should evolve spiritual values out of the very suffering which their position as a minority brings them. *Just as in olden times the Jews countered the imperialism of might with the imperialism of the spirit, so should they at present counter the nationalism of might with the nationalism of the spirit.* It should be the mission of the Jew to challenge the braggart nationalism and chauvinistic patriotism of the modern nations as being merely camouflage for the domination of the privileged classes, and to point the way to a nationalism which is based upon social justice and equitable opportunity for all, a nationalism which does not have to thrive upon the hatred of all other nations, but which sees itself best realized through comity and cooperation with all other peoples. Let the Jew not be afraid of accepting the title of internationalist, and let him foster that international-mindedness which, it is hoped, will ultimately cure the peoples of their national exclusiveness and megalomania.

To do that effectively, Jews have to go back to their spiritual heritage and relearn it, and then reinterpret and apply it to the problems of industry, exchange and government. The causes, the history and the implications of anti-Semitism must become an integral part of the education of the Jew. This is the modern analogue of the traditional behest to remember what Amalek had done unto Israel. The evil of Jew-hatred must be traced to its roots, and the spiritual values of Judaism must be set off as its foil, not in a spirit of self-glorification, but so that the Jew might learn to plead guilty to the very ideals with which he is so often charged and for which he is hated. If he is taunted with internationalism, let him respond not by trying to out-Herod Herod in demonstrative assertion of chauvinistic national patriotism, but by doing all in his power to promote better international relationships. If a State seeks to eradicate from its life every evidence of "Jewish intellectualism," let the Jew regard such an accusation as an unconscious tribute to the part played by Jews in the quest for reasonableness and truth, and let him seek to merit the unintended compliment. The inculcation of such an attitude through Jewish education will immunize the Jew against the virus of self-hatred and prevent it from entering the souls of his children.

Direct action designed to defend the economic and political status of the Jews is not by itself adequate to counter the evils inherent in their situation as a minority group. In Jewish tradition, Amalek, who cruelly attacked the Israelites in the wilderness, is regarded as the prototype of Israel's deadliest enemies. The manner in which the Israelites met Amalek's attack may well symbolize the manner in which Jews should meet anti-Semitism. Joshua's active defense should be paralleled by active measures on the part of the Jews to ward off the dangers of loss of self-respect and of economic deprivation to which they are exposed. Yet such defense is to no purpose, unless the action of Moses in holding up his hands while the battle raged serves as a reminder that the courage to bear the brunt of the attack and the ability to ward it off depend, in the last resort, upon the spiritual ideals for which Jews insist on retaining their national individuality.

If Jews do not wish to have recourse to delusions of grandeur by way of compensation, the only means which will enable them to transcend the persecutions and discriminations to which they are subjected is Jewish creativity. If Jewish existence will be redeemed from its cultural, intellectual and spiritual poverty, it will be immune to the bombardment of hate. This is why Jews as a group must add to the cultural and spiritual values of the world. They must enrich the sum of esthetic, ethical and religious achievements. As Jews, they must produce ideas, arts, literature, music. The sense of latent and dormant powers, the realization of enormous forces that plead for expression, the very act and product of expression—it is these, the fruit of creative genius, that will give Jews a sense of legitimate standing in the world.

That loyalty to God renders the Jewish people impregnable to all assaults on its honor and its life was clearly set forth about twenty-five centuries ago by an anonymous prophet, when he said:

> No weapon that is forged against you will succeed;
> And every tongue that will rise against you in judgment you will confute.
>
> This is the heritage of the servants of the Lord,
> And their due reward from Me, saith the Lord.[11]

[11] Is. LIV :17.

Index

187, 295, 316, 367; cultural and spiritual creativity—281; Creator —164

Cynicism—29, 89

D

Daniel—141
Daramulun—299
David—208, 231
Day of Atonement (see Yom Kippur)
Debs, Eugene V.—350
Decalogue—91, 267
Declaration of Independence—83, 215
Democracy—124, 214, 217, 270, 278, 357; industrial democracy —236; democratic nationalism— 313
Demons—1, 305; demoniac powers —164
Destiny; historic destiny—100; human destiny—27, 46, 64, 70, 95, 123, 245, 353, 357
Dewey, John—230
Dionysos—226, 269
Divine—12, 25, 72, 87, 89, 108, 122, 146, 161, 164 f., 167, 170, 182, 184, 194, 261, 269, 329; divine aspect of life—107; divine goal—125; divine grace—26; divine immanence in human life —120; divine in man—113, 182, 290; divine intervention—360; divine judgment—143; divine king—124; divine law—144, 164; divine origin of laws—299, 310; divine phase of reality—62; divine power of intelligence—267; divine presence—48, 138, 225 f.; divine principle in man—215; divine principle of creativity—61, 77 ff.; divine process—284; di-

vine purpose of life—173; divine purpose with man—282; divine right of kings—57; divine ruler —119; divine sanctions—164, 306-315; divinity—78, 293; double divinity—71
Dreiser, Theodore—66
Dualism—73 ff.

E

Ecclesiastes (see Koheleth)
Education—125, 185, 217, 359, 367
Egypt—70, 142, 159, 220, 231, 242, 272, 292 f., 338 f.; Exodus from— 91, 192, 194, 201, 203, 265-267, 286, 310; Egyptian Kings—190; Egyptian religion—300; Egyptians—284, 300
Einstein, Albert—28, 328
Eldad and Medad—231
Elijah—143, 284
Elisha—348
Elohim—4, 305
Emancipation—43, 92, 156, 352
Emerson, Ralph Waldo—60, 259, 260, 341
Emmaus—331
English; English children—191; English civilization—341; English Puritans—191
Enlightenment—43, 55
Ephraim—242
Epstein, Isidore—12
Equality—215-225, 281, 295
Eros—227
Esau—231
Esther—360-362
Esthetic; esthetic improvement of Jewish liturgy—352; esthetic reconstitution of Jewish religion— 358 f.; esthetic self-expression— 217; esthetic values—217
Ethics—84, 126, 244, 256, 307;

372

Gentile—98, 159, 352; Gentile society—349

Germany—226; German children—191; German people—226; German persecution of Jewry—95

Gezerah Shavah—5

God; God's sovereignty over Israel—45; God's throne—132; God a righteous judge—7; God and man—14, 187, 212, 215; God as a cosmic monster—68; God as creator—61-68; God as creator of world—46, 154; God as King—104-148, 314; God as source of evil—76, 168; God as source of goodness—26, 168; God as liberator—265-296; God as magic power—25; God in history—13 ff.; God of Israel—23, 101, 106 f., 191, 203, 263, 266 ff., 277, 284, 301, 330, 335 ff., 344; attributes, nature of God—20, 182, 193, 269, 295, 303; belief in God—25-30, 72, 302, 326; communion with God—25, 58, 153, 243 f., 264, 337, 360; confidence in God—73; definitions of God—26, 30, 52, 58, 76, 104, 107, 109, 133, 160 f., 165, 175, 178, 244, 248 ff., 268, 270, 287, 293, 305 f., 309, 321, 323 f., 329; duality of God—71; existence of God—76; grace of God—55; gratitude to God—226-228; immanence of God—119, 214, 248, 295; justice of God—283; kingdom of God—57, 84, 101, 104-148, 346, 364; knowledge of God—40, 272; law of God—73; mercy of God—46, 283; personal God—87; presence of God—2, 170, 172, 242-264, 318, 327; reality of God—252 f., 272 f.; return to God—184, 187; self-revelation of God—297; sovereignty of God—104-148; traditional conception of God—76, 328; transcendence of God—258, 294; voice of God—48, 177; will of God—1

God-awareness—30, 33, 193, 244, 249

God-consciousness, (see God-awareness)

Godhead—1

Godhood—23, 29, 61 f., 76, 106 f., 154, 190, 193, 267 f., 303-306

God Idea—vii, 15, 18-21, 28 f., 87, 108, 158, 195, 244, 303-306, 320 f., 323

Godless—217

Godliness—227

Gods—21, 25, 65, 87, 107, 146, 171, 193, 196, 267, 276, 300 f., 304, 328, 334-336, 363; gods of Canaan—193, 334-336; Aryan god—226; Babylonian gods—336; false gods—284; Greek gods—333; national god—102

Gog and Magog—141

Gomorrah—182

Good and Evil—27, 46, 50, 63, 67, 71, 72, 75, 78, 168

Good, True, and Beautiful—173

Good Yezer—168, 286

Greco-Roman; Greco-Roman culture—302; Greco-Roman world—22

Greece, (see also Hellas)—131; Greek(s)—64 f., 190, 226, 316, 330; Greek art—338 f.; Greek civilization—323, 334, 338-345; Greek gods—333; Greek literature—338; Greek mythology—65; Greek philosophy—22 f., 48, 68, 198, 253, 338 ff.; Greek religion—65, 338; Greek rule, ruler-

M

Maccabees—330-360; Maccabean period—105

Macedonian Empire—364

Machiavelli—211

Maimonides—12, 49, 87, 203, 347

"Main Institutions of Jewish Law, The"—318 (n. 22)

Malraux, Andre—290

Man—51, 70, 77 f. 80, 86, 114, 123, 135, 161 f., 170, 195, 213, 251; man and God—14, 189; man created in image of God—85, 87, 89; ancient man—327; biological nature of man—121; fall of man —47, 135 f.; modern man—1, 53, 76, 165, 186; nature of man— 129 f., 212, 214; natural man— 214; primitive man—226, 260; religious man—145; social man —214; Western man—65

Mandeville, Bernard de—89

Manetho—365

Manna—47

"Man's Fate"—290

Marx, Karl—284 f.

Marxists—283

Matter—61

May Day—82

Megillat Esther—361

Memory—97

Memshelet Zadon—118

Mennonites—125

Menorah—331

Messiah—47, 346; Messianic movements—125; Messianic redemption—158

Metaphysics—29, 64, 75, 292, 303 ff.

Michaelangelo—281

Midrash—5, 42, 74, 118, 130, 142, 169, 181, 210

Mind—15, 246; Occidental mind— 67; Western mind—66

Miracle(s)—20, 45, 61, 74, 80, 111, 126, 266

Mishkan—152

Mishnah—12, 71, 156, 187, 225

Mizvot—108 f.

Modern approach to problems of life—128; modern civilization— 209 f., 275; modern conception of God—79, 94, 166; modern experience—107; modern Jew— 57, 80, 98, 243; modern man— 1, 53, 76, 165; modern-minded— 11; modern nationalism—191; modern psychology—255; modern religion—14, 129; modern science—88; modern thought— 10; modern world—34, 199; modernist—10, 12 f.

Mohammedanism—22, 253, 279, 300 f.

Monotheism—4, 21, 23, 74, 108, 148, 227; ethical monotheism— 198

Moody, Vaughan—288

Mordecai—362

Moses—40, 48, 114, 127, 207 f., 231, 260, 285, 293; Mosaic law —41, 319, 367

Murray, Gilbert—7, n. 13

Mysticism, Jewish—78

N

Naboth—284

Napoleon—295

Nathan—232

Nationalism—147, 311-315, 330-360; chauvinistic nationalism— 230; democratic nationalism— 313; Jewish nationalism—100, 330-360; secular nationalism— 353 f.

Printed in the United States
16031LVS00001B/37-153

9 780814 325520